...ion
of Force

The Application of Force

An Introduction

to **Army Doctrine**

and the **Conduct of Military Operations**

London : The Stationery Office

Published by The Stationery Office and available from:

The Stationery Office
(mail, telephone and fax orders only)
PO Box 29, Norwich, NR3 1GN
Telephone orders/General enquiries: 0870 6005522
Fax orders: 0870 6005533

You can now order books online at **www.tso.co.uk**

The Stationery Office Bookshops
123 Kingsway, London, WC2B 6PQ
020 7242 6393 Fax 020 7242 6394
68-69 Bull Street, Birmingham B4 6AD
0121 236 9696 Fax 0121 236 9699
9-21 Princess Street, Manchester M60 8AS
0161 834 7201 Fax 0161 833 0634
16 Arthur Street, Belfast BT1 4GD
028 9023 8451 Fax 028 9023 5401
The Stationery Office Oriel Bookshop
18-19 High Street, Cardiff CF10 1PT
029 2039 5548 Fax 029 2038 4347
71 Lothian Road, Edinburgh EH3 9AZ
0870 606 5566 Fax 0870 6065588

The Stationery Office's Accredited Agents
(see Yellow Pages)

and through good booksellers

ISBN 011 772983 3

Contents

Chapter 1 Defence Perspectives

Section 1 Introduction

"Our security and defence policies are rooted in assessments of our national interests; and of how those interests can be best promoted within the domestic and international setting, now and in the future, in conjunction with our Allies and partners where it is sensible to do so."

STATEMENT ON THE DEFENCE ESTIMATES 1996

Background

Many major factors have influenced defence policy and these have helped to determine the types of forces the nation requires to meet its national and defence commitments. Historically, the United Kingdom has been concerned to prevent a major power, or group of powers, from establishing a position of dominance on the European Continent which could have threatened the security, freedom and economic prosperity of the nation and Empire. This generally meant contributing ships and troops to allies on the Continent. At the same time the United Kingdom was interested in protecting and promoting its own national interests at home and abroad and thus had a vested interest in ensuring that continental states did not threaten these interests.

Alliances were formed with other threatened nations on the Continent to meet each separate menace on a contingency basis. Alliances were often temporary. Some did not survive the duration of a single war. All lapsed at the peace treaty ending each war, or soon after, although the arrangements set in hand by the Congress of Europe (1814–15) endured for several decades after the Napoleonic Wars.

European Security

After the First World War, British troops remained in the Rhineland until 1929, but apart from this instance Britain avoided committing forces on a permanent basis to an alliance in peacetime. Such forces as were maintained in peace were dedicated to purely national tasks and, in the case of the Army, the security of the Empire had first call on its resources.

The Second World War and its aftermath have altered this long-standing perspective of national defence. After the War it became plain that while the

United Kingdom continued to have a major voice in the international world it did not have the resources to act without allies. There was a growing direct threat to Europe from the Soviet Union and its satellites coupled with many separate and individual threats to various parts of the British Empire.

All this began to be recognised and there was a deliberate and significant reversal of previous British policy in 1949 when the United Kingdom joined the North Atlantic Treaty Organisation (NATO) to counter the growing threat from the Soviet Union. As a consequence of the North Atlantic Treaty, following on the more limited Brussels Defence Treaty of the previous year, an increasing proportion of the armed forces were declared to NATO. With the gradual reduction of imperial responsibilities the Army became increasingly structured to meet the new continental commitment. Never before had so many European states combined in a peacetime alliance with such a wide measure of agreement as to the origin and nature of the threat and on the need to provide forces to meet it.

The growing stockpile of nuclear weapons created by America and Russia (joined by the UK and later France) added new factors into the political and military balance involving both NATO and the Soviet Union (later the Warsaw Pact). Popular concern over their possible use in Europe was complemented by a similar reluctance on the part of the Warsaw Pact to initiate any aggressive conventional move which might subsequently lead to the use of nuclear weapons and from this developed the strategy of deterrence for NATO in the mid-1960s. The development of the adversarial relationship between the two main power blocs and the aims of national and NATO strategy to overcome this are covered in later Sections of this Chapter.

Control of the Armed Forces

The Higher Management of Defence. The main principles of policy are decided by the government. Major questions of defence policy are dealt with by the Defence and Overseas Policy (DOP) Committee of the Cabinet which is chaired by the Prime Minister and includes senior ministers with responsibilities relating to defence. Within these broad guidelines, defence policy issues are resolved by the Secretary of State for Defence, his ministers and his two principal advisers: Chief of the Defence Staff (CDS) and the Permanent Under-Secretary (PUS). Under the control and direction of the Secretary of State, the MOD ensures effective co-ordination of all policy and administrative matters affecting the fighting Services. This includes:

Formulation and Execution of Defence Policy.

Conduct of Operations.

Manpower Planning.

Equipment Requirements and Procurement.

Detailed Financial Control.

Co-ordination of Business. The Central Staffs of the MOD are responsible for advising ministers on, and co-ordinating, defence-wide policy determining priorities and allocating resources. They are also concerned with common arrangements and planning for operations, intelligence, logistics and pay and personnel matters. The single-Service staffs are responsible for the management of their Services and execution of delegated operations. The Procurement Executive is responsible for the development, production and purchase of all warlike equipment and stores.

Budgets. Top-Level Budgets (TLB) are now held by senior commanders and civil servants throughout the Ministry of Defence in order to meet the costs of their organisations, and a hierarchy of Higher Level Budgets Holders and Basic Level Budgets Holders ensure that budgets are delegated as far down the chain of command as possible. Commanders of stores depots, repair workshops and frontline units have their own budgets and have to ensure value for money in day-to-day business.

Financial Planning. The overall mechanism for planning defence expenditure is the Long Term Costings (LTC) process which provides a framework for up to 10 years ahead. Defence policy, commitments and capabilities are decided by ministers. They are set out in the Departmental Plan, and reflected in the form of increasingly detailed objectives through the Army Plan, the TLB plans and lower level plans to the units that have to fulfil them. Budget holders at all levels use their own planning as a framework for constructing the LTCs. LTCs are submitted up the budgetary hierarchy and scrutinised at each level for realism and compliance with agreed plans and assumptions. Proposed changes to the programme are set out in Alternative Assumptions. The Central Staffs at the MOD compile the overall Defence Programme, embracing both the TLB costings and the equipment programme, and adjust it to fit within the resource levels agreed by the government. After approval by the Secretary of State the plans are adjusted to take account of agreed changes to the pro-gramme and the finalised LTC programme forms the starting point for the next annual costing review.

Command

The command of the Services formally rests with the Crown. In practice the authority of the Crown is represented by the government of the day and responsibility for the Armed Forces is delegated to the Secretary of State for Defence, supported by the Defence Council which is the legal authority for all three Services. Command over all officers and soldiers and the detailed administration of the Army is delegated by the Sovereign, through Letters Patent to the Defence Council and the Service Chiefs. Each is fully responsible for the fighting effectiveness, management, overall efficiency and morale of their Service. They normally report and tender advice through the Chief of the Defence Staff (CDS) to the Secretary of State while retaining their right of direct access to him and to the Prime Minister. The Chief of the General Staff (CGS) directs the work of the Army in accordance with policy directives and budgets for the main areas of expenditure. Detailed management of the Army is controlled by the Executive Committee of the Army Board, chaired by the CGS.

Each year the MOD publishes a Statement on the Defence Estimate which details British defence planning based on mission types, military activity over the past year and procurement plans for all three Services. It also details expenditure and covers other defence related topics such as arms control and the environment. These annual Statements provide a regular update on the UK's overall defence policy as it develops and describe clearly the influences that affect the defence programme such as the Tri Service nature of defence, the varied roles of the three Services and the cost effectiveness of the resources available. Parliament also obtains information about defence issues in the following ways:

Parliamentary Questions and Parliamentary Enquiries. MPs may ask Parliamentary Questions on any aspect of defence or may write to a defence minister.

The Public Accounts Committee (PAC) and the National Audit Office (NAO). The NAO, headed by the Comptroller and Auditor General (C&AG) and independent of ministerial control, audits departmental accounts to see that public funds have been managed efficiently and for the objects specified by Parliament. These reports are submitted to the Public Accounts Committee.

Select Committees. In addition to the Public Accounts Committee, the House of Commons Defence Committee is the committee principally concerned with the three Services.

Ministry of Defence headquarters, Whitehall, London.

Section 2 National Defence

The purpose of the Ministry of Defence is to define the strategy and maximise, within resources allocated, the defence capability required to:

> Deter any threats to and, if necessary, defend the freedom and territorial integrity of the United Kingdom and its Dependent Territories, including providing support as necessary for the government in countering terrorism;
>
> Contribute to the promotion of the United Kingdom's wider security interests, including the protection and enhancement of freedom and democratic institutions and free trade.

There are some nine overall standing objectives which are set to achieve this aim. Two objectives that affect the Armed Forces directly are to:

> Provide by the most effective means, Armed Forces of appropriate capability, readiness and sustainability to implement our defence strategy, through national, NATO, United Nations, Western European Union and other allied operations as necessary.
>
> Provide the strategic direction on behalf of Her Majesty's Government for the operation of the United Kingdom's Armed Forces, ensuring that the contributions of all three Services are brought together to maximum effect.

There are seven types of mission which the government considers British forces may be engaged in future. They are sub divided into 30 military tasks. The missions are deliberately not placed in any order of priority and comprise:

> Security of the United Kingdom and its citizens in peacetime.
>
> Security of the Dependent Territories.
>
> Defence support to wider British interests.
>
> Support to international order and humanitarian principles.
>
> Regional conflict outside NATO.
>
> Regional conflict inside NATO.
>
> Strategic attack on NATO.

Current Defence Policy

Defence policy forms a key component of a wider security policy. Its purpose remains to contribute to maintaining the freedom and territorial integrity of the United Kingdom and its Dependent Territories, and its ability to pursue its legitimate interests and activities at home and abroad. Since the end of the Cold War there have been welcome reductions in the direct and immediate threat to the UK and that of our allies in Europe; the Armed Forces remain however a standing insurance against the uncertainties of a rapidly changing world.

National security remains inextricably bound up with that of other partners in Europe and the Alliance. It remains an important feature of national defence to sustain the present network of multinational security arrangements. The principle of collective security within the North Atlantic Alliance remains a key element in providing stability and security in Europe and beyond. This is firmly established in Article 5 of the North Atlantic Treaty which quotes that "an armed attack against one or more ally in Europe or North America shall be considered as an attack against them all." This has been recently invoked following the terrorist attacks in New York and Washington in September 2001.

Flexibility, willingness and political will to work with other nations are important factors in achieving collective security. They will be reflected in a need to establish common doctrine and working practices with allies and on interoperability of communications and equipment. Most British forces have primary tasks within the Alliance, but forces assigned to NATO's force structure could be deployed outside the NATO area under national or multinational command should the need arise. Our forces have to be strong enough to deter but also, if deterrence fails, to succeed in all types of conflict including general war. Since 1982 operations in both the Falkland Islands and the Gulf War have under-lined the need to be able to respond to the unexpected.

This need for security continues to have a prior call on the resources including reserves available to meet our defence commitments. Principal concerns for the Army are the provision of forces for the defence of the United Kingdom and those assigned to NATO's Reaction Forces. The latter includes the Headquarters of the ACE Rapid Reaction Corps (ARRC), an Armoured Division based in Germany, and a Mechanised Division and an Airmobile Brigade based in the UK. Both forces are assigned to the Allied Command Europe (ACE) Rapid Reaction Corps (ARRC).

Outside the NATO area threats may arise to our national interest, or military action may become necessary as a result of treaty obligations with other friendly states. The United Kingdom has been and would be prepared to join a United Nations' mandated operation for peacekeeping duties or for the provision of an observer mission where this is appropriate. It may also be in the interests of the Alliance, as well as for the UK, to respond to other challenges overseas. The Fleet reinforced by shipping taken up from trade, long range transport aircraft, a few remaining staging posts, a mid-air refuelling capability and airportable reserves in the United Kingdom provide a limited capacity to operate outside the NATO area of responsibility. For the rapid deployment of a major formation, additional aircraft and strategic shipping would be required in order to deploy a more capable armoured force. At a lower level, duties in the few remaining overseas garrisons, exercises and limited forms of military aid such as sec-onded personnel, training teams and sales groups provide economic but effective ways of promoting and protecting national interests outside the NATO area.

Deploying Military Capabilities

General. The effective conduct of future operations will also depend on all three Services working together in a cohesive joint force. A number of initiatives have been set in hand to enhance this aspect of interoperability. Two of these have come to fruition in the creation of a Permanent Joint Headquarters and of a Joint Rapid Deployment Force. Taken together with other measures, such as the establishment of a Joint Services Command and Staff College, they will over time have a major impact on the way in which the Armed Forces train, prepare and plan for future operations and on the way in which such joint operations are mounted and conducted.

The Permanent Joint Headquarters (PJHQ). The establishment of PJHQ for joint operations enhances the capability of the United Kingdom to respond to the variety of challenges that are likely to be faced in the future. There will, no doubt, be a number of calls upon the United Kingdom to respond to a range of crises and the ability to react swiftly to stabilise a situation before it deteriorates have already been put to the test. PJHQ draws together contingency planning, co-ordinates joint operational activities, joint training and exercises, and is a focus for joint doctrine. Concentrated within PJHQ are those staff required for the planning and execution and budget control of operations.

Operations Room, Permanent Joint Headquarters.

The Joint Rapid Deployment Force (JRDF). The JRDF strengthens the United Kingdom's existing capability to project military power quickly, at short notice worldwide in support of British interests. The core of the JRDF comprises maritime, land and air combat forces, and a variety of Combat Support and Combat Service Support units. Planning to define its missions, concept of operations and core capabilities continues. As 'rapid deployment' implies, elements of a JRDF have to be at high readiness, with a capability for strategic deployment by air or sea. Once in theatre, the Army element of the JRDF relies heavily on the support provided by other elements of the Armed Forces, particularly for firepower and mobility. In principle, any element of forces could be drawn on to contribute to a JRDF operation, and the combat capability (and hence composition) of any deployed force would have to be carefully matched to meet the specific requirements of a particular operation. The key to the JRDF's success is its potential flexibility and responsiveness. These will be improved by extensive joint training and improved interoperable communications. The United Kingdom's armed forces already have a great deal of experience of joint warfare; the JRDF builds on this experience.

Future Planning

Within the MOD there are planning teams working for the CGS who review and evaluate current doctrine, military commitments and force structures. This work is necessary to take account of the changing nature of international security obligations, government policy and the availability of resources to keep up to date with technological research and development. These planning teams make use of operational analysis, war games, developments in foreign armies and lessons learned from current and previous operations. The result of this planning is evaluated and, where appropriate, is endorsed as policy or doctrine and placed in the Army programme for resources and budget allocation.

The Territorial Army (TA)

The TA and the Regular Army are now almost totally integrated together and in recent times this has resulted in TA servicemen and women being employed on operations and taking their part in duties in the Gulf and on NATO operations elsewhere. Training is conducted in the same manner as for the Regular Army except that it will be over a longer period.

There has always been some natural political reluctance to resort to compulsory call-out in circumstances short of general war and this has often precluded the call-out of formed units. This, however, has not prevented the use of substantial numbers of volunteers for duty when needed, particularly in the Gulf and in Bosnia. Changing strategic circumstances, particularly the reduced need for forces to defend the territory of the United Kingdom, have led to a reappraisal of the roles of the Reserve Forces and the overall number of reservists. As a result, the Territorial Army (TA) has been restructured to give it a wider range of capabilities for the range of operations they now expect to face.

The Officer Training Corps (OTC) and the Army Cadet Force (ACF)

The OTC. There are nineteen University-based Officer Training Corps. These aim to give an understanding of the Army, including the TA, to undergraduates and to provide initial training for potential officer recruits for the Army.

The ACF. The Army Cadet Force (ACF) is a voluntary organisation, whose role is to inspire young people between the ages of 13–18 to achieve success for themselves and their local community, and to develop the qualities of good citizenship, responsibility and leadership. The ACF is run by voluntary leaders, part trained by the Army, who manage a broad programme of military, sporting and adventurous training activities and skills attracting vocational qualifications, all designed to help the cadets gain employment and improve the quality of their lives.

SECTION 3 NATO

Background

Since NATO's foundation in 1949 all developments in its strategic doctrine have been geared to the fulfilment of its essential role: to safeguard the freedom and security of its member nations by political and military means in accordance with the principles of the United Nations Charter. The Alliance's primary task, as a purely defensive organisation, has always been and will continue to be that of deterring aggression against its members. Article 5 of the Treaty, spells out in unambiguous terms the nature of this deterrence. Deterrence is the thread which runs unbroken through NATO's history, adapted as necessary to meet changing threats and risks.

A strategic concept underlines NATO's core security functions. The Alliance continues to serve as the principal foundation of security in Europe, to deter aggression, mainly in the form of a general war offensive against its members individually and collectively. It also acts as a forum for transatlantic co-operation on security matters in Europe. In future though, these functions will be fulfilled by a greater emphasis on the political aspects of security, with increased dialogue and co-operation, enabling additional member nations to build on the benefits gained in the West by the commitment to collective defence. The credibility of NATO's military strategy, developed to reflect the improvements in the Alliance, however remains the ultimate guarantor of the security of its members and the basis for their ability to make still wider contributions to peace and liberty in Europe.

The Alliance's military strategy continues to be based on the principle that any aggression will be met with the minimum force needed to restore territorial integrity. The nature of this response, which includes a nuclear deterrent force[1], depends on the political and military circumstances. Force levels are smaller in total than those of the Cold War era and it is not necessary to station so large a proportion as hitherto in forward deployments, especially in the Central Region. Forces are more flexible, to meet the wider variety of possible threats which now include peace support operations and will become more multinational to underline Alliance solidarity in a crisis. This post Cold War era strategy provides the principles and guidelines which underpin the Alliance's new force posture.

[1] Nuclear forces belong to sovereign members of the Alliance and remain at all times under national control.

Force Structures for NATO Forces

General. The agreement reached between Presidents Bush and Yeltsin in 1992 to decommission all land-based ICBMs, to reduce strategic nuclear warheads to between 3000–5000 and for all tactical nuclear missiles to be withdrawn from deployed locations and destroyed, established a new East–West relationship. Conventional arms control agreements (CFE and others) have also helped to establish a new security environment. NATO's former strategy of flexible response was no longer necessary and a new military strategy has been fashioned for NATO assigned forces.

NATO Air Defence. NATO has for many years fielded an Alliance-wide air defence system, NATO Air Defence Ground Environment (NADGE) stretching

NATO headquarters, Brussels, Belgium.

SHAPE headquarters, near Mons, Belgium.

from Northern Norway to Eastern Turkey. This system maintains a continuous early warning of potentially hostile aircraft or missiles approaching NATO's air space. The NATO Airborne Early Warning force (NAEW) complements the NADGE by deploying aircraft to fill the gap in radar capacity which may exist at low altitudes and to control any interceptor aircraft sent to challenge potential intruders.

NATO Communications. An effective system to give early warning of any form of attack needs efficient and secure communications. An Alliance-wide system in which every NATO capital and major NATO Command Headquarters is linked with a computerised network of secure teleprinter links and a satellite system is now in place. This is complemented by a Situations Centre located at Brussels which is the focal point for all NATO communications.

The Operational Framework. Strategic nuclear forces, albeit reduced, are still necessary to deter a major war and to counter possible threats from states outside the NATO area which either possess or may develop a nuclear capability. NATO forces will no longer be tied to the defence of specific areas in peacetime nor will they rely on tactical nuclear firepower. Instead, NATO forces will be organised for conventional defence in three echelons:

- Reaction Forces.
    - Immediate Reaction Forces (IRF).
    - Rapid Reaction Forces (RRF).
- Main Defence Forces.
- Augmentation Forces.

Immediate Reaction Forces. A constant problem facing NATO during the Cold War was the threat of a limited attack on the flanks which could have destablised the cohesion of the Alliance. To offset this risk NATO created the allied force known as the ACE Mobile Force (AMF). It is still extant and comprises both a land component (AMF(L)) and an air component (AMF(A)). The AMF(L) has a permanent allied commander responsible directly to SACEUR and a small headquarters located at Heidelberg in Germany staffed by allied officers. Six or more allied battalion groups are assigned to the force which can be airlifted at short notice to any threatened area to present an aggressor with a military force which indicates the cohesion of NATO's resolve. On deployment the AMF(A), with up to four squadrons of aircraft, is placed under command of the senior NATO air commander of the area in which it is to operate. All but the US units are based in their own countries in peacetime. NATO maintains a standing naval presence in the Atlantic (STANAVFORLANT). The force comprises a squadron of frigates or destroyers with afloat support; as crews and ships rotate periodically, the training and value of this combined force is appreciated throughout the Allied navies. NATO also maintain a Standing Naval Force in the Mediterranean, known as STANAVFORMED and a Standing Naval Mine Countermeasure Force (SNMF). These naval forces also form part of NATO's Immediate Reaction Forces.

Rapid Reaction Forces. The forces will include naval and air units but the land element consists of the Allied Command Europe (ACE) Rapid Reaction Corps (ARRC), available for deployment. The ARRC can command up to four divisions and combat support units. There are permanently assigned divisions and other assigned allied formations which the ARRC can deploy to suit the type of operation to be undertaken. Both British divisions, (1 (UK) Div and 3 (UK) Div), are permanently assigned. Another permanently assigned division is the Multi National Division (MND) (C). A further brigade-sized formation, the United Kingdom–Netherlands Amphibious Force, normally assigned to SACLANT, may be available to augment the ARRC should the Force not be needed in the Northern Region of NATO. A division drawn from Southern Command (AF SOUTH) is also planned to be assigned to the ARRC.

Main Defence Forces. Seven other corps, all except for 3 (GE) Corps based in what was Eastern Germany with divisions drawn from different nations, make up the Main Defence Forces for NATO in Europe in the event of major aggression. Together they represent about 65% of NATO's forces in Central Europe.

Augmentation Forces. A further 25% of NATO's forces are held at lower states of readiness within the member states of Europe and the United States. Consisting of reserve as well as regular units, they will require some time to mobilise.

Partnership for Peace

The objective of Partnership for Peace (PfP) is to enhance security in Europe by deepening the political and military ties between NATO and Central and East European states. The PfP programme offers close co-operation in fields such as the preparation of forces for use in peacekeeping and humanitarian operations. Participation in the programme also assists those Partners who aspire to NATO membership in the evolutionary process leading to their integration. By 1995 25 states had joined the Allies in the programme, which now has a broader membership than the North Atlantic Co-operation Council from which PfP was developed. Detailed Individual Partnership Programmes have been agreed with Albania, Bulgaria, Estonia, Finland, Latvia, Lithuania, Romania, Slovakia and Sweden. There are Partnership Offices at NATO Headquarters in Brussels and in the Partnership Co-ordination Cell at SHAPE (Supreme Headquarters Allied Powers Europe) which co-ordinates practical co-operation activities.

Non Article 5 Operations

General. In other areas of the world outbreaks of violence in unstable areas may jeopardise a fragile status quo and pose further threats to regional stability. During the Cold War the Soviet Union was able to exploit unrest outside NATO's defensive area by use of the veto within the UN. While the East–West nuclear balance led to an uneasy truce it was difficult to resolve conflicts which involved states closely connected by other links with the Soviet Union. Countries in less

Partnership for Peace signing ceremony.

stable regions such as the Middle East acquired massive quantities of arms from individual states in both the East and West. While the Soviet Union's successor states are currently preoccupied with their internal problems and super power relations remain at a friendly level, it is possible to resolve some of the world's serious problems without the risk of an East–West crisis. The allied build-up in the Gulf and the United Nations Security Council Resolution of November 1990 authorising the use of force if Iraq did not withdraw from Kuwait would not have been possible during the Cold War.

NATO Operations Outside the Alliance Area. With, its Intervention Force (IFOR) NATO deployed for the first time outside the Alliance area in December 1995. This deployment in Bosnia replaced UN Forces and was to carry out certain particular military tasks while other diplomatic and political initiatives were set in hand. This is an example of the sort of involvement by NATO, which includes non NATO forces, outside its territorial boundaries, acting on behalf of the UN for a specific period of time and may well be the forerunner of other similar types of activity.

Developments within NATO

Changes in structure and command arrangements are now being developed within NATO as a result of these new tasks. Command headquarters, which previously were static and in hardened bunkers' may well need to be capable of deployment to locations outside NATO's traditional boundaries. The establishment of Combined Joint Task Force HQs is under active development and the level and status of other HQs may well change altogether.

A potential change in the overall structure of the NATO Alliance could now occur because Poland, Hungary and the Czech Republic have joined the Alliance and more nations could join in the next few years. This action could well alter the overall strategic role for NATO and its security arrangements over the next few years.

SECTION 4 OTHER INTERNATIONAL OBLIGATIONS

Background

The United Kingdom also has other international defence obligations which stem from treaties, formal commitments with other Allies and informal arrangements developed since the end of the Second World War. In most embassies there are Defence Sections which provide military contact with a host nation. Staff talks are held regularly with allied partners and there are many other bilateral and multilateral military meetings with Allies in which defence business is conducted. The most important of these international obligations are listed in the next paragraphs.

Western European Union (WEU)

Under the arrangements agreed at Maastricht in 1991, the Western European Union (WEU) began to be developed in a dual capacity: as the defence component of the European Union; and as the European pillar of NATO. It has created links with the countries of Central and Eastern Europe, with the offer of 'Associate Partner' status to Bulgaria, Hungary, Poland, Romania, the Czech Republic, Slovakia, Estonia, Latvia and Lithuania. The new status gives these nations the opportunity to participate in WEU Council meetings, to contribute forces to WEU operations and to establish links with WEU planning bodies. The WEU now has ten 'Full Members', three 'Associate Members', five 'Observers' and nine 'Associate Partners'.

The WEU has developed an agreed position on the formulation of a common European defence policy and has continued work on the further development of its operational capability to carry out peacekeeping, humanitarian relief and other tasks. The WEU has been closely involved in work at NATO Headquarters on a project which will provide NATO facilities for operations under WEU direction and control. Multinational exercises play an important part in developing the WEU's capabilities. It is clear that there will be more progress towards the harmonisation of defence issues between NATO and the WEU over the next few years as closer and more integrated links within Europe are achieved.

America Britain Canada Australia (ABCA) Basic Standardisation Agreement

The ABCA Standardisation Agreement was started in 1947 by the first three named nations (Australia joined in 1964 and New Zealand joined as observers in 1965), to continue the standardisation of equipments and procedures within their national armies. This agreement preceded the forming of NATO in 1949 and although operating in the shadow of NATO since then has produced significant levels of standardisation and co-operation particularly during the Korean War of 1950–53. In recent years, exercises have been added to the programme of work and a system of common procedures for use when operating in coalitions has been adopted.

The need for this standardisation work has become more obvious since the Gulf War (1991) and its overall value appreciated in an era when coalitions and groupings of nations perhaps operating on behalf of the UN are seen as a major method by which the resolution of conflict and peace support operations can be achieved.

FINABEL

FINABEL is an informal grouping of European nations set up by France in 1953 (France, Italy, Netherlands, Allemagne (Germany), Belgium and Luxembourg). The UK joined in 1973, Spain in 1990 and Greece and Portugal in 1996. The army staff of each nation meet regularly to discuss topics of mutual defence Interest. The aim for FINABEL is the harmonisation of ground forces' practices, procedures and doctrine across the spectrum of military conflict, but principally at the tactical level.

Currently emphasis is given to multinational and peace support operations. Some of the British Army's current influence in Europe in the promulgation of its work on a doctrine for peace operations has been facilitated by its membership of FINABEL. It should be noted that member nations are not bound by treaty or agreement to the organisation. Implementation of any FINABEL study recommendations is thus entirely voluntary. In practical terms the studies tend to be viewed as providing insight into European views on particular military ideas and developments without any political overtones.

Five Power Defence Arrangements (FPDA)

The FPDA was established after the British withdrawal from the Far East in 1971. The nations involved are the United Kingdom, Malaysia, Australia, Singapore and New Zealand and the defence arrangements cover the commitment of these nations to the defence of Malaysia and Singapore.

The FPDA is co-ordinated by the High Commissioners and Defence Attachés of the five nations in a co-ordinating committee (FCC). Military activity is covered by the MODs of the five nations with their in-country Defence Attachés' meeting every six months in Singapore or Malaysia. All three Services of the five nations take part in an annual combined exercise hosted by one of the participants.

Political Control

Just as armed force is the servant of policy so the use of military force is a matter for political control at the highest levels of government. Military operations can never be divorced from political control. The government selects and defines the security and defence aims. The MOD then has its own defence objectives to give effect to these aims. It identifies forces and capabilities to carry out military tasks. There is thus an explicit link between policy goals and forces to achieve them.

In peacetime, defence policy is designed to support the overall security policy which the government designates and is normally based on those international security structures (NATO, WEU, UN) and other institutions which promote peace and international stability. In war or times of national emergency the government will decide on the overall political aim. To fulfil the government's intentions the MOD selects a military aim, or perhaps a series of aims, designed to achieve a favourable military situation to support the overall aim. This in turn should allow the government to negotiate or to impose a settlement to accomplish national security aims from a position of strength.

The next stage would be the production of a broad strategic plan incorporating the government's political guidance within which a military commander should be free to exercise control over the operational employment of the allocated forces. A clear understanding of the political objectives is essential to the proper conduct of operations. The government may impose some restrictions on the use of force which reflect political considerations, such as the need to ensure domestic support for the war effort, to make a favourable impression on world opinion in general and our allies in particular, or to avoid unnecessary civilian casualties. When there is a possibility that the level of conflict may escalate, especially if there is a risk that nuclear weapons might be used, major military decisions will require political clearance. Internal security and counter-insurgency operations will normally be conducted within a very tight political framework and with Rules of Engagement (ROE) to control the use of force. Regional war, by definition, implies a clear measure of political control.

Consequently, political aims and restraints will determine strategy. These restraints may impose restrictions on the use of certain weapons and so influence tactics. While military commanders have to accept political direction and constraints on the application of force, should these restrictions hazard the safety of their troops or jeopardise the achievement of an aim they should point this out to the political authorities through the appropriate ministers. When British forces are acting within the framework of an alliance such as NATO, the military chain of command would be through the Supreme Allied Commander to the appropriate political authority although a British subordinate commander would always retain a national channel to the MOD. Similar arrangements would be made if a coalition of allied partners were formed to deal with particular circumstances.

Modern communications enable a government to exercise close control over the conduct of a campaign once R has been launched. Commanders have to appreciate the political pressures which will influence the conduct of military operations. They have to keep their military superiors in the chain of command fully aware of their future intentions in time to obtain political guidance, should this be necessary. Similarly, they have to report their operations in sufficient detail to enable the government to assess the political as well as the military implications. There may be occasions when, in the light of these broader considerations, a commander in the field is urged to adopt a course which he considers to be unsound on military grounds. Given tact and understanding of both points of view, such problems can be resolved with the minimum of friction, although this has caused real problems for military commanders in the past.

Political Advice

As can be seen from the preceding paragraphs a military commander has to be fully aware of the political implications (both to the United Kingdom and internationally) of all his military actions. In general war the need for political advice will probably only be necessary at the higher levels of command. In other types of conflict, and particularly in Operations Other Than War (OOTW) political advice, even at a lower formation level, may well be necessary for a commander when dealing with a complex and difficult situation involving many parties and potential belligerents. The operations in Bosnia are a good example of this requirement. In multinational operations a suitably qualified political adviser able to assist a commander and his staff will be an essential part of any future formation staff.

Public Opinion

In no other national enterprise is public support more important for success than in the prosecution of war. Unity and resolution within the UK are essential if it is to withstand the shocks, accept the casualties and bear the privations involved. By bringing the war to every household, the media exercises a powerful influence on public opinion. Modern technology and the international profusion of media channels means that the commander and even a national government cannot exercise any significant degree of control over the contents of broadcast material and programmes. All servicemen have to be aware that any loose talk or unfavourable activity can and probably could be on the world's TV screens within minutes. This is particularly important to appreciate because once military operations have started well handled public relations could play an important role in influencing opinion and make a major contribution to the morale of the nation and the Armed Forces. Reports from the theatre of operations have to be quick and accurate so that the nation's position can be put convincingly to both domestic and foreign audiences.

The sympathy of allies and friendly states is indispensable for international, diplomatic, economic and financial support. Influencing public opinion amongst neutral and potentially hostile nations is equally important if they are to regard our actions favourably or at least remain neutral. Public opinion in a hostile or neutral nation should not be neglected. Military action likely to inflame it unnecessarily and harden an enemy's resolve should be avoided. On the other hand everything should be done to undermine an enemy's resolution and to enlist international sympathy for national objectives. This is the task of diplomacy and, where appropriate, information operations. As an adjunct of overall policy, this would be controlled by the appropriate government agencies, although the Army may be called upon for assistance.

A military commander will receive political guidance on these matters through the Chief of Defence Staff. He will be supported by a public relations staff and, where necessary, by a political adviser. He can contribute by being fully aware of the problem and by making sure that nothing is done which might prejudice national and world opinion. As a corollary he will do everything possible to present the actions and attitudes of his forces in a favourable light to the public and agencies of the media.

Since it is unlikely that the UK would be acting alone but alongside other partners (such as UN, NATO or OSCE), many of the issues of public concern and opinion will be the responsibility of the multinational organisation controlling the Theatre of Operations and hence there may well be differing controls and restraints on the means available to influence public opinion.

Relations with the Civil Authorities

Military commanders at every level have to be prepared to co-operate harmoniously with their allies and the Civil Authorities at home and abroad. When a force is operating in support of the latter the situation may be very delicate. In general the paramountcy of the Civil Authorities has to be recognised. Commanders should advise them as to the best military course of action, meet their wishes whenever possible but bear in mind their responsibilities for those they command. Good relations with the Civil Authorities require tact, tolerance, understanding, persuasiveness and, especially when a vital principle is at stake, honesty and firmness. In counter-insurgency and internal security operations a similar close and cordial relationship with the police and other security authorities is just as necessary because their active and willing co-operation is essential to the success of any such operation. Links between the Army and the security authorities should be established and maintained on a routine basis when conditions are normal so that when an emergency arises a good working relationship and procedures already exist.

Wherever the Army operates overseas, whether within the context of a NATO operation or in support of the UN or an ally elsewhere, it will expect to receive host nation assistance. Help may range from the use of port, airport, rail and transport facilities, the provision of accommodation, the employment of local labour and access to the telecommunication network and to the supply of rations, fuel and common user items. Such assistance is arranged by formal agreement between the United Kingdom and the host nation government, either in advance in furtherance of an established treaty commitment, or at the time in the case of an unforeseen emergency.

Within the Army, government civil servants work alongside their military counterparts at many headquarters and other establishments, Army schools and in training establishments. At the MOD, civil servants work in an integrated organisation alongside Service colleagues to monitor and develop the government's defence policies and to keep control over public funds. These responsibilities are reflected down the chain of command. Commanders at almost all levels have access to advice on civil affairs, the law, budgetary and financial matters, public relations and links with media agencies.

SECTION 6 LEGAL CONSTRAINTS ON THE USE OF FORCE

Background

All too often, the law of armed conflict is seen as at best irrelevant and at worst a positive hindrance to the effective conduct of military operations. Yet this law is of the greatest importance to a commander. If he orders his troops to take action contrary to the Geneva Conventions or any of the other protocols and agreed conventions he exposes them to the risk of reprisals by the enemy and makes himself liable for trial as a war criminal. In an era when most conflicts are fought in the full glare of the media, allegations of atrocities can alienate important allies and neutral governments and undermine support for the Armed Forces amongst the public within the UK.

Moreover, the assumption that the law of armed conflict is an obstacle to the effective conduct of military operations is a misconception. It is true that the law imposes important limitations on a commander, requiring him, for example, to accept constraints on the conduct of operations in order to spare the civilian population. For the most part, however, the law of armed conflict reinforces, rather than contradicts, good military practice. Attacks against civilians, the ill-treatment of prisoners of war, the looting of enemy property are not only wrong, they are actions which make no military sense, diverting resources from the effective conduct of operations and frequently having a corrosive and serious effect upon discipline.

International law today generally forbids a State to initiate hostilities, yet the law of armed conflict then lays down how those hostilities have to be conducted in the event that this occurs. Moreover, the law of armed conflict applies with equal force to both sides in a conflict, irrespective of which side is the aggressor. The equal application of these laws to aggressor and victim alike reflects the fact that, since no State involved in a conflict will normally concede that it is the aggressor, any attempt to apply different rules to the aggressor and thus to benefit the victim would be likely to end in a total disregard for the law of armed conflict by both parties.

Unlike the United Kingdom, international society has no parliament which can create new rules for international law binding on the entire international community. Rules of international law are derived for the most part from treaties – agreements between States – and 'custom' – law which has been created over time by the practice of States. Most of the law of armed conflict is now the subject of treaty provisions but these treaties are binding only in conflicts between States which have become parties to the treaties concerned.

In the case of the Geneva Conventions of 1949 this causes no problems, because virtually every State in the world is party to the Conventions. The 1977 Additional Protocols to the Geneva Conventions are a different matter, since a number of major States have not yet ratified these Additional Protocols. The same applies for the UN Conventional Weapons Convention 1977 and 1980. Even though a treaty may not be binding as such, however, its provisions may still be important if they are regarded as authoritative statements of customary rules, ie of rules which have come to be accepted in State practice as part of the unwritten body of customary law, since customary law is binding upon all States.

Apart from their continued obligation to military law, covered in the Manual of Military Law, servicemen and women are also subject to the law of armed conflict as expressed in various Conventions, Treaties and Protocols. The details of these obligations are recorded in an Army publication *A Soldier's Guide to the Law of Armed Conflict*. There is a mandatory requirement for these provisions to be included in all military training programmes and widely disseminated throughout the Army.

General Principles

The principle that the choice of means and methods of warfare is not unlimited became firmly established in the 20th century. The principle is not related to any particular weapon system. The regulations involved in the law of armed conflict cover many areas of combat and the conduct of belligerents and others in wartime. In outline these cover such matters as:

- Limitations on the Means and Methods of Warfare.
- Unnecessary Suffering.
- The Principle of Humanity.
- Distinction between Combatants and Non Combatants.
- Treatment of Prisoners of War.
- Treatment of the Civil Population.
- Limitations of Attacks on Military Objectives.
- The Rule of Proportionality.
- Indiscriminate Attacks.
- Reprisals.

The Geneva Conventions

In international law the Geneva Conventions are probably the most widely known. The 1949 Geneva Conventions deal with persons likely to be affected by war and their protection from the effects of hostilities. Their main relevance for the combatant is in respect of prisoner of war rights and conditions, and the status of protected persons.

Additional Protocol One is principally concerned with international conflicts, including wars of national liberation, and the protection of civilians. It defines the limitations on the conduct of operations and imposes a number of prohibitions and restraints on combatants, infringements of which are classified as grave breaches and regarded as war crimes. The Protocol also requires that commanders ensure their subordinates are aware of the law of armed conflict and that they are obliged to prevent breaches of this law. In the latter case commanders at all levels could be held personally responsible for breaches committed by their subordinates. Additional Protocol Two is a declaration of principles relating to the protection of victims of non-international armed conflict.

The Geneva Conventions and the Additional Protocols have been incorporated into two Acts of Parliament – the Geneva Conventions Acts of 1956 and 1995 respectively. Thus non-compliance would represent a clear breach of United Kingdom law.

Law of Armed Conflict

The law incorporates the four Geneva Conventions of 1949 and the two 1977 Additional Protocols to the Convention. Nations which have ratified the Conventions and Additional Protocols are required to comply with these, which now form part of international law.

The fundamental concept of the law is the direct relationship between military objectives and humanitarian concerns, known as the doctrine of proportionality (Additional Protocol One). Nations should refrain from attacks which may be expected to cause collateral damage which would be excessive in relation to the concrete and direct military advantage anticipated. Commanders have to recognise that military necessity is the benchmark against which to assess the likely humanitarian consequences of an attack.

Treaties

With the passage of time a number of treaties have been drawn up, normally in peacetime, to take account of events, developments and experience of hostilities with a view to ameliorating unnecessary suffering. These treaties are normally a compromise between military and humanitarian interests.

Some of the more prominent, and recent treaties are listed below:

Geneva Convention I for the Amelioration of the Condition of the Wounded and Sick in Armed Forces in the Field, 1949.

Geneva Convention II for the Amelioration of the Conditions of Wounded, Sick and Shipwrecked Members of Armed Forces at Sea, 1949.

Geneva Convention III Relative to the Treatment of Prisoners of War, 1949.

Geneva Convention IV Relative to the Protection of Civilian Persons in Time of War, 1949.

United Nations Convention on the Prohibition of Military or Any Other Hostile Use of Environmental Modification Techniques, 1977.

Convention for the Protection of Cultural Property in the Event of Armed Conflict, 1954.

Convention on the Prohibition of the Development, Production and Stockpiling of Bacteriological (Biological) and Toxin Weapons and their Destruction, 1972.

Geneva Protocol I Additional to the Geneva Conventions of 1949, and Relating to the Protection of Victims of International Armed Conflicts, 1977.

Geneva Protocol II Additional to the Geneva Conventions of 1949, and Relating to the Protection of Victims of Non-international Armed Conflicts, 1977.

United Nations Convention on Prohibition or Restrictions on the Use of Conventional Weapons Which May be Deemed to be Excessively Injurious or to Have Indiscriminate Effects and Protocols, 1977 and 1980. (Protocol I, which covers the use of laser-blinding equipments and Protocol II which covers the use of anti-personnel mines.)

Chemical Weapons Convention, 1992.

Rules of Engagement (ROE)

Rules of Engagement (ROE) define the degree and manner in which force may be applied and are designed to ensure that such application of force is carefully controlled. ROE are approved by ministers and issued to operational commanders by MOD before operations begin. Changes to ROE can only be approved by ministers. ROE authorising messages will contain guidance on government policy and intentions, to assist commanders with regard to their plans.

ROE inform commanders of the limits or constraints imposed, or of freedom permitted, to carry out their assigned tasks. If a commander at any level considers he requires a change to the extant ROE profile in order to carry out his task he should request a change, with justification. This request should be made as soon as the need is identified. It should be noted however that the inherent right of self-defence is not affected by any ROE.

Status of Forces Agreement

For a national, or international, military force to have a lawful presence within a particular State requires the consent of that State. That consent should be formalised by an agreement between the nation, or international organisation, providing the force and the host nation through a Status of Forces Agreement (SOFA).

The SOFA regulates in detail the activities of the force and individual members of the force concerning freedom of movement, use of host nation facilities, liaison and any privileges and immunities for the members of that force. Normally arrangements for any SOFA would be handled by the Army Legal Service on behalf of the MOD.

Legal Advice

Experience has shown that it is essential for a commander to have a legal adviser to act in a similar manner to that of the political adviser. Both advisors should be fully involved in all significant decisions made by a commander. The difficulties of charting a sensible military course of action through the potential political and legal minefields cannot be overstated. Recourse to legal advice before military actions are set in hand is essential, particularly in a multi national environment.

CHAPTER 2 THE DOCTRINAL BACKGROUND

Section 1 The Relevance of Doctrine

Background

Military doctrine can guide commanders in their military thinking, its purpose being to teach soldiers how to think, and not what to think. The Army definition states that 'military doctrine is a formal expression of military knowledge and thought, that the Army accepts as being relevant at a given time, which covers the nature of current and future conflicts, the preparation of the Army for such conflicts and the methods of engaging in them to achieve success'. Military doctrine lies at the heart of the Army's business. Its ultimate purpose is success on operations. If it is to have any utility it has to be effective in all parts of the Army, and also provide the rationale for the research and development, operational analysis, equipment procurement, organisations and structures, leadership and training. Doctrine gives all these functions a sense of direction - a common purpose. It is described in a series of publications, manuals, handbooks and *aides-mémoire*.

The Importance of Doctrine

"The central idea and purpose for an army is known as its doctrine, which to be sound has to be based on the principles of war, and which to be effective has to be elastic enough to admit of mutation in accordance with change in circumstance. In its ultimate relationship to the human understanding this central idea or doctrine is nothing else than common sense - that is, action adapted to circumstance."

MAJOR GENERAL F C FULLER[1]

The relevance and importance of doctrine is hard to overstate and it is appropriate to reiterate that the Army, like many comparable organisations, has a requirement to be able to resolve complex activity. Warfare is an activity for which few hard and fast rules can exist. At low levels activities can be reduced to a number of drills. An Army that is to succeed in war has to have the ability to adapt rapidly to changing circumstances to endure chaotic conditions. For

[1] Major General F C Fuller, *The Foundations of the Science of War*, 1926.

this mere drills will not suffice. If it is to represent an effective deterrent in peacetime, an army has to be seen to be physically capable of fighting and mentally and morally prepared to do so. Such an army has to be clear how the complex situations, difficulties and hardships that will inevitably arise in war are to be tackled. Conduct of war is a matter of applying both science and art. Captain Liddell Hart explained that, 'war is a science which depends upon art for its application. The Army's doctrine has to attend to both aspects, but military doctrine should seek primarily to influence the way in which its officers and non-commissioned officers think. Hence the function of any military doctrine is to establish the framework of understanding of the approach to warfare – not a set of rules but to provide direction as an aid to understanding.'

The major component of any military doctrine is past experience and it is important that there is a proper awareness of how the doctrine has been developed over time. It should be noted that doctrine should be relevant for the past, the present and the future in the following ways:

The timeless, intellectual component – those enduring tenets, the lessons from history and experience embodied in the Principles of War.

The practical and dynamic component – which takes those timeless elements, and interprets and applies them in the light of current circumstances.

The predictive component – which takes the current element, and the trends in operations, technology and the potential for future warfare in order to apply them to force development.

The Place of Doctrine

While military doctrine can be described as what is taught there are major and distinct differences of content between, for instance, the application of the principles of war in a theatre of operations, and the tactical techniques needed to set an ambush. Doctrine splits naturally into principles, practices and procedures and the British Army makes use of this natural split to assign a form of hierarchy to their doctrinal publications.

Within the Army at the highest command level doctrine carries the authority of the Chief of the General Staff (CGS) and covers strategic and operational level issues recorded in an Army Doctrinal Publication (ADP). At the tactical level, doctrine provides the main body of instruction within the Army. This normally appears in publications sponsored by the Ministry of Defence (MOD). The Army Field Manual (AFM) series, together with the range of subsidiary handbooks and Tactical Aides Memoire, provides the core of tactical doctrine.

The diagram below shows these levels of doctrine related to the functions they perform.

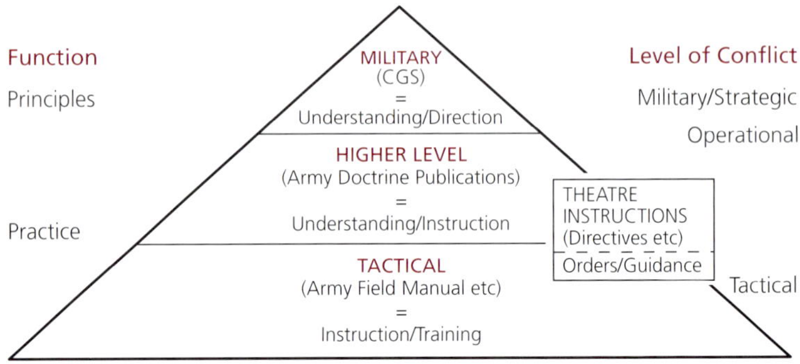

The application of doctrine does not imply the formulating of rules and regulations that have to be followed, but establishes a framework of understanding and is an aid to thinking, often in situations that can change rapidly and has a natural tendency to degenerate into chaos. The value of doctrine lies in the mechanisms it provides to incorporate change. It also encourages continuity and consistency to military thinking and to articulate, discuss and determine relative priorities.

Development of Doctrine

A military doctrine cannot be regarded as absolute or set in tablets of stone, but if properly founded on principles it will be enduring and have authority and substance. It should however be responsive to changing situations and the development of both the science and the art of warfare. Military experience provides doctrine's enduring quality but resources, technology, experiment and the changing nature of alliances and social developments are factors that could affect the context of doctrine and thus lead to its alteration or replacement.

Military doctrine is applicable to all types of warfare. It is as relevant to peace support operations and counter-insurgency as to general or regional conflict. While there is very little evidence concerning the nature of nuclear, chemical or biological operations, no specific doctrinal guidelines can be set, although there is no reason to suppose that the current doctrine would not be suitable for such operations if they occur.

For a more complete understanding of doctrine and its development it is necessary to be familiar with the current doctrine and more particularly how this has been developed from hard won experience gained in conflict.

Section 2 The Concept of Fighting Power

Introduction

Fighting embraces more than just physical contact with an enemy or disrupting the enemy's will and cohesion. It also involves surviving in different types of environment. While resisting the stress that an opponent is attempting to impose, a military commander has to impose on an enemy so great a degree of physical and moral stress that he is compelled to abandon his objective. To succeed, an army needs to be able to rationalise and to work through the chaos of war. A clear doctrine and all that stems from it is an important ingredient in that success. Many point to the role that luck has to play in the outcome of conflict but luck tends to favour those commanders who have prepared themselves and their soldiers both mentally and physically for what they have to do.

The Components of Fighting Power

The term 'fighting power' defines an army's ability to fight. These components of Fighting Power are reproduced below:

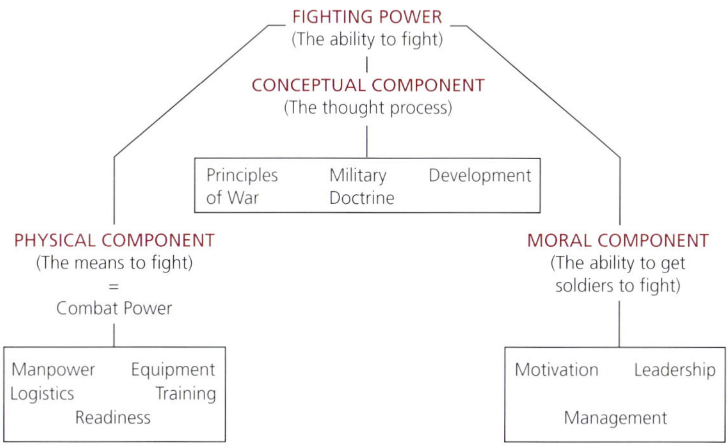

In outline the three components of fighting power are:

> *The Conceptual Component.* The thought process behind military actions that involve the Principles of War, doctrine and development of military forces and equipment for the future.
>
> *The Moral Component – the Ability to get Soldiers to Fight.* The ability to get soldiers to fight has four fundamental elements: the motivation to achieve the task in hand; effective leadership from those placed in authority; adequate and appropriate welfare provision; and sound management of all personnel and resources.

The Physical Component – Combat Power. Combat power furnishes the means to fight; the equipment, resources and organisation which are needed to be employed in combat. It should be created in peace, adjusted and enhanced for a specific operation when conflict threatens and committed and sustained once conflict is joined.

The Development of Fighting Power

All three components have to be adapted and developed as time passes and circumstances change. The conceptual component is particularly important because although fundamental principles do not change, doctrine has to reflect the conditions and constraints applicable to the Army at the time. How doctrine has changed and develops is covered in the subsequent Sections of this Chapter.

Aspects of the moral component and the ability to get soldiers to fight are covered in Chapters 6 and 7 which deal with command, training, provision of operational welfare support and the effective management of soldiers. Examples of achieving good morale and leadership are given in Annex A at the back of the book.

The physical component is indirectly covered in the Chapter on training, but as can be noted by a reading of the 10 examples of the Principles of War in Annex A it is not difficult to see the conceptual, moral and physical components of fighting power in all the examples chosen. Perhaps the breakout of 1st Panzer Division at Moscow in December 1941 exemplifies this best in conditions that almost defy belief and which goes well beyond most modern day experience for British soldiers.

In national terms, achieving better combat power is the essence of British defence procurement policy. This seeks to improve the resources and equipment available to the Army in order to provide the appropriate capability to carry out these defence policy commitments. The Army have adopted a matrix system of evaluation to measure fighting power within formation and this is the basic management tool for planning deployments and fresh commitments. The funding and allocation of resources are recorded in the annual Statement of Defence Expenditure (SDE) which is published each June. These Statements give an updated picture on the current and projected funding and allocation of those resources which, in turn, have a direct bearing on combat power in the Army and hence its future capability to operate effectively.

Section 3 The Principles of War

The Art of War

A study of the history of war reveals that its conduct is influenced by certain broad precepts which have come to be recognised as Principles of War. Revolutions in technology, developments in weaponry and improvements in mobility have wrought changes in the application of these principles without detracting from their general validity. Dissimilarities in scale, geography, history and commitments colour the manner in which different nations conduct military operations. Aside from these differences, war is a part of human behaviour where personality and emotion play a large part. In theory subject to the political and legal restraints indicated in Chapter 1, a commander is able to deploy and employ forces and resources in any suitable way to achieve his military aim. Warfare changes and develops as politics, technology and perceptions change everyday life and conditions. The British Principles of War reflect the particular circumstances of the United Kingdom. Ten separate Principles were codified and established by Field Marshal Montgomery as CGS soon after the Second World War ended. These have been used by the Army since then and have in recent times been endorsed by the two other Services. Other nations make use of some or all of these Principles of War, often with different titles and emphasis.

The principles influence the conduct of operations in their widest sense. They are especially relevant at the strategic level where they provide criteria against which courses of action affecting the national interest or the planning of a campaign may be tested. They also have a direct application at lower levels where they provide a guide for the planning and conduct of operations on the battlefield. However, they are not like the laws of natural science, where the observance of specific conditions produces a predictable result; nor are they like the rules of a game, a breach of which entails a prescribed penalty. Rather they are guides to action or fundamental tenets forming a basis for appreciating a situation and planning, but their relevance, applicability and relative importance change with the circumstances. In the past their application with judgement and common sense has led to victory. Disregard for them involves risk and could lead to failure.

In Annex A there are examples for each Principle of War taken from the Second World War onwards, which cover several different armies and situations. These demonstrate the international applicability of the principles even though techniques and tactics may vary. Success in the future will however not be gained by a slavish imitation of the past. Rather the lessons of history should serve to illuminate the present and inspire future commanders to conceive original ways of applying the principles to defeat an enemy. The ten principles are explained here in more precise detail. With the exception of the first principle, undue emphasis should not be accorded to the order in which the others are placed. Indeed their application should be viewed in a collective manner and not individually. Only when treated in this way will the principles become dynamic and have positive application rather than as a check list to ensure tactical compliance.

The Selection and Maintenance of the Aim

In the conduct of a war as a whole, and in every military operation, it is essential to select and define the aim clearly. The ultimate aim could be the complete overthrow of a hostile government, or it may be more limited, such as the recovery of disputed territory. Within the political framework set by the government a commander may have a choice of courses of action, each of which would fulfil the aim. The commander's estimate will determine which of the possible courses is most likely to succeed. This will be expressed as a mission and plan.

The operation could be broken down into phases and again into particular forms of operation. While planning in outline will continue for the long term it may be contingent on achieving success in the current phase. Only in the current phase will intelligence normally be sufficiently detailed and reliable to produce a specific and clearly realisable initial aim for which a firm plan can be made. The selection of the aim is thus one of a commander's most important duties, demanding clear and logical thought. Depending on the operation the aim may be very precise, as for a deliberate attack, or it may be expressed in broad terms, as in the case of a pursuit. Whatever the circumstances the aim has to be unambiguous and attainable with the forces at the commander's disposal. A commander has to constantly reassess the means of achieving the aim and ensure that this overall aim is maintained throughout all the phases of operation. Once the aim has been decided there should be no doubt as to what a commander is trying to achieve.

The implications of this principle for a commander are that:

Ideally the right aim will be selected and events so directed that the aim is achieved without deviation. It would, however, be a poor idea to go to war with a narrow vision of the possibilities about to unfold. What is required is a hierarchy of aims at different levels. There should be a strategic aim, supported by a number of operational aims, themselves supported by an array of tactical aims which are steps on the path towards that strategic aim. Aims will tend to change more often with events the lower down the hierarchy they appear. The extent to which aims higher up the hierarchy change will probably be a measure of their original merit, or the degree of competence displayed in executing those lower down.

Given that an aim is still appropriate, it should be the focus for all activity. Deviating from the aim is likely to create the circumstances in which it will be necessary to replace it with a less advantageous, if more readily accomplished one. If an aim is valid but the method of achieving it unsuccessful, it is the method not the aim that should be changed.

Maintaining the aim does not imply blinkered rigidity. Having the imagination to recognize when to select a fresh aim will often be more important than stolid adherence to one whose course has run. The ability to do this will depend on many factors, but primarily on an educated judgment. In the first instance this relies on an adequate supply of information about the current circumstances.

A change of aim is likely to be fatal if your own force cannot itself cope with sudden change and achieve it successfully. Given a new aim, subordinates have to be capable of extracting and identifying further aims for their own subordinates and be trained to expect and meet such demands. Equally, higher commanders have to respond to changes below and reassess their own aims, for example to grasp the opportunity made possible by an unexpected tactical success.

An army will be best able to select and maintain the aim in changing circumstances if it has a system of orders which transmits this hierarchy of aims clearly, while ensuring that it recognises the appropriate moment to modify the aim or method, and has the doctrine and training to do so successfully. This will be more easily achieved if an army has been trained to focus its efforts on this style of command and control.

The Maintenance of Morale

Because success in war depends as much on moral as material factors, morale is probably the single most important element of war. Napoleon's dictum, 'Moral is to physical as three is to one', reflects the value he placed on this intangible asset. High morale fosters the offensive spirit and the will to win. It should inspire an army from top to bottom, from commander to private soldier.

Although morale is a mental state, it is sensitive to material conditions and a commander should look after the well-being of his men. Good morale is based on a widely shared sense of purpose, a clear understanding of the aim, discipline and self-respect, confidence in weapons and proficiency in their use, provision of appropriate welfare support, sound administration and, above all, on trust in the leadership right through the chain of command. Public opinion plays an important part in sustaining morale. Recognition of his successes in the media and public appreciation of his endeavours hearten the soldier.

The implications for the commander of this principle are that:

The value of high morale is validated by historical experience. It is best achieved by ensuring that men have a cause and an aim in which they believe and confidence in their ability to achieve it – faith in themselves and the plan they are to execute. The latter is fostered by a sense of belonging to an organisation which they believe to be cohesive and superior. This can often be achieved by ensuring that troops are well organised, equipped, sustained, trained and above all led.

To build high morale a commander will need close personal knowledge of his own men and their circumstances. This mirrors the need for information about the enemy which permits the seizing of the initiative and the taking of offensive action - both of which usually engender high morale.

High morale is not dependent on the combination of all these factors, and historical examples can be found where only few existed. To ignore the need for these factors is to introduce risk. However, numbers, armament and resources cannot compensate for lack of courage, energy, determination, skill and a bold offensive spirit, which springs from a determination to conquer.

Offensive Action

Offensive action is the chief means open to a commander to influence the outcome of a campaign or a battle. It confers the initiative on the attacker, giving him the freedom of action necessary to secure a decision. A successful defence, unless followed by offensive action, will only avert defeat temporarily. The principle of offensive action embodies a state of mind which breeds the determination to gain and hold the initiative and to create opportunities to harass and defeat the enemy. It does not imply attacking indiscriminately and regardless of casualties. The morale of an army which is continually on the defensive will suffer. Offensive action is essential to create confidence and to establish an ascendancy over the enemy.

The implications for the commander of this principle are that:

> The ultimate overthrow of the enemy demands offensive action, but offensive action may also play an important part in defensive and delaying operations. Offensive action is most likely to succeed when the balance of mutual information between the commander and his enemy is in the commanders favour. This enables him to be ahead in the thought and action, but this will probably be useless unless the command and control mechanisms exist to exploit the knowledge in the form of a suitable plan. If in doubt over what course to adopt, take the most aggressive. This wins the initiative and provides information.
>
> This action depends upon a material offensive capability: mobile weapon platforms to bring direct fire to bear on the enemy and long range indirect weapons to reach and attack the enemy at any time or place – fire mobility. Both manoeuvre and firepower will depend upon logistic sustainability.
>
> Offensive action requires an offensive spirit at all levels. Except in cases of extreme disparity of forces, it is most likely to succeed where the attacker has developed the ability to concentrate his effort at the decisive point and has a system of control that allows him to exploit tactical opportunities as they arise for operational advantage.

Surprise

Surprise is a potent psychological weapon. It causes confusion and paralysis in the enemy's chain of command and destroys the cohesion and morale of his units. The shock may not last long but, while the enemy's equilibrium is upset, the initiative may be seized to neutralise or destroy his forces at the cost of relatively few casualties. Surprise may be accomplished strategically, operationally and tactically, either by a ruse such as deception or good operations security, or by exploiting new equipment and techniques. Even if lost at the strategic level it may still be achieved at one of the lower levels. The elements of surprise are security, concealment, deception, originality, audacity and speed. Because it is such an essential condition for victory commanders must specifically aim for it in their planning. 'Stonewall' Jackson always adjured his officers, 'Always mystify, mislead and surprise the enemy'.

The implications for the commander of this Principle are that:

Surprise is a most effective and powerful influence in war and its moral effect is very great. It is most likely to be achieved when considered at the outset of planning rather than as an afterthought. By the use of surprise, results out of all proportion to the effort expended can be obtained. The success resulting from surprise is relative to the enemy's rigidity in responding to it. Surprise will depend largely upon the successful collection of information about the enemy and the ability to exploit that information. Physical surprise can be achieved by manoeuvre – appearing and attacking at unexpected places on the battlefield, and by fire mobility – striking the enemy without warning. Both of these will be even more surprising if their effect is multiplied by deception.

The ability to surprise an enemy is dependent upon his ability to react. In the cycle of action and reaction the more flexible army has the advantage. An army will therefore be more likely to achieve surprise if its command and control is structured to transfer quickly from one activity to another. Such a structure will combine the advantages of a centralised command with clear intentions transmitted to subordinates, and the delegation of authority to subordinates to allow them to respond to changing situations as quickly as possible. This implies the need for subordinates to be given the maximum freedom of action and a concept of command where there is a clear focus or point of main effort.

If the enemy can be outpaced mentally, he will probably be surprised physically. On the other hand it is the mark of a good and resilient army that it can respond to the unexpected without collapse (rather as a fit man's pulse will return to normal more quickly than an unfit man's). However alert and flexible the mind of an army may be, this will count for little if the organisation of any army leaves its equipment out of balance with regard to the threat. Equally, an army may keep up the virtuous circle of surprise if it is well informed, well balanced and pays regard to its own security.

Concentration of Force

Military success will normally result from the concentration of superior force at the decisive time and place, whether material or psychological or a combination of both. Concentration does not imply that there should never be dispersion. A carefully organised distribution of troops and firepower, accompanied by feints and a convincing deception plan, helps to balance our own forces and confuse the enemy. Once a concentration has achieved its aim, dispersion may be necessary to avoid retribution. Knowing when to concentrate and when to disperse is a matter of timing and judgement depending on a careful appreciation of the situation. Rapid concentration and dispersion demand good control and communications, mobility and an efficient traffic control system and procedures. They also depend on balance and cohesion, the essence of the next two principles.

The implications for a commander of this principle are that:

To concentrate force, both moral and material, implies having a main effort necessarily matched by a relative weakness. The success of this depends upon a number of factors. Among these are the possession of a force which is strong enough in absolute terms to make the concentration significant against the threat. The selection of the main effort will be reliant on timely information and a command and control system capable of recognising where the point of decision lies and exploiting that judgement. The execution of the plan will depend upon the ability to move forces to create or shift the main effort. This will require equipment mobility, fire mobility and flexible logistics to sustain them.

Concentration has to be matched by a corresponding lack of concentration elsewhere. This involves risk which will be reduced according to the quality of decision making.

Concentration does not necessarily imply a massing of forces, but rather having them so deployed as to be able to deliver the decisive blow when and where required.

Concentration is not necessarily in itself advantageous and should be seen always in relation to the enemy's capabilities and concentration of force. A concentration can become a focus of vulnerability (bunching) against some threats, for example, concentrations of troops in forward trenches hit by artillery fire in the First World War. A concentration of force can also be a cause of collapse if the logistic means do not exist to sustain it. Many forces have defeated themselves in circumstances of their own making by their own weight. It is therefore essential that an army be designed and organized to sustain what may appear to be a deliberate imbalance in deployment.

The benefits of concentration can also be achieved in relative terms by preventing the enemy from concentrating. A decisive advantage can be gained at the point of decision if the enemy is denied the means of knowing where this point lies and can be prevented from moving his forces to it and sustaining them once they are there. Deception, counter mobility and attrition in depth will help to achieve this.

It will not be so easy to concentrate forces if they do not share common doctrine and equipment.

Economy of Effort

The corollary of concentration of force is economy of effort. It is impossible to be strong everywhere and if decisive strength is to be massed at the critical time and place there must be no wasteful dispersal of resources or expenditure of effort where they cannot significantly affect the issue. This involves risk, but as General Wolfe observed, 'War ... is in its nature hazardous, and an option of difficulties.' In order to gain a substantial advantage a commander will accept a calculated risk in a less vital area. Those forces which are not assigned to the main effort may be required merely to hold their positions defensively, to fight a delaying action or to act offensively in a feint or holding attack. The application of the principle may be summed up as planning for a balanced deployment combined with a prudent allocation of resources which are strictly related to the aim of the operation.

The implications for a commander of this principle are that:

> If resources are not used economically, in the sense of frugally, concentration of force cannot be optimised. The greatest economies will be achieved if the point of decision is identified and the main effort directed accordingly. Economic use of resources is dependent upon knowing where and against whom to apply them, making an efficient and effective plan and having a well trained force to carry it out. Over-insurance and hoarding are to be avoided.
>
> Economies can be achieved by ensuring that there are the minimum levels of command (bureaucracy) between the decision taker and the man required to execute the mission, allowing for some built-in redundancy and resilience. Such a system will tend to delegate decision-taking to the lowest possible level. Economies become more important the scarcer the resources.
>
> Armies should adopt a style of warfare befitting their means. For some, prophylactic firepower may be seen as a 'cheap' and economic alternative to risking the lives of soldiers. For others, manpower may be plentiful and the need to be economic with firepower a greater concern.
>
> Economies of effort can be achieved by establishing commonality in doctrine training and equipment.

Security

Every military operation requires that degree of security which will both deny information to the enemy and enable our forces to achieve their aim despite the enemy's interference. Active measures, which includes the use of technical security devices, should cover the defence of bases and entry points, the maintenance of a favourable air situation, the protection of flanks to secure freedom of action and the availability of an adequate reserve. At the lower level it implies constant alertness. The denial to the enemy of information on our own forces and intentions entails unceasing vigilance to safeguard classified information and equipment, prevent infiltration and sabotage and to conceal combat units and logistic installations from enemy observation, air reconnaissance and other collection sensors. Security measures should, however, be based on an accurate threat assessment derived from up-to-date intelligence on the enemy's capabilities, or else valuable assets (both men and materiel) can be tied up protecting every location and installation against an exaggerated threat. There are two components of security. The first is the standing measures given above, which are common to all military operations. The second is the specific overall plan covering the operation in hand; this is known as Operations Security (OPSEC), which is described in Chapter 7 in greater detail.

Security is not merely defensive. Attempts to guard against every threat would result in weakness everywhere. Bold measures to seize and hold the initiative are one of the surest ways of achieving security. In operations at all levels commanders establish a balance between offensive action and security by a judicious allocation of troops and resources. The three principles of concentration of force, economy of effort and security are all closely interrelated.

The implications for the commander of this principle are that:

A sufficient degree of security is essential in order to obtain freedom of action to launch a bold offensive in pursuit of the selected aim. It does not imply undue caution and avoidance of risk, for bold action is essential to success in war. Security wards off unexpected developments that might interfere with the pursuit of a vigorous offensive. Security itself can be enhanced by taking offensive action against potential threats.

Security depends largely upon having superior information to the enemy, anticipating and pre-empting his actions. This implies not only that information must be gathered aggressively but also that information should be denied to the enemy by means of deception at all levels.
It may be that the success of the main effort in one place requires greater security efforts, perhaps deception, in another – the main effort is clearly not to be confused with a location. It may well be that resources are diverted from security to some other activity but this is a matter of risk.

Flexibility

No plan of campaign can look with any certainty beyond the first engagement with the major forces of an enemy. A commander will often be compelled to reach decisions on the basis of incomplete information about the enemy. This does not imply that a commander should alter his aim, but that he should exercise judgement and flexibility by modifying his plan to meet changed circumstances, taking advantage of a fleeting opportunity or shifting his effort to a more promising sector. A commander has to keep his forces well balanced so that he can switch quickly from one course to another with the minimum of regrouping. The ability to react rapidly depends on mental qualities such as elasticity of mind to discern a new situation, rapidity of decision to alter the plan in time and determination to pursue the aim to a successful conclusion. It also depends on good training, efficient staff work, sound organisation, reliable communications and a high degree of mobility. There is a premium on simplicity; elaborate and complicated plans will not survive the stress of battle, nor can they be modified readily to meet the unexpected. An uncommitted reserve is an essential element in the maintenance of flexibility to enable a commander to exploit a new axis or to regain the initiative after a setback. Once committed, a fresh reserve should be created. Above all, flexibility demands accurate and timely intelligence.

The implications for the commander of this principle are that:

Flexibility is required to modify a plan in changing circumstances and on occasions the aim. This requires a command and control system and a balanced force structure trained to react to change, and timely information to know when change is appropriate.

Without information a main effort could become an unbalanced and inflexible liability.

A force will be most flexible if its components share a common doctrine, training and equipment.

Co-operation

Military operations are joint enterprises involving co-operation with all parts of the Army, between the three fighting Services, between allies and, particularly in peacekeeping and in counter-insurgency operations, between the Army and the Civil Authorities. Co-operation is based on team spirit and training, and entails the co-ordination of all activities to achieve the optimum combined effort. Three elements are essential to co-operation: a common aim and a clear division of responsibilities and goodwill. A force commander will normally be appointed from the Service making the largest contribution to the operation. Subordinate to the joint headquarters the individual Services will usually run their own chains of command in parallel. From time to time one Service has to be prepared to place itself under the operational control of another. The closest co-operation between commanders and staffs has to replace parochial Service attitudes without sacrificing legitimate Service interests. The kind of co-operation which makes for efficiency between arms, Services and allies is born of a thorough understanding of each other's capabilities and limitations obtained during joint training and exercises in peacetime.

The implications for the commander of this principle are that:

Concentration of force, economy of effort and flexibility will depend largely upon co-operation between formations, services and allies. By co-operation with other forces, synergy can be achieved.

Other Principles are reliant on co-operation to a lesser degree but co-operation is enhanced by common doctrine, training and equipment and is effected by an efficient liaison mechanism and a spirit of goodwill.

Sustainability

Sustainability is a pre-requisite for the success of any operation and embraces both the physical and moral components. Logistic and administrative considerations are often the deciding factor in assessing the practicability of an aim or the feasibility of an operation. A clear appreciation of the potential constraints of logistics is as important to a commander as is his ability to make a sound analysis of an operational situation. No tactical plan can succeed without a degree of administrative support commensurate with the aim of the operation. From this premise, flows an essential pre-requisite for a commander to have a level of control over the sustainability plan proportionate to the level of his responsibility for the operation.

Logistic resources take time to generate, both in the UK base, and in any theatre overseas. Requirements can only be foreseen and provided for if the logistic staff are involved right from the beginning of the planning process and thereafter work closely with the operations staff. The art of administration lies not in over-insurance but in making the most economical use of the available assets. Scarce resources have to be controlled at the highest level. The logistic organisation has to be flexible enough to react quickly to changes in the situation; to meet the unforeseen; to provide for interruptions in the supply chain due to enemy action, and to meet expenditure rates due to enemy action; mechanical, physical and psychological attrition. All movement resources, road, rail, water and air, must be carefully co-ordinated and fully exploited in the interests of economy and flexibility.

The implications to a commander of this principle are that:

Sustainability will depend upon an organisation which is designed to maintain and to use its resources efficiently and economically.

The balance between 'Teeth and Tail' has to be appropriate and operations tailored to logistic capability or acceptable risk. Sustainability has also be flexible.

Flexibility and efficiency will best be achieved if logistic doctrine, equipment and training are common.

Both the physical and psychological needs of soldiers have to be sustained in order to maintain morale.

Section 4 Military Doctrine Since 1990

Background

It is always difficult to alter and change doctrinal thinking, particularly if this has been in place for many years; furthermore the United Kingdom continues to have the same overall commitment to NATO's defensive alliance. What has changed is that the major threat from the Soviet Union has disappeared, the Warsaw Pact has disbanded and the relationship between Europe and North America has changed because of this. This has led to a change in doctrinal thinking.

Since 1990 some NATO Forces have collectively operated outside NATO's traditional areas (Gulf War and Bosnia). Resources, technology and operational thinking have comprehensively changed the conditions in which the previous doctrinal thinking was relevant. More importantly, the US Army and Marine Corps moved away from their previous doctrinal thinking. Economic restraint coupled with subsequent reductions in the strength and capability of the Army (Options for Change 1991) indicated clearly that British military influence abroad would, in future, be tied to coalitions or other international groupings – probably with US forces. In these radically altered circumstances where operations are not envisaged on a linear scale and where the battlefield is less dense, a review and renewal of doctrine were necessary and was probably overdue.

More practical evidence to support these views were highlighted in the operations during the Gulf War of 1991. A doctrine based on a manoeuvrist approach to warfare was subsequently fashioned and promulgated during the early 1990s. This manoeuvrist approach is not a modern concept; history shows that many of its component parts have been used frequently from classical days to the present time. The essential feature of the manoeuvrist approach is that it is designed to teach commanders and soldiers alike how to think and not what to think.[2]

The Manoeuvrist Approach to Operations

British doctrine stems from the manoeuvrist approach to operations which is examined in detail in the ADP series of publications. The manoeuvrist approach involves an all-encompassing attitude to the conduct of military activities and specifically to the conduct of operations in which commanders attempt to defeat the enemy through a variety of means and not simply by the attritional destruction of his force. Indeed, the highest and purest application of this approach is to pre-empt an enemy, that is to defeat him without engaging in combat and to defeat his will to fight. If this is not possible then the manoeuvrist seeks to dislocate an enemy. If an enemy cannot be defeated by pre-emption or dislocation then the manoeuvrist commander will endeavour to seize and hold the initiative thereby disrupting the enemy ideally by destroying his centre of gravity[3] – his critical weakness – preferably by attacking a point of vulnerability with considerable strength. In its simplest form, a manoeuvrist approach involves using a part of one's force to find, then fix or contain the enemy, while the remainder of the force attacks – or strikes – his weakest point. The purpose is to mass sufficient combat power at the critical place and time to defeat the enemy or threaten him with destruction, while preserving one's own freedom for future action. This approach applies at every level of command and includes all types of operation within the spectrum of conflict.

Before embarking on any operation the commander will understand the intent and overall concept of operations of his superior commander so he can properly employ his own forces. The commander develops his own intent and concept and accepts calculated risks to achieve decisive tactical results in the outcome of the current or immediate battle. He will strive to seize the initiative early on in any engagement, and conduct offensive action regardless of the overriding operation of war in order to impose his will on the enemy. The objective of any plan will ultimately be to position his strength against the enemy's weakness,

[2] An SCSI Occasional Paper (No 26) entitled The British Army and Approaches to Warfare Since 1945 by Major General John Kiszely provides a much more detailed and comprehensive analysis of British military doctrinal thinking since 1945. Occasional Papers are sponsored by Colonel Defence Studies at the Joint Doctrine and Concepts Centre.

[3] The 'centre of gravity' is that aspect of the enemy's overall capability which, if attacked and eliminated, will lead either to the enemy's inevitable defeat or his wish to sue for peace through negotiation.

to throw the enemy off balance and aggressively follow up, whenever possible, to complete the defeat or destruction of the enemy.

Ultimately the style of any operational activity, be it attrition or manoeuvre based, has a considerable influence on the tactics of the Army. On the battlefield, at the tactical level of conflict, the elements of attrition and manoeuvre exist simultaneously. Obviously attrition, the physical destruction of the enemy, must occur in manoeuvre warfare just as manoeuvre often occurs in the deadliest war of attrition. However, an element of attrition remains the more likely method of contributing to the defeat of the enemy at the lower tactical level. This means that manoeuvre and firepower are inseparable and complementary elements of tactical combat. Although one characteristic might dominate a particular period of the battle, the co-ordinated use of both typifies all operations. At the sharp end of combat, amongst the battlegroups, war fighting is inevitably characterised as a combination of fire and movement – of killing and moving – which remains a bloody business.

In summary the British Army have adopted a philosophy which seeks to defeat an enemy by shattering his moral and physical cohesion – his ability to fight as an effective and co-ordinated whole, rather than to destroy him physically through attrition.

Mission Command

One of the major prerequisites in the application of this manoeuvrist approach is the concept of mission command with the aim of getting within an opponent's decision cycle. This concept has three enduring tenets: timely decision-making, the importance of understanding a superior commander's intention, and, by applying this to one's own actions, a clear responsibility to fulfil that intention. The underlying requirement is the fundamental responsibility to act (or, in certain circumstances, to decide not to act) within the framework of a commander's intentions which, at the lower tactical levels, will be expressed as a concept of operations and associated mission statements. Together, this requires a style of command which promotes decentralised control, freedom and speed of action, and initiative at all levels.

This style of command is defined as Mission Command which is designed to promote a robust system of command and to achieve unity of effort at all levels; it is dependent on decentralisation. Historically, this approach has proved to be the most appropriate to contend with the demands, uncertainties and frictions of command in war. It requires the development of trust and mutual understanding, based on a common doctrinal approach, between commanders and subordinates throughout the chain of command, and timely and effective decision-making, together with initiative at all levels: the keys to unlock and obtain access to the enemy's decision-action cycle. Mission Command provides a common base-line: it applies not only to operations but also to much of the regu-lation of the Army's affairs in peacetime. It is to be used at all levels of command. Mission Command should also remain a dynamic component of doctrine and not become dogma; as new technology becomes available, its principles and application should be re-addressed as necessary.

Section 5 The Spectrum of Conflict

Background

There have been many attempts to codify the nature of conflict. After 1945 the two main types of conflict were nuclear and non nuclear or conventional conflict and each had their own specific terminology.

Later on the term 'limited war' was widely used to denote all combat operations where there was no recourse to nuclear weapons although this lost credibility as more nations acquire the means to develop or obtain nuclear weapons. There are always some limitations inherent in any conflict short of general war. Four of these cover the limitations on objectives, the means, the geographical area and the time factor.

The intensity of fighting is another means by which conflict can be described – both to the degree of intensity or the frequency in which conflict is encountered.However, descriptions like 'low intensity conflict' to denote operations such as counter-insurgency activity and 'high intensity conflict', to denote general war can be very misleading especially to the soldier involved in the fighting. A useful guide is to assess intensity by the rate of consumption of men, equipment or materiel. In this way the measure of intensity can be related to the battle or campaign, as opposed to other yardsticks which may lead to false deductions about the type of campaign being fought.

The three main categories are described (in ascending order of escalation).

Military Activities in Peacetime which include the role and function of military deterrence and Military Aid to the Civil Authorities (MACA).

Operations Other Than War (OOTW) which include Peace Support Operations (PSO) and Counter Insurgency (COIN).

Regional Conflict and General War.

A diagram to illustrate the connections between all three categories is given below:

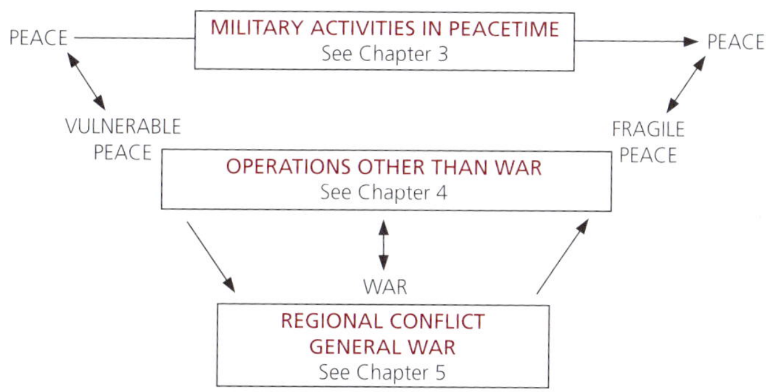

CHAPTER 3 MILITARY ACTIVITY IN PEACETIME

Section 1
Deterrence

"To be prepared for war is one of the most effectual means of preserving peace."

GEORGE WASHINGTON

General

In simple terms any nation, state or definable group can be said at any particular time to be at peace (stability) or in conflict (at war). Since the end of the Second World War in 1945, British forces have been involved in a large variety of military operations at home and in many parts of the world. While the prospect of an all-out major war against a super-power opponent has receded with the ending of the Cold War, the possibility of more military involvement by British Forces has increased albeit, at levels below that of general war. The Gulf War of 1991, and operations in former Yugoslavia from 1993, are suitable examples.

The present size and commitments for the United Kingdom's armed forces show that there is little chance of these forces being able to muster any numerical military superiority in most types of conflict on their own; and there is clear rationale to have the political support of other nations. There is also a need to retain strong links with allies, and to continue to show publicly that the United Kingdom is capable of honouring its treaty obligations and other military responsibilities. In this respect it is advantageous to have military capabilities across all types of conflict so that allies and potential enemies alike can observe that national forces are available to protect the United Kingdom's vital interests at whatever level of combat. In this way overall national deterrence can be achieved, and by means of alliances and support for UN commitments a similar British contribution can be made to deterring or preventing conflict outside the United Kingdom.

The Role of Deterrence

Deterrence is not absolute but rather a relative concept; it is also, above all, proportional. No threat is credible unless it is proportionate to the action it purports to deter: if the anticipated pain is smaller than the expected gain, then deterrence is not likely to succeed. Deterrence aims to present a potential aggressor with an unacceptable degree of risk and damage in proportion to any potential gain. For such a concept to succeed it is essential that two conditions are met. The potential aggressor has, firstly, to be aware that such a concept exists, and secondly, that the concept is matched by both the political will and the physical means to carry it out effectively.

Readness.

In more straightforward terms British forces need to be seen to be capable, credible and competent. This implies the continuation of high standards of soldiering and a professional approach to all military matters coupled with the provision of modern and up-to-date equipment, effective training and an ability to deploy quickly with the appropriate support to sustain military operations.

Aspects of Deterrence

Training. Training provides the means to practise, develop and validate, within constraints, the practical application of a common doctrine. Equally importantly, it provides the basis for schooling commanders and staffs in the exercise of command and control respectively. Well trained units and formations make a vital contribution to deterrence in that they increase the commander's ability to conduct sophisticated military operations when required, thereby enhancing the potential of that force, and hence its deterrent value.

Readiness. A key feature of credible deterrence is the ability to provide formations and units at a high state of readiness to deploy on operations. Troops cannot be at high states of readiness for prolonged periods, and thus an effective system of rotation, for well trained troops, can further contribute to providing general deterrence to any would-be aggressor or by way of enhancing credibility within an alliance.

Deployability. Similarly the ability to deploy forces over long distances in support of allies adds significantly to the role and function of deterrence. If a potential aggressor perceives that United Kingdom forces can deploy quickly to threatened areas, operate effectively when there, and have the ability to fight across a wide spectrum of military operations, this could well cause him to think again. An example of preventive deterrence is the move of British forces to Kuwait

Deployability.

in 1994 (Operation DRIVER). When Iraq moved two armoured divisions close to the Kuwait border, British forces, together with those of Coalition partners, were deployed rapidly to Kuwait to demonstrate an international determination to maintain both Kuwait's sovereignty and integrity, and the authority of the United Nations.

Conflict Prevention

Since the formation of the UN in 1945, many attempts to anticipate or forestall conflicts around the world have been made. The prevention of conflict has become a feature of UN military and civil activity and there have been various means by which this has been attempted. An example of this type of activity has been the UNPROFOR operations first established in 1992 to facilitate, in co-ordination with the UN, the delivery by the relevant organisations of humanitarian assistance to the people of Bosnia.

Other examples of operations undertaken independently of the United Nations are:

The Commonwealth Ceasefire Monitoring Force in Rhodesia (CMF) to keep the peace during the transition to the internationally recognised independent state of Zimbabwe from December 1979 to March 1980.

The Multi National Force in Lebanon (MNF). Contingents from the USA, France and Italy arrived in August 1982 and were joined by a British contingent in February 1983. The Force was withdrawn in March 1984.

The Sinai Multi National Force and Observers (MFO) established in April 1982 with contingents from eleven nations, including the UK.

Military Aid to the Civil Community (MACC).

Section 2 Contingency Planning within UK

General

Contingency Planning is the overall term for planning the graduated military responses to a wide range of contingencies that may occur within the UK in peace, times of tension or crisis, and war. This covers the activities of Military Aid to the Civil Authorities (MACA), less those military operations in Northern Ireland, Military Support to the Mounting of Operations at home or abroad, and Military Home Defence (MHD) in times of general war. It is a national responsibility provided by the three Services and is directly related to the Home Office provision of integrated emergency management. Contingency planning in the UK is now conducted at all levels down to formation (Bde) level. A diagram of all the types of contingency planning is given at Annex A to this Chapter.

Military Aid to the Civil Authorities (MACA)

Introduction. The Services, and in particular, the Army, have traditionally been involved in the provision of aid to the Civil Authorities in the United Kingdom or any of the Dependent Territories. The term 'Civil Authorities' covers local authorities, such as magistrates and police forces, District and County Councils and central government Departments of State. Military aid takes three separate forms:

Military Aid to the Civil Community (MACC). Military aid to the civil community is the provision of Army personnel and equipment both in emergencies, such as natural disasters, and in routine situations to assist the community at large. Aspects of MACC have also been a useful tool in certain categories of UN operations such as in Bosnia under the auspices of the Overseas Development Agency. Examples of this role are the use of EOD bomb disposal units and assisting the community during a civil emergency such as flooding and control measures during the recent foot and mouth crisis.

Military Aid to Government Departments (MAGD).

Military Aid to Government Departments (MAGD). This encompasses the use of military forces for non-military government tasks, including assistance to maintain public services and the essentials of life in a community or to undertake urgent work of national importance. Recent examples include firefighting and providing emergency ambulance and prison support services. In modern times it should be noted that the Armed Forces are not in a position to provide the appropriate support for some of the more sophisticated public services and industries; most of the public services are now in private hands which would inevitably change the nature of how the government would deal with such forms of support for essential industries. Contingency planning for such support and assistance will however still be necessary.

Military Aid to the Civil Power (MACP). The Army may also be called upon to help maintain public order and security when the police are unable to control the situation. In the United Kingdom and its remaining dependencies the principle of the supremacy of the civil authorities normally precludes the introduction of any form of martial law to deal with civil strife. The military force always remains subordinate to the civil authority. It may be necessary to introduce special legislation or declare a state of emergency in order to invest the security forces with the necessary powers. The rescue of the diplomatic staff at the Iranian embassy in Knightsbridge by the Special Air Service in 1980 is an example of the temporary, small scale and selective use of military aid to the civil power (MACP) on the mainland of Great Britain. The employment of the Army since 1969 in support of the Royal Ulster Constabulary in Northern Ireland is an example of a wider more sustained, but careful controlled, application of MACR. There are various contingency plans controlled by the Director Military Operations (DMO) which govern the precise conditions and circumstances in which the Army will be employed on MACP duties.

*MACP.
Northern Ireland
1970's.*

*MACP.
Northern Ireland
2000.*

Military Support for the Mounting of Operations (MSMO)

Contingency Planning covers the planning necessary to mount a variety of operations at home and overseas. These include:

Selective Mobilisation. The selective mobilisation of individuals and small units for duties and tasks, normally abroad. The use of TA volunteers for duties in Bosnia and the Falklands Islands are examples of this.

Deployment of Forces. Contingency planning for the deployment of national and allied forces from the UK to overseas theatres of operation.

Joint Theatre Plans. Contingency planning for the mounting of specified Joint Theatre Plans and Joint Logistic Plans to support operations world wide. These could include Allied or Coalition deployment plans.

Casualty Reportinq/Reception Plans. These would include contingencies for the reporting of casualties, the reception of casualties entering the UK, and the evacuation of non-combatants from a threatened area.

The Joint Planning Staff (JPS) at PJHQ are responsible for the planning and integration of all these military operations.

Military Home Defence (MHD)

Military Home Defence would embrace all military activities in time of general war connected with the protection and survival of the UK Home Base. It is a Joint Service operation and the Army would be involved in:

Guarding of specific Key Points (KPs).

Assisting in the full mobilisation of military manpower.

Guarding all types of KPs.

The territorial defence of the UK.

Assisting in nuclear survival and recovery.

ANNEX A TO CHAPTER 3

CONTINGENCY PLANNING WITHIN THE UK

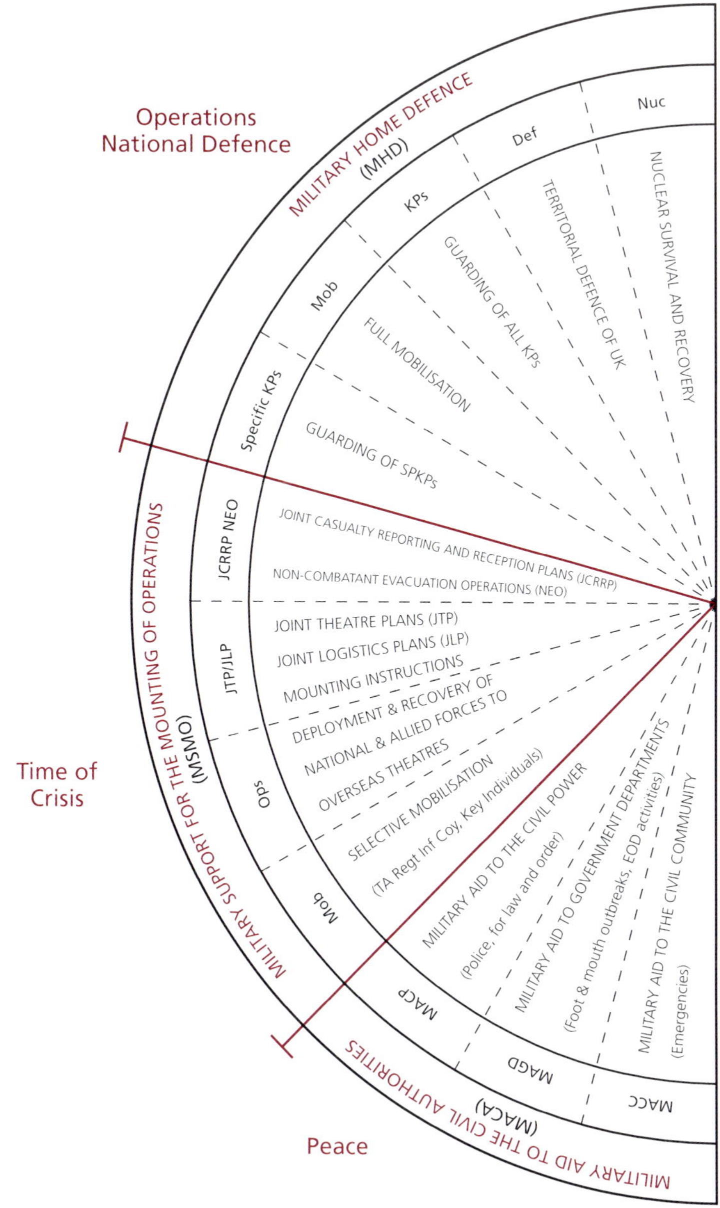

CHAPTER 4

OPERATIONS OTHER THAN WAR (OOTW)

Introduction

For many years the term Operations Other Than War (00TW) has been used to describe those military actions that fall short of general or regional war, but do not fall into the category of MACA which normally cover military activity in the UK only. The term OOTW is gradually failing out of use as a catch-all term because of its lack of clear focus and definition. Nevertheless, OOTW continues to have currency within the Army as a whole and in this publication is used to describe Counter Insurgency (COIN) and Peace Support Operations (PSO). Both these military activities fall well short of general and regional war, but are activities in which the application of military force may well have to be considered. The term OOTW is now being replaced by the term 'Other Operations' (OO).

Section 1 Counter Insurgency

Insurgency

Insurgency is generally defined as the actions within a state of a minority group who are intent on forcing political change by means of a mixture of subversion, propaganda and military pressure, aiming to persuade or intimidate the broad mass of people to accept such a change. It is an organised armed political struggle, the goals of which may be diverse. Some insurgencies aim for a straightforward seizure of power through a complete revolutionary takeover, while others attempt to break away from state control and establish an autonomous state within traditional ethnic or religious bounds.

Insurgencies tend to arise when the state authorities are unable or unwilling to redress the demands of significant social groups. Insurgencies could therefore be coalitions of disparate forces sometimes united by a common enmity towards a government, and a willingness to use violence to challenge its legitimacy

Crises often develop quickly, particularly in parts of the world left unstable by the demise of empires or power blocs, and in other areas, where a combination of overwhelming political, cultural, economic, ethnic and religious forces could threaten the stability of a state and possibly its neighbours. The patterns of this sort of activity are likely to vary from a spontaneous uprising, caused by some real or perceived injustice, to a carefully prepared insurgency organised by a revolutionary style cadre in furtherance of its aims and ideals.

External influences are present in most insurgent situations and inspire many of them. Outside powers provide material aid and assistance in training, organisation and propaganda to insurgent movements. In more recent times revolutionary terrorists such as Carlos Marighella in Brazil and Abimael Guzman in Peru have provided political inspiration and instruction on insurgent tactics for other

PALESTINE 1946–47

The King David Hotel, Jerusalem, bombed by Jewish Insurgents, 1946.

MALAYA EMERGENCY 1948–60

SAS patrol and boatmen.

terrorist groups. Nearer home certain terrorist groupings have received political, financial and material support from sympathisers outside Northern Ireland.

Counter Insurgency

The British Army has for over 100 years been involved with insurgency of one type or another and from this experience has evolved a practical doctrine for countering insurgency. No one can forecast what future situation British forces may have to face at home or abroad. While each new threat arises in its own context to present a fresh set of problems, there are certain operational principles that remain valid for countering any type of insurgency, acts of terrorism or civil disorder.

ADEN 1963–67

Patrolling in the Crater.

SARAWAK 1964

Ghurkas prepare to deploy.

DHOFAR 1965–75

Briefing a firqat patrol.

The three broad fundamentals of doctrine developed and adapted by the British for counter insurgency, that is minimum force, civil/military co-operation and tactical flexibility, also provide an essential backdrop for the newer and more recent forms of peace support operations. The way in which these fundamentals are applied would have to be adjusted to suit the particular circumstances, but it is apposite to note that the experience gained by the British Army from previous counter insurgency campaigns should not be forgotten or overlooked when considering potentially new or unusual situations.

Service in Northern Ireland has also provided many in the Army with basic experience at tactical level but this in itself may tend to constrain military thinking on the subject because of its national context. There are many military lessons that can be learnt because of the similarities between the MACP campaign in Northern Ireland and other COIN campaigns which have been conducted elsewhere. There are also significant differences. Tactics, such as cordon and search operations and some forms of convoy anti-ambush drills, which from the perspective of Northern Ireland, may seem to be relics of a colonial past, could well be very relevant and necessary in a different operational and environmental setting.

The Army has not developed a general antidote to the problem of insurgency but has made use of guidelines and practices to conduct counter insurgency operations which includes counter terrorist action. Not only is the threat changing, but so too is the environment in which an insurgent has to be confronted. For example, as in all future operations, military action will be conducted under the critical scrutiny of the law, the media, human rights organisations and other international bodies such as the European Court. This will be particularly so for COIN operations where the media organisations will inevitably have wider access to the Civil Authorities and the general public.

It is necessary to appreciate that although military forces may have a crucial role to play in restoring and maintaining government control, military force is not an end in itself, but always a means to achieve a wider political purpose. This implies that the military commander will have a far from free hand, and indeed, in a well orchestrated COIN strategy a military commander is unlikely to direct the overall campaign. Acceptance of this fact has deep implications for the part that military forces will be given (and should seek) to play in COIN, and of any military approach to the situation.

Section 2 PEACE SUPPORT OPERATIONS

Peace Support Operations

The term peace support operations covers both peacekeeping and peace enforcement. The word 'support' is used deliberately to emphasise the subordination of the military operation to political objectives. Military activities have to complement diplomatic, economic and humanitarian efforts, which should combine to pursue the political aim for the operation. These operations are generally multinational; authorised by the United Nations or NATO; and normally involve a number of civil and military national and international

UNPROFOR,
YUGOSLAVIA 1994

Peace support operations.

KFOR,
KOSOVO 1999

Intervention.

agencies. Military actions will be designed principally to create or sustain conditions in which diplomatic, economic and humanitarian activities can proceed towards the political resolution of a conflict or hostilities. Peacekeeping and peace enforcement require different approaches even though they share many practical applications at the tactical level.

Peacekeeping

Peacekeeping consists of operations carried out with the general consent of the disputing parties, as part of the peace process agreed by those parties, in support of efforts to promote security and confidence, in order to bring about a long-term peace settlement. They are based on the common attributes of consent, legitimacy, impartiality and the minimum necessary use of force.

Peacekeeping operations are normally authorised by the United Nations or an appropriate regional organisation. Experience has shown that the United Nation's most successful peacekeeping operations have been deployments in support of previously agreed peace settlements. In general terms force may be used only in self defence. In practice this need not preclude the robust use of force provided it is legitimately applied, proportional and allows for some form of consent to be maintained or rebuilt taking full account of the implications for all the civil and military agencies involved.

Peacekeeping tasks could include observation and monitoring, supervision of truces and ceasefires and placing peacekeeping forces between belligerent forces. Other tasks could be demobilisation and disarmament, transition operations, humanitarian relief and its protection, operational mine clearance and community projects to support a civilian authority.

Designated peacekeeping forces operating by consent will normally be relatively small and dispersed, with only sufficient combat capability for use in self defence.

Peace Enforcement

Peace enforcement operations are generally carried out under the authority of the United Nations Security Council to maintain or restore peace between belligerent parties who may not all consent to any intervention. Enforcement action authorised by the United Nations, without the consent of North Korea in 1950, set in train the Korean War 1950–53 in which British and Commonwealth troops took part. This rapidly developed into a regional war controlled on the UN's behalf by the USA.

Peace enforcement operations are coercive in nature, using force or its threat against any party to enforce norms, sanctions, or agreements reached by the parties themselves. These operations are designed to create conditions that could lead to political progress, as an enforced pacification operation is unlikely to produce a long term resolution of a conflict.

Peacekeeping: UNFICYP, Cyprus 1974–9.

Checking weapons in Macedonia.

Peace enforcement tasks could include the restoration of peace by impartial actions, such as the application of military deterrence within the theatre, conflict containment by the interposition of military forces and the forcible separation of belligerent factions. Other supporting tasks could be the establishment and protection of safe areas, controlling movement on the group and the enforcement of sanctions. A peace enforcement force may not necessarily be large but should be equipped, organised, deployed and sustained to enable it to achieve its operational objectives in the face of real or potential threats. It should also have the capability to conduct full scale military operations and to increase the intensity and scale of its military activities if necessary.

A volatile geostrategic situation implies that any peace enforcement operation could be mounted in a situation that has the characteristics of civil war or insurgency. The cause of any conflict is likely to be complicated and not easy to resolve. The belligerents may well use unconventional military tactics, and there is likely to be rapid variation in the intensity of activity. Random atrocities and

Mine clearance training, UNTAC, Cambodia.

UNPROFOR, YUGOSLAVIA 1994

Convoy protection.

large scale human suffering are possible, compounded and exaggerated by ineffective local government and the lack of infrastructure. The issue of consent may be difficult to establish properly; manifest and public consent at the strategic and operational levels could easily be fragile, patchy or non existent at the tactical level. If not carefully managed the repercussions of any enforcement action at local level could rapidly affect the overall military situation.

The general response from the international community to any situation is bound to be mixed, and the decision to commit military forces will require clear instruction about the use of force beyond that of self defence. Once deployed any subsequent transition from a peacekeeping role to a peace enforcement role would require a new mandate from the United Nations.

Section 3 Other Forms of Intervention

In some circumstances it may be necessary to provide a military force to intervene or assist in a potentially warlike or dangerous situation. The military evacuation of British citizens caught up in a civil war or a *coup d'état* abroad is such an example where only British interests may be directly involved. These situations and the contingency planning necessary to prepare for them would be controlled by PJHQ and may well be carried out by components of the JRDF.

Other similar forms of military activity either in support of UN, WEU or NATO could also easily occur again in the future. An example of this type of activity is the British military force temporarily based in Congo-Brazzaville to stand by for the evacuation of British nationals from Kinshasa before and after the departure of President Mobutu of Zaire.

16 Para Brigade deployed in Jordan during 1958.

British troops in Brazzaville, May 1997.

CHAPTER 5 REGIONAL CONFLICT AND GENERAL WAR

Section 1 The Characteristics of Conflict

"Four elements make up the climate of war: danger physical exertion intelligence and friction are the elements that form the atmosphere of war and turn it into a medium that impedes activity."

VON CLAUSEWITZ[1]

The Features of the Modern Battlefield

The principal features of a modern battlefield have been described in other military publications. In addition other factors should also be considered such as:

The need for a joint approach by the three Services to all military operations.

A fluctuating rate of military activity.

The increasing availability of information.

Operations over extended areas with fewer forces.

Increased range, precision and lethality for all types of weapons.

These features and many other subsidiary factors will have their effect on the soldier in one way or another and will continue to be just as physically and mentally demanding for soldiers on operations as in the past.

The Psychological Effects

Danger and Fear. 'War is the realm of danger; therefore courage is the soldier's first requirement.' Courage is of two kinds: physical in the presence of danger and moral in the face of responsibility. Fear is the natural human reaction to danger and to a degree it is essential for survival. An excess of it paralyses the will, the ability to reason and to make rational decisions. Fear cannot be eliminated; it can only be controlled by an act of will. Selecting men with this quality in peacetime is not easy but a man of character in peace is likely to be a man of courage and resolution in war. Discipline, pride, comradeship, esprit de corps and worthwhile activity all help the individual soldier. A commander can sustain his men's courage with positive leadership, by earning a reputation for not squandering his soldiers' lives recklessly, by ensuring that his troops are well supported in battle and by giving them tasks at which they can succeed in order

[1] von Clausewitz, *On War*, edited and translated by Michael Howard and Peter Paret, Princetown University Press, New Jersey, 1976.

to build up their confidence. Moral courage and nerve are the intellectual equivalents of bravery. They are essential qualities for any commander but the higher the level the more necessary they are; Commanders need strong nerves to endure the tension of waiting for news and to withstand the shock of a setback.

Exhaustion. A tired man is normally a less brave man. A weary commander is a less resolute one, his reactions are slower and he is more prone to make mistakes. Technical advances enabling troops to fight by night almost as easily as by day could benefit an attacker with superior forces who can commit successive echelons to maintain continuous pressure. To prevent the exhaustion of units and the collapse of any defence, a commander will have to fight the battle in considerable depth and with a plan for the relief of exhausted troops. The forming and reforming of reserves or second echelons will be a constant preoccupation of commanders at all levels. In prolonged periods of contact with the enemy, casualties, including trusted leaders, and the accumulation of months of fear and fatigue will erode the courage, resolution, stamina and fighting efficiency of any unit. In a long campaign formations have to be taken out of the line periodically to rest and absorb reinforcements. There has in the past been a temptation to rely on experienced units and formations to execute the most demanding tasks indefinitely. Gradually, leadership at unit level will become diluted, the troops become more cautious and the units will lose their cutting edge. There comes a time when tired units and long serving commanders have to be withdrawn permanently.

The Fog of War. War is the realm of uncertainty; three-quarters of the factors on which action in war is based are wrapped in a fog of greater or lesser uncertainty. Reports originating from units in contact with the enemy are often inaccurate, incomplete and misleading. They may be distorted and misinterpreted on the way up the chain of command. First reports and first impressions are often over

57th Regiment of Foot (The Middlesex Regiment) under fire at Albuhera, 1811.

sanguine or unduly pessimistic. Some time will elapse before even a partial impression of the situation will emerge at corps and higher headquarters. Modern surveillance devices, reconnaissance, and communications notwithstanding, doubt, uncertainty and error will often cloud the commander's perception of the battlefield. With only a partial picture of the situation he may have to make his decisions on inaccurate or incomplete information and intelligence, relying on his judgement and a 'feel' for the situation based on experience and knowledge of the enemy, the quality the Germans call *Fingerspitzengefühl*[2]. The more modern phenomenon of data overload also adds complications to a commander's decision making process.

The Friction of War. 'Everything in war is very simple, but the simplest thing is difficult. The difficulties accumulate and end by producing a kind of friction that is inconceivable unless one has experienced war'[3]. This quotation summarises the cumulative effects of danger, exhaustion, uncertainty, chance, accident and other imponderables inseparable from conflict, which render the execution of a plan less perfect than the concept. Some friction is due to causes outside human control, such as the weather and mud which reduce mobility, and could preclude air and aviation support, but the fallibility of human nature lies at the root of the problem. However well trained an army, misunderstandings, misinterpretations, mistakes, hesitations and dilatoriness will occur. In the stress of battle a recognition signal is forgotten and a commander is killed. A convoy goes astray and ammunition vital for the defence of a key crossroads is lost. A liaison officer carrying orders dies in a road accident, or there is a computer breakdown. The well ordered routine of peacetime breeds a habit of regularity. While essential to the smooth running of headquarters and units on operations, so reducing the friction of war, routine and habit may render commanders and staffs more vulnerable to the unexpected and any deception plans. Apart from the accidents of war the enemy's actions and initiatives constantly impose a measure of uncertainty, surprise, disorganisation and delay. Commanders and staffs have to allow for the element of friction in war by ensuring that their plans are flexible and simple. Only plans which fulfil these two criteria are likely to survive the hazards of war.

Sustaining the Man

The soldier is the most important resource in war. So much depends on the morale of the soldier that nothing should be neglected which fosters his fighting spirit and promotes his well-being. It is the task of the logistic services to sustain the man in battle. In the past sickness has claimed more casualties than wounds. Awareness and training in hygiene to combat disease and in first aid to save life are essential to the efficiency and well-being of formations and units in the field.

[2] A German term that does not translate easily but can be described as 'a feeling in the fingertips'.
[3] von Clausewitz, *On War* (see note 1).

During and after the Second World War soldiers had many certainties to sustain them in battle, such as the just and right nature of the state, the monarch and church: and the unjust and evil nature of the enemy. Many of these personal certainties have gone. Soldiers are now very conscious of their own mortality and frailty when faced with the loneliness of the battlefield. Additionally, their experience of death, particularly death of the young, is now infrequent. The manoeuvrist approach to warfare seeks to exploit, and target, human frailties. The moral component of fighting power has to be sustained. High quality medical support which promises speedy and expert treatment and relief from the chaos and violence of the battlefield makes a substantial contribution to sustaining this very fragile human factor.

Section 2 The Environment

General

In addition to the dangers and difficulties described in the preceding paragraphs there will be the added hazard of combat in particular environments where the weather and terrain can increase these dangers and difficulties for the soldier. Bad weather has a restricting influence on men, equipment and terrain. Men are affected physically and psychologically. The performance of equipment is degraded and movement can be difficult or temporarily impossible. In conditions which are manifestly different such as mountains, jungles, deserts and sub-arctic conditions, tactical guidance will vary from that required for operations in temperate climates.

Weather

Effect on Men. A man's natural reaction to severe rain, snow and dust storms is to take shelter, shield the eyes, cover the ears, withdraw into himself and become far less alert and effective. The supervision of sentries and observation posts is less easy. Bad weather places a premium on physical fitness, morale, vigilance, training and leadership.

Effect on Equipment. Surveillance equipment, such as infrared, image intensification, thermal imaging and radar can redress these difficulties but are subject to varying degrees of degradation in adverse weather conditions. Cloud, rain and mist impede the use of instruments in air operations and aviation support and may preclude their use altogether. Minor obscuration could prevent the observation of fire on targets in depth and thus restrict the operation of terminally guided munitions. Modern communication equipment can be similarly affected by attenuation during poor weather.

Effect on Tactics. Darkness, mist, fog, heavy rain and dust reduce visibility, restrict fields of fire and conceal movement. Wind and rain muffle the sounds of moving men, wheels and tracks. The cumulative effects of bad weather and poor visibility are to erode security and enhance surprise. The defender could lose many of the benefits of a prepared position, an integrated surveillance system and a co-ordinated fire plan. The advantage passes to the attacker and

Cold Weather: Skioring, North Norway.

Long-range Patrolling in Snow.

a surprise attack under cover of bad weather, especially at night, may breach a strong defensive position and achieve such depth of penetration, by assault or infiltration, as to unhinge the defences. The attacker's problems are maintaining control, accurate navigation and bringing down fire on targets from a pre-arranged fire navigational and sight instruments plan when in reduced visibility. Success may depend on a familiarity with night and bad weather conditions gained on peacetime training, the availability of suitable navigational and sighting devices, and careful planning. Commanders have to allow for the weather factor in appreciating the situation and formulating their plans.

Terrain

Military operations are quite likely to take place in areas that are very different geographically from those in Continental Europe. The UK could offer troops to support UN, NATO or Coalition operations almost anywhere in the world, and thus there is a need to be aware of and train to operate in many different

Mountains,
Falklands 1982.

Built-up Areas,
Italy 1944.

Desert: Digging out.

conditions of terrain and climate. The growth of urbanisation worldwide and a demographic shift to towns and cities also increases the importance of a military capability to operate across the spectrum of conflict in built up areas.

In all severe and testing conditions the most important factor is morale. Only forethought, good training, fitness, acclimatization and discipline can give troops the confidence to face battle in unfamiliar and arduous conditions with any prospect of success. Once troops have mastered the initial fear of the difficult and unfamiliar they take great pride in overcoming hardship. Formations and armies can develop a singular esprit de corps which sees them through the hazards of war in harsh environments. The problems of operating in difficult terrain are compounded by extremes of climate and health risk but few of them are beyond the capacity of any fit man or well trained properly equipped unit. However, psychological adjustment and mental robustness are required of the soldier in addition to special training and acclimatisation.

A long air move to a distant operational theatre will involve changes in the human body's metabolism while it adjusts to the new conditions. Acclimatisation, in-country training, suitable preventive medical treatment, such as inoculations and steps to avoid dehydration can significantly offset these effects. These important factors will all compete for time during any immediate predeployment period but deployment timescales may severely constrain the opportunity to conduct such training adequately.

Section 3 Operating in NBC Conditions

The Proliferation of Weapons of Mass Destruction (WMD)

The ending of the Cold War and the lessening of superpower constraints has encouraged the further proliferation of WMD among other nations and has enhanced the likelihood of their use in regional conflicts. Increased openness in the exchange of scientific knowledge, commercial and sometimes criminal transfers of manufacturing technology and materials, coupled with the growing availability of long-range delivery systems (including ballistic and cruise missiles), has tended to promote the adoption of WMD as a cheap and accessible means of acquiring substantial political and military leverage. The UK continues to co-operate with allies in efforts to prevent the proliferation or use of WMD while recognising the need to provide its forces with appropriate means of defence against this form of attack. It should be noted that the UK has no offensive chemical or biological capability.

In addition to the development and possible use of fully engineered WMD, there is also a significant and growing risk that future operations could involve exposure to toxic hazards of industrial origin. The globalisation of the chemical industry and the increasing employment of radioactive materials in the generation of power, industrial processes and medical treatment compels a recognition of the possible release into the environment of toxic chemical and radiological contaminants. This may arise through collateral or incidental damage to facilities in the course of military operations or via the deliberate misemployment of such materials by insurgent or other ad hoc groups, unconstrained by traditional attitudes towards the use of WMD.

The Utility of WMD

Background. Nuclear, biological and chemical weapons and, more recently, industrial chemical and radiological devices have generally been considered to form a single class of threat, encompassed by the term 'WMD'. While this is appropriate as an expression of the political divide that has to be crossed by a state when introducing such weapons into a conflict, it is also deceptive insofar as it implies that the individual weapons effects are more-or-less comparable. In fact, the triad of these weapons with their surrogates vary greatly in form and application.

Nuclear Weapons and Radiological Devices. Nuclear weapons are unique within the NBC spectrum of hazard in inflicting both massive physical damage to men and materiel at the moment of detonation (flash, blast, heat, initial nuclear radiation, electro-magnetic pulse, and transient radiation effects on electronics) while also posing an enduring hazard to persons over a sustained period thereafter, in terms of radiological fallout. The scale of damage arising from even a single detonation together with the enduring environmental effects of fallout serve to ensure that nuclear weapons have either operational or strategic value in their application or effect. It follows that these weapons are most likely to be used where the military benefit is perceived to be so great as to outweigh the inevitable political costs. Such moments might arise when a deploying force is concentrated around its point of entry or at a moment prior to defeat when an initiator judges he has little left to lose. It is also potentially feasible to make use of nuclear radiological devices which would allow for the deliberate spread of radioactive materials. This form of nuclear weapons use might be employed by insurgent groups who may have less concern for the precise timing of their action.

Biological Weapons. While the use of biological agents overtly or covertly to contaminate food and water supplies cannot be ruled out, the military employment of BW is more likely to focus on the use of aerosols. Disseminated from land, sea or air platforms, aerosol clouds of biological agents may cover a large part of a theatre of operations. The principal limiting factors in the employment of BW aerosols are: decay as time passes, progressive destruction through environmental factors, and time to take effect within the infected individual. This last limitation, involving a delay of hours or days, together with the likely impact on a civilian population, will tend to place the use of BW in the same strategic setting (politico-military frame) as the employment of nuclear weapons.

Chemical Weapons. Chemical weapons are, in the purely military sense, tactical instruments operating over limited areas (tens of square kilometres) and readily countered by the use of appropriate equipments and procedures. However, the very use of these defensive techniques, either on a precautionary basis or as a direct response to an attack, will impose inefficiencies in performance that degrade military activity. In general, an opponent may be expected to employ chemical weapons to satisfy the following tactical aims:

Decontamination.

Attrition. Persistent and non-persistent chemical agents may be used in an attempt to generate casualties and lower morale, by employing the element of surprise. Non-persistent agents (especially Blood agents) could be selected where there is an intention to launch an attack subsequent to their use and to seize ground. The focus of this form of employment will be the close battle. Attacks on depth targets with chemical weapons that have the aim of creating casualties is considered less likely.

Harassment. Persistent agents could be employed across the depth and breadth of a theatre of operations to impose disruption and chaos. Airfields, ports, HQs, logistic sites and fire support bases are good potential targets. Missiles will offer the most effective and economical delivery method, particularly where sub-munition warheads are available, but aircraft can also be used.

The Creation of Obstacles. Ground features of tactical significance, such as choke points, the flanks of advancing forces and ground abandoned in the wake of a withdrawal could be contaminated with persistent agents to canalise movement and deny the occupation of ground vital for future operations.

Wider Employment and Hazards. While CW in their military application are a tactical weapon they could offer wider strategic utility when employed to terrorise unprotected civilian populations and thereby to exert political leverage on their governments. In consequence, an enemy might identify targets of advantage within a theatre of operations that do not accord with the strictly doctrinal approach to their military use. This, together with uncertainties concerning the persistency of, perhaps, poorly manufactured agents and misemployed Toxic Industrial Chemicals (TIC) changing weather and the dangers of accidental TIC release all highlight the possibility that chemical agents, once used, may be encountered at any place or time across the breadth and depth of a theatre of operations.

The First Use of Chemical Weapons. Experience has shown that no matter how well equipped and trained a force may be, the first use of CW against it will be most unsettling and disruptive. A military enemy is likely to follow up this first attack with further attacks in order to gain the maximum advantage from this first use of CW. Subsequent use of CW will, or should have, less and less effect.

The Aim and Structure of NBC Defence

It is a defence policy requirement that UK forces should be able to survive and fight in an NBC environment. This is accomplished by equipping and training individuals and units to respond to actual or immediately threatened hazards whilst also furnishing formations with specialist crew-served systems to accomplish the more complex tasks of biological detection, nuclear and chemical survey and the decontamination of major equipments. These functions of detection and protection are complemented by the use of intelligence to identify particular weapons or agents in the enemy's inventory and his intentions for their use. Moreover, resistance to NBC hazards is part of the design process for new equipments. Deployed forces would also be supported by a range of medical countermeasures, comprising both pretreatment and post medication.

NBC defence planning and preparations are put into effect by formation staffs utilising a warning and reporting system based on agreed NATO procedures. These are recorded in both manual and automated form, the latter in the form of the Biological Radiological and Chemical Information System (BRACIS). The timely and accurate operation of this reporting structure enhances the commander's understanding of the impact of the enemy on the battlefield while allowing for the application of a 'risk taking' philosophy, to avoid unnecessary performance degradation during operations.

NBC Publications

The NBC defence of land based forces is dealt with on a Tri Service basis by the Defence NBC Centre at Winterbourne Gunner on the edge of Salisbury Plain. In addition to its training role, this Establishment is responsible for the development and publication of operational NBC defence procedures, while a collocated element conducts trials and staff studies on behalf of MOD staffs.

Section 4
Joint Operations

"Operations in which elements of more than one Service of the same nation participate."

JOINT WARFARE PUBLICATIONS

Joint Operations

Background. Major operations involving the Army will invariably be joint; they are very likely to be both joint and combined. The doctrine, capabilities and practices of the other Services and allies will influence any approach to operations and may well have a significant effect on the planning and execution of any campaign plan. The Army has a long tradition of working with the other two Services but the expertise necessary for such operations is only acquired through the development and practice of joint procedures in peacetime in a spirit of unselfish co-operation. When the forces committed to a joint operation come from more than one Service, a Joint Force Headquarters (JFHQ) will normally be deployed to exercise command over all single Service components and to control all aspects of staff work and land, air maritime, logistic and SF components of the force. The establishment of the Joint Services Command and Staff College to provide joint staff training for officers of all three Services is a further recognition of the integrated nature of future operations.

Air Support. In addition to its main task of providing a favourable air situation, which in itself requires that counter air operations are successful, the Royal Air Force can assist the Army in the following ways:

> *Close Air Support (CAS).* The use of offensive aircraft to provide additional firepower in close proximity to friendly ground forces is known as CAS. These missions have to be closely integrated with any ground fire plan and positively controlled: this is achieved through Forward Air Controllers (FAC) who may be ground based or airborne, in helicopters or fast jet aircraft. Laser target marking equipment may be used for this purpose because targets in the immediate battle area are usually well concealed, dispersed and protected. CAS is difficult to conduct and poses high risks to the pilot and aircraft. However, in an emergency or when ground force weapons are either not available or unsuitable, CAS may be the only means of destroying or neutralising a target. It is particularly valuable in support of formation attacks or deep operations.
>
> *Air Interdiction (AI).* One of the most effective ways in which the Royal Air Force can support the Army is the destruction of enemy tanks, vehicles, equipment and supplies along road, rail and inland waterway systems behind the immediate battle area. Enemy forces are at their most vulnerable when moving along canalized routes, particularly through choke points in towns and at river crossings; such points can be destroyed, halting movement into the battle area, and greater damage can be inflicted against an enemy force on the move than when it is dispersed in assembly areas or deployed and dug in. Such attacks are likely to affect a commander's ground force operations, and will have to

HMS *Hermes*: passage to the South Atlantic, 1982.

be co-ordinated between the land and air component HQs. The enemy's command and control installations are also a prime target for AI tasking. The land commander will identify a Fire Support Co-ordination Line short of which AI sorties have to be co-ordinated with him; such sorties are termed as Battlefield Air Interdiction.

Air Reconnaissance. The Air Force provides photographic electro-optical and electronic reconnaissance. Aerial imagery includes oblique and vertical panchromatic photography, infrared, thermal and radar imagery. Used singly or in combination these provide a virtually all-weather capability. The results of recce sorties are provided to the intelligence community for analysis and distribution as intelligence products. Air reconnaissance is not normally tasked directly by a land commander. Where the anti aircraft threat is low, aerial reconnaissance can also be provided by Aviation resources.

Transport Support. The Air Force provides strategic and tactical lift, resupply, casualty evacuation and airlift for airborne and airmobile assaults with fixed wing and rotary aircraft.

Airborne and Air Assault Operations. Airborne and air assault operations include the delivery of troops by air-landing, parachute or helicopter. Such operations may involve troop-carrying and attack helicopters and fixed-wing aircraft. They will require the close co-ordination of aircraft with ground forces either for rapid deployment across the battlefield or for manoeuvre in ground operations. Once deployed, the ground force will need significant air support and resupply until a ground link-up is achieved.

Amphibious Operations. In addition to its main tasks of protecting sea lines of communication and exercising overall sea control around the theatre of operations, the Navy has the ability to mount limited amphibious operations. These operations

Movement of equipment.

Joint force training in the UK.

comprise assault ships. All these can be utilised to land troops on undefended or lightly defended coastlines. Aircraft and helicopters based on a carrier may also be part of any amphibious landing force. Although the Royal Marines Commando Brigade is especially trained for this role there could be occasions when Army units are required to undertake similar tasks. The Navy's fleet of Landing Ships Logistic, Landing Craft Logistic and the Ramped Powered Craft are available to help bridge the water gap to land vehicles and stores once a beach-head has been secured. Further reinforcements are likely to be moved to the theatre of operations in merchant ships taken up from trade. Naval ships can provide gunfire support and naval or air force aircraft operating from carriers can provide the types of support provided by shore-based aircraft but on a more limited scale.

Command of Joint Operations. For national and ad-hoc contingencies command of any joint force deployed for operations will be vested in the Commander Joint Operations (WO) at the Permanent Joint Headquarters (PJHQ) at Northwood near London. There will also be a Joint Force Commander (JFC) in theatre once the joint force has reached its area of operations. Further information is available in the current Allied and Joint Service Publications.

Service Doctrinal Publications

The publication JWP 0-01 *British Defence Doctrine* describes the national and grand strategic framework in which all three Services play a part. Each Service has its own major doctrinal publications. These are:

For the Navy. BR1806	*The Fundamentals of British Maritime Doctrine*
For the Army. AC 71451	*The British Military Doctrine (BMD)*
For the Air Force. AP3000	*Air Power Doctrine*

These publications are widely distributed throughout the three Services and are available through Command and Service libraries.

Section 5 Combined Operations

"An operation conducted by forces of two or more allied nations acting together for the accomplishment of a single mission!"

NATO DEFINITION

Allies

In the future as in the past it will be normal for the United Kingdom to operate in concert with other allies in any future general war. Overseas it will be unusual to operate alone except in defence of particular national interests (Falklands War). It should be noted that terms such as 'Allied, or Alliance Operations' refers to operations conducted together by NATO partners. Multinational or Coalition operations would be the appropriate term for any combined operations conducted outside the NATO Alliance – such as the Coalition formed for the Gulf War of 1990/91.

Practices and Procedures

Some of the difficulties in working together with new allies in any coalition are the nomination of a common language and the use of common or similar practices and procedures for all aspects of military business; this applies particularly for CIS matters. Decisions on these two important topics will be necessary at an early stage of setting up any coalition of partners. It is in this area that NATO procedures, the English language and, in some cases, common doctrines have their greatest advantage. In an era of increased UN led operations, and with NATO forces acting outside traditional areas, it is of real advantage for the United Kingdom to be actively involved with other international military organisations.

States of Command and Control

In all alliances and coalitions there is, naturally, much staff attention paid to the conditions and the provisions of command and control relationships. It is important to agree these relationships before the assignment of forces and the subsequent commitment of troops to task. There are no precise and abiding criteria for applying the operational states of command and control, but NATO definitions have proved workable over many years within the Alliance and have been used as a basis for coalition working in other theatres, such as in the Gulf War and in UN operations in Bosnia. They are:

Full Command (Full Comd). The military authority and responsibility of a superior officer to issue orders to subordinates. It covers every aspect of military operations and administration and remains a national responsibility which cannot be delegated.

Operational Command (OPCOM). The authority granted to a commander to assign missions or tasks to subordinate commanders, to deploy units, to re-assign forces, or elements of forces, and to retain or delegate operational and/or tactical control as may be deemed necessary. It does not include responsibility for administration or logistics.

Operational Control (OPCON). The authority delegated to a commander to direct forces assigned so that the commander may accomplish specific missions or tasks which are usually limited by function, time or location; to deploy units concerned, and to retain or assign tactical control of those units. It does not include authority to assign separate employment of components of the units concerned. Neither does it, of itself, include administration or logistic control.

Tactical Command (TACOM). The authority delegated to a commander to assign tasks to forces under his command for the accomplishment of the mission assigned by higher authority.

Tactical Control (TACON). The detailed and usually local direction and control of movement and manoeuvre necessary to accomplish missions or tasks assigned.

Each campaign situation will be different and many nuances in effecting these states of command can be developed given co-operation and goodwill at all levels. Even bilateral arrangements can be fashioned that work within a coalition. The Russian troops committed for IFOR operations in Bosnia operate bilaterally with American troops within a NATO led alliance. Great care is needed when assigning forces to ensure an appropriate level of command is given for the mission. That done, flexibility and co-operation are essential to ensure that command arrangements are effective in practice.

In principle, all national governments have a right to be informed and consulted about the assignments for their troops in forthcoming operations within any coalition. Thus military planners have to be aware of this obligation and to be aware of national sensibilities, cultures and religions when committing troops to tasks and missions.

CHAPTER 6 THE CONDUCT OF OPERATIONS

"I was poring over the principles of war, listed in the old Field Service Regulations, when the Sergeant-Major came upon me. He surveyed me with kindly amusement. 'Don't bother your head about all them things, me lad,' he said. 'There's only one principle of war and that's this. Hit the other fellow as quick as you can and as hard as you can, where it hurts him most, when he ain't looking'."

FIELD MARSHAL SLIM

Section 1 Strategy, Operations and Tactics

Background

Hostilities are conducted of four different levels; grand strategy (Government Level), military strategy (MOD/PJHQ), operational (Corps, Div/Bde in some cases) and tactical (lower formations). These are reflected in the diagram in Chapter 2. It should be noted that tri-Service planning and operations are now common features of joint military activity particularly at the military strategic and operational levels of control.

Grand Strategic Level

As a facet of national policy, grand strategy is a function of government, although the government will seek the opinion of its military advisers. There are two main types of grand strategy; a deterrent strategy to keep the peace and a war strategy to impose the Nation's will on the enemy should deterrence fail. Details of the mechanics of how grand strategy is put into effect are given in *British Defence Doctrine* and is beyond the scope of this publication.

Military Strategic Level

Military strategy embraces the functions of organising, distributing and applying military resources to fulfil the political aims of national or alliance grand strategy. It involves the allocation and disposition of military forces to obtain an advantage which can be exploited to achieve a decision on the battlefield. As such it is the province of the theatre commander, who works within the parameters of political direction, to set the stage for success at the operational and tactical levels. In the context of a counter-insurgency campaign, military strategy involves the controlled application of force in conjunction with the Civil Authorities to implement government policy.

Operational Level

The operational level of command is concerned with the concept and conduct of operations at formation level where the tactical battles fought by lower formations are controlled and co-ordinated. The term applies particularly to the command levels above division but may equally apply at the divisional and possibly at brigade level when two or more separate but related tactical battles are being fought to achieve one objective, although a brigade sized force is not normally in a position to conduct more than one major task at any one time. In regional or general war the Joint Force Headquarters (JFHQ) is normally the formation which is responsible for the design and control of operations, allocating specific tactical missions to the Service components under its control. The division is the appropriate headquarters which is responsible for the design and control of operations, allocating specific and limited tactical missions to the formations under its control.

Tactical Level

Tactics for the Army is the art of disposing the appropriate forces on the ground, deploying them for combat and handling them on the battlefield to achieve a decision which furthers the operational aims. The term relates particularly to combat at brigade, battle group and below.

Applying the Principles of War

The Principles of War which are described in Chapter 2 are abstractions which acquire practical relevance only when related to the realities of specific military operations. They have to be considered in the context of the functions in combat which together form the basis of operational capability. The application of the Principles of War has to be continually examined in the light of new technical and scientific developments.

Evolution of new weapon systems can tend to emphasise the importance of some principles, while obscuring that of others. Although the relative importance of the Principles of War may vary with scientific developments it has to be noted that the real art of war is to apply the principles in combination, and with due regard to the circumstances. The conflicting claims of the various principles can often be balanced by applying the Principle of Economy of Effort.

Calculating Risks

Principles are easier to formulate than to apply. In practice it is difficult to assess their relative value, to perceive the one or two which might be of overriding importance, to decide which ones might reasonably be discounted and to judge how they might be affected by political factors. Many of the circumstances which influence a decision are not precisely quantifiable either because information is lacking or because there is no way of measuring intangibles like morale. A commander has to draw on his experience, insight and deductive powers to conceive the plan which is most likely to succeed in the uncertainties of war. In every situation there is an element of risk. Calculating risks, weighing up the chances of success and accepting the cost in terms of casualties are the inescapable responsibilities of command. There will be times when boldness will pay off and occasions when caution may be more prudent.

By drawing on the Principles of War it is possible to derive particular functions in combat which if adhered to by commanders will in consequence comply with the Principles of War. These functions in combat and their relationship to the Principles of War are described in the next Section. The associated Principles of War are underlined in the text.

Section 2 The Functions in Combat

Command

Successful command will take account of human, organisational and procedural factors.

Human Factors. Everything possible has to be done to ensure and sustain a high Morale. For with high morale comes the ability to endure the shock of battle, and other assaults on the spirit, such as might occur from the media in circumstances short of total war. Other aspects are:

A discipline based on self discipline has to be inculcated and leaders selected who are brave, calm, aggressive and decisive in a crisis, or Morale will suffer, the Aim will not be maintained and Offensive Action not taken.

Commanders have to be trained to take calculated risks, or the correct balance between Concentration of Force, Economy of Effort and Security will not be struck.

Organisational Factors. These include:

Forces allocated a particular mission should be grouped under a single commander otherwise the Selection and Maintenance of the Aim and the Concentration of Force become difficult to decide and to co-ordinate and in any event extra time will be needed to achieve this co-ordination.

The allocation of a balance of forces capable of taking independent action. If this is not done, in the chaos of battle they will not be able to take advantage of circumstances quickly nor will the effect of one arm complement that of another. Correctly balanced groups will be able to take Offensive Action and Flexibility thus achieving Surprise and Security by Co-operating quickly and by being able to Administer themselves. They will achieve this Co-operation the better if they have trained together.

Procedural Factors. The object of procedural measures is to make and disseminate appropriate decisions rapidly amidst the chaos of battle.

To do this, decision levels should be as low as possible, thus reducing the need to pass information and ensuring information is more nearly up to date. In this way commanders can react quickly and Flexibly and take Offensive Action.

By taking Offensive Action the initiative is seized and the situation changed, at least locally. The faster this tempo of change the greater the ability to Concentrate Force and to take the risk of further Economising of Effort without undue risk to Security.

There should be no planning without the responsibility of execution. The commander has to be committed to his own plan or his own Morale may suffer and by involving men in the decision-making process they become committed to the plan, which enhances Morale.

Orders should be issued so that subordinates are aware of the commander's overall intentions and the result desired from their successful execution. A secondary objective should be set. In these circumstances subordinates can pursue the Aim tenaciously while reacting Flexibly in a changing situation.

To focus subordinates' decisions in the desired direction the commander should state his priorities in advance. The Germans encapsulate this idea in Schwerpunkt which can be termed as Main Effort. Subordinates can then take quick and independent action while still Maintaining the Aim, Concentrating Force and Co-operating with each other.

Deception, either positive or passive, is to be included early in the planning process. Measures to Economise on Effort and Secure the force are then balanced with other elements of the plan.

The need to Co-operate and to operate Flexibly demands that procedures be common throughout any military grouping and that they be thoroughly practised.

Information and Intelligence

Information and intelligence is required before formulating an Aim. It is required to achieve Surprise, to plan Offensive Action, to reinforce Morale and to assess Sustainability requirements. It enables a commander to plan and act Flexibly and to strike the balance between Concentrating Force, Economising on Effort and Security. To this end:

Reconnaissance and surveillance have to be carried out at every level of command, even if dedicated resources are not available.

Reconnaissance and surveillance resources should be grouped with weapon systems of a similar range and be commanded at the same level to reduce the passage of information and improve Co-operation.

Firepower

The Aim is achieved by applying Concentrated firepower to destroy and break the will of the enemy. Concentrated firepower is required if Offensive Action is to succeed and in active (as opposed to passive) Security measures.

As a rule weapons should be commanded at the highest level that in the circumstances matches their range. The commander of the weapon system can then Concentrate Fire at a point and be able to shift this concentration Flexibly. The fire has to be directed at the lowest possible level by those who are moving in concert with it otherwise the fire will not be applied most effectively and Co-operation will break down.

Concentrate Fire rather than Forces. Because this is quick to do, it can achieve Surprise. Economise on Effort and is more Flexible. Remember the weight of fire is directly proportional to what can be supplied. It has to be possible to Sustain the fire plan.

If the balance has been struck correctly, Concentrating Fire on the Main Effort leads to defeating the enemy at that point; this is good for Morale and allows for Force to be concentrated elsewhere. Done quickly and Flexibly this achieves Surprise and overall an Economy of Effort.

Manoeuvre

The object of manoeuvre is to Concentrate Force at a point and to exploit the consequence of that action in furtherance of the Aim. For reasons of Security and Surprise it is important to concentrate only at the last minute and then as rapidly as possible. By denying or delaying the enemy's ability to move and deploy we can achieve Economy of Effort. Manoeuvre may also be required if adequate Co-operation is to be maintained with flanking formations or units.

To be Secure, manoeuvre must take place in conjunction with fire or fire on call. This applies at all levels of command.

Groups should be so organised that they have similar movement characteristics; failure to do this reduces the speed of the group as a whole to the speed of the slowest, and in consequence reduces Flexibility.

Commanders at every level should deploy according to their mission, while one may deploy on a broad front, his subordinate may deploy more narrowly. However, reserves or forces in depth have to be capable of moving in time to reinforce success, otherwise the commander will fail to Concentrate Force to take Offensive Action.

Protection

Security results from taking various passive and active measures to deny information to the enemy, to reduce the consequence of his actions and to deceive him of our intentions. The Aim should ideally be Secure the enemy. This is achieved by concealment, by silence, by reducing communication, by taking Offensive Action against enemy reconnaissance and surveillance units and by dispersal. Security will be enhanced if the enemy loses the initiative and he is Surprised. Equally our own Security will be threatened by the unexpected. A commander should be Flexible in order to react to this. Forces should only be concentrated to the density required to bring the necessary fire to bear at the time required.

Security results from seizing the initiative by Offensive Action. With the initiative a commander can dictate the tempo of the battle, he can afford to Economise on Effort to a greater extent in order further to Concentrate Force, thus increasing the tempo further. So reinforce success rather than failure.

A force, uncommitted to any mission critical to the plan (it might be used on secondary tasks without compromising its primary function), should always be held, capable in the circumstances of reacting to the unexpected or reinforcing success. If this force is not available it may not be possible to seize the opportunity to take Offensive Action and achieve Security.

Good Security depends on those in the surrounding area. Co-operation is essential. The ability to Secure ourselves will be impaired if Sustainability fails. Logistic and administrative plans should therefore, be made Secure.

Combat Service Support (CSS)

Logistics will regulate the Aim and the ability to Concentrate Force will be dependent upon Logistic installations. Logistics have to be Secured, for manoeuvre depends on them. They should be reduced to the minimum. Frugality or Economy in this field will allow greater speed of manoeuvre overall, leading to an enhanced ability to take Offensive Action. Logistics have to be Flexible enough to respond to changes in plans and attrition.

Combat units have to be confident of the logistic arrangements or hoarding will take place which is not Economic. Morale will suffer if faith is lost in the suitability and reliability of equipment vis-à-vis that of the enemy, and if the casualty evacuation and treatment arrangements are considered in the circumstances to be inadequate. Logistics will be improved if Co-operation is achieved at various levels of command and with flanking formations and allies. This will be more easily achieved if they share a common doctrine and interoperable equipment.

Summary

The collective expression of the six functions in combat is combat power - physical capabilities. When guided by doctrine and with trained and effective troops, the overall result is fighting power which defines an army's ability to fight. While the relative importance of the functions in combat may vary according to the purpose of an operation, they collectively provide the coherence and balance with which a commander can conduct operations successfully.

Section 3 The Operational Framework

The Core Functions

It is necessary to place the manoeuvrist approach to operations described in Chapter 2 into its full context in order to understand the basic elements of military operations. The three elements of manoeuvre, are those of finding, fixing and striking which are outlined in the three paragraphs below.

Finding the Enemy

Finding the enemy is a basic function which endures throughout an operation. It spans locating, identifying and assessing an enemy. At lower tactical levels the effective use and co-ordination of all intelligence, surveillance, target acquisition and reconnaissance (ISTAR) assets in the commander's overall Intelligence Preparation of the Battlefield (IPB) and its associated surveillance and target acquisition plan (STAP) form a fundamental part of this function. The principal tool to achieve this is reconnaissance. This should seek to find the gaps or weaknesses in an enemy's forces and then exploit them.

Fixing the Enemy

To gain freedom of action, a commander has to deny the enemy the opportunity to achieve his goals and put him in a reactive frame of mind. The aim is to throw the enemy off-balance and the principal means to achieve this are surprise, deception and lure. Fixing the enemy has a physical and psychological requirement. In military terms to fix the enemy is to:

Deny an enemy his goals (this includes physical action).

Distract an enemy (which includes psychological action).

Deprive an enemy of freedom of action in order to gain the necessary freedom of action for successful operations.

Striking the Enemy

To strike an enemy is to use that freedom of action to:

Manoeuvre – that is to get into a position of advantage in respect of an enemy from which force can be threatened or applied.

Hit an enemy unexpectedly, or in superior force, at the point selected in order to destroy or defeat him.

Striking is the conclusive and final part of the three elements, although finding and fixing are essential prerequisites. At the higher strategic and operational levels all three are joint activities, requiring the synchronisation of land and air power. Such synchronisation makes the most of the complementary characteristics of the different capabilities within a combat force to concentrate sufficient superior force at the selected point to guarantee a favourable outcome.

Deep, Close and Rear Operations

At both the tactical and operational levels, operations to find, fix and strike the enemy may well be simultaneous and should be closely integrated. The operations should be organised within a framework of deep, close and rear operations. The terms deep, close and rear are used to describe how these three operations relate to each other primarily by function (ie what they are to achieve) and by geography (ie where they are to achieve it). These three operations have to be considered together and fought as a whole at both the operational and tactical levels. They require continuous and careful synchronisation and, where necessary, integration between levels of commands. While finding the enemy is a function common to all operations, fixing and striking him may be achieved by either deep or close operations, according to the overall design for battle. In order to achieve concentration of force, one of them will be designated as the main effort at any one time. Rear operations will invariably protect and sustain the force, while ensuring that freedom of action for future operations is maintained.

The simultaneous prosecution of deep, close and rear operations requires a decentralised philosophy of command – Mission Command which has been described in Chapter 2. The essence of Mission Command is decentralisation of command which rests on initiative, timely decision-making and unity of effort. To be successful, it also requires an unbroken chain of trust and mutual understanding throughout the span of command. Command is decentralised to allow subordinates to use their initiative within their delegated freedom of action, to fulfil their commander's intention without constant reference to him. Underlying this approach to command are two beliefs: that forces act with greater cohesion and effect if they know not only what to do but why; and that the man best placed to decide how to act is the one with the best information who may be the one closest to the action.

The diagram overleaf provides, in outline, the general sequence of how doctrinal principles and concepts turn into practical tenets that can be understood and applied. The diagram also places into a dynamic context the relationship between defence policy, government commitments, fighting power and capability.

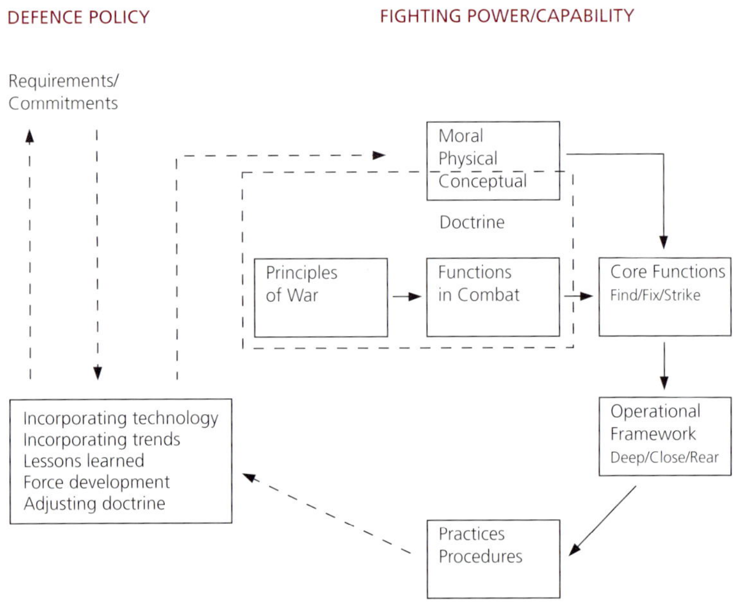

Section 4 Intelligence

Background

The aim of intelligence is to assess the enemy's capabilities and forecast his intentions in terms of what he will do and how, when, where and in what strength he will do it. The task of the intelligence (G2) staff is to meet its commander's needs for timely intelligence so that he can make a plan to carry out his mission.

A distinction has to be made between information and intelligence. The former is unprocessed data of every description which may be used in the production of intelligence. It is provided by many different sources and agencies, such as air reconnaissance, radio intercept and prisoners of war. The latter is the product obtained by processing information, which involves collation, evaluation, analysis, integration and interpretation. A plain fact is information, its significance becomes intelligence.

At the start of operations most of the information flowing in intelligence channels will be in the form of contact reports from forward troops either observing or fighting the enemy. Much of it will rapidly become out of date in a fast-moving situation and, since there will be no time to process it in the heat of the battle, it will not be intelligence. It is thus known as combat information. A great deal of it will be used immediately by units engaged with the enemy. Relevant combat information should be transmitted swiftly to those who need it to fight the current battle and through intelligence channels to higher headquarters for processing. It is equally important to control the flow to avoid choking communications and burdening staffs with information which is of no concern to them.

There are two types of intelligence:

Basic. Permanent or semi-permanent background material which forms the basis for planning operations.

Current. The topical material related to what is happening now. Current combat intelligence is usually short-lived but its value depends on basic intelligence which involves a detailed knowledge of the enemy, and which cannot be acquired overnight.

It is partly on long-term basic intelligence that the army plans its equipment programmes and formulates the tactical doctrines which are practised and developed in peacetime. The competence of the intelligence staff and its knowledge of potential enemy methods, strengths and weaknesses, so essential in war, can be acquired only before its outbreak. The foundations of good military intelligence in war are normally laid in peacetime.

Principles of Intelligence

Eight principles govern the organisation, activities and production of intelligence. These are:

Centralised Control. Intelligence must be controlled centrally to avoid unwarranted duplication, provide mutual support and ensure the efficient, economic use of all resources.

Timeliness. The most accurate and reliable information or intelligence is useless if it arrives too late. By the same token, the tasking system must be capable of reflecting without delay any significant changes in the situation.

Systematic Exploitation. Sources and agencies must be systematically exploited by methodical tasking, based on a thorough knowledge of their capabilities and limitations.

Objectivity. Any temptation to distort information to fit preconceived ideas must be resisted.

Accessibility. Relevant information and intelligence must be readily available to intelligence staffs and to users. All information and intelligence must be processed by intelligence staffs, and this includes comparison with previously acquired data. Intelligence is of no value if it is not disseminated or accessible to those who require it.

Responsiveness. The intelligence staff must be responsive to the intelligence requirements of the commander.

Source Protection. All sources of information must be adequately protected. In extreme cases action may not be taken as a result of specific information, purely to protect the source.

Continuous Review. Intelligence must be reviewed continuously and where necessary revised, taking into account all new information and comparing it with what is already known.

The Intelligence Cycle

General. A logical and methodical system is required for the production of intelligence and the revision of previous intelligence estimates. The need is met at all levels of command by the intelligence cycle which has four stages and is illustrated at Annex B to this Chapter. The stages are:

Direction.

Collection.

Processing.

Dissemination.

Direction. There are two aspects to direction:

That given by the commander to his intelligence staff in the form of intelligence requirements, in order of priority and with a time limit to provide the necessary intelligence for operational planning. This is an essential command function.

That given by the intelligence staff to their sources and agencies.

Collection. This involves the exploitation of sources of information by collection agencies and the delivery of collected information to the appropriate processing unit for use in the production of intelligence.

Processing. Processing is the system of converting information into intelligence in the following closely related steps:

Collation – the routine office work of the registering and recording of all incoming information. Depending on local circumstances this may range from brief entries in a log and map-marking to computer inputs.

Evaluation – determining the reliability of the source and the credibility of the information.

Analysis – identifying significant facts, comparing them with existing data and drawing conclusions from them.

Integration – putting all the analysed information together to form a pattern of events or to build up a picture of the subject being studied.

Interpretation – deciding what the collated, evaluated, analysed and integrated information means in terms of what is likely to happen in the future.

Dissemination. This covers the timely conveyance of intelligence in an appropriate form and by suitable means to those who need it. It can take the form of oral briefings, at which questions can be asked and problems resolved, or by reports and summaries.

Summary. The intelligence cycle system enables an intelligence officer to:

Meet the intelligence requirements of his commander.

Assess the enemy's capabilities.

Forecast his probable intentions and plan.

Reveal any enemy vulnerabilities and highlight any already suspected.

Intelligence Preparation of the Battlespace (IPB)

The development of the manoeuvrist approach to operations and advances in military technology have resulted in an increase in the tempo of operations. At the same time, these changes have improved the ability to collect, process and disseminate large amounts of information and intelligence very rapidly. In parallel with these enhancements, there have also been developments in the way in which a commander carries out the decision-making process leading to his plan. The effect of all these changes has been to highlight the need for Intelligence staffs to be able to provide accurate information and intelligence in a timely manner.

The commander needs information and intelligence in order to conduct the Estimate process which leads to his Decision and ultimately to his Plan. He will need information about his own forces, other friendly forces and the enemy, and about the battlespace environment within which both he and the enemy will conduct operations; these are the Commander's Critical Information Requirements (CCIR). He will need timely intelligence about an enemy and an accurate assessment of his intentions; these are the commander's Priority Intelligence Requirements (PIR). In order fully to meet these requirements, a method of assessing and presenting large amounts of information and intelligence quickly is needed.

Formal consideration of two principal components of the CCIR and the PIR, the enemy's course of action (COA) and terrain, is not new. The Appreciation of the situation, which took these factors into account, was used in the British Army for many years. IPB, however, is a process which takes a structured approach to the assessment of these influences on operations and produces the answers graphically. Experience gained in teaching IPB has shown that the process is valid, has considerable utility and has now been adopted as a part of tactical doctrine.

IPB is a command and staff tool which allows systematic, continuous analysis of the threat and the battlespace environment to be carried out and which presents the results in a graphical format. It assists in determining the threat's most likely, or worst case, COA, enables assessment of the effects of the battlespace environment on the commander's own COA and highlights points in time and space at which decisions critical to success have to be made. In addition to assisting the commander with his estimate, IPB is also a significant tool in the production and synchronisation of component plans. These include the Reconnaissance Plan, the Operations Security (OPSEC) Plan and Counter

Surveillance Control Measures, the Deception Plan and others appropriate to the operation.

Surveillance and Reconnaissance

Surveillance and reconnaissance are essential tools of intelligence. The resources for carrying out these functions fall into four categories.

Control of the electro-magnetic spectrum.

Other forms of electronic surveillance.

Imagery and observation obtained from overhead platforms such as satellites, aircraft, drones and remotely piloted vehicles (RPVs).

Ground observation and reconnaissance.

Control of The Electro-Magnetic Spectrum

The Electronic Battlespace. As opposing forces increasingly rely on electronic systems control of the electro-magnetic spectrum is becoming vital to the successful prosecution of the commander's plan. Without a clear understanding of who is occupying which part of the spectrum and for what purpose it will be impossible for friendly EM systems to be used to best effect. Control of the EM spectrum is achieved by a thorough reconnaissance of the spectrum, including an in-depth exploitation of some transmissions, followed by selective, offensive action to influence or deny hostile use. At the same time protective measures are necessary to ensure the survival of friendly systems from similar hostile activities. These processes, together with precise assignment of friendly frequencies, will lead to an effective management of the EM spectrum to friendly advantage.

Reconnaissance of the EM Spectrum. Methods include:

Signal Intelligence (SIGINT). SIGINT operations are strategic activities and cover the interception and exploitation of electro-magnetic emissions for the purpose of producing technical information and intelligence. They comprise two elements:

Communications Intelligence (COMINT) – is defined as the gathering of technical material and intelligence information derived from electro-magnetic communications and communications systems (eg Morse, voice, teleprinter and facsimile) by other than the intended recipients.

Electronic Intelligence (ELINT) – is defined as technical material and intelligence derived from electro-magnetic non-communications transmissions (eg radars, navigation aids and jamming transmissions) by other than the intended recipients.

Electronic Warfare (EW). EW is conducted at the tactical level and relies in part on a database provided by SIGINT.

EW Support Measures (ESM) – is defined as the search for, interception and location of radiated electro-magnetic energy for the purpose of immediate threat recognition. It provides a source of information required for immediate decisions involving electronic countermeasures, electronic protection measures and other tactical actions. This activity is carried out by specialist troops and is the principle EW activity in support of the Intelligence process.

Electronic Counter Measures (ECM) – again specialist activities to prevent an enemy's effective use of the EM Spectrum. These include jamming, deception and neutralisation.

Electronic Protective Measures (EPM) – Measures taken by everyone to ensure that they are protected against enemy ESM and ECM.

Other Forms of Surveillance

Ground Radar. Ground radars detect and locate movement and provide early warning of hostile intentions. Though not affected by darkness, smoke or bad weather, they are active systems and work on line-of-sight only. Weapon locating radars determine the positions of mortars and guns by observing the trajectories of their projectiles. This information is used for counter-battery shoots.

Remote Sensors. Remote sensors are divided into categories in accordance with their method of positioning or delivery and their system of detection:

Delivery. Sensors may be:

Emplaced by troops around their defensive positions to give warning of local enemy movement.

Positioned by patrols on enemy routes in depth to give information and provide target acquisition on enemy operational and supply activity.

Delivered by artillery or dropped from aircraft.

Types of Sensors. There are six main types, each with its own system of operation and relying on radio links for the transmission of data to the control monitor:

Seismic. Vibrations may be detected at distances depending on the type of soil. A skilled operator can determine from his monitor the number of men and the number and types of vehicles passing the seismic sensor.

Acoustic. Movement detected by seismic sensors can be used to activate microphones for general surveillance purposes. Sound ranging equipment can be used to locate guns or mortars for counter-battery purposes.

Magnetic. Magnetic sensors may also be used to confirm seismic detections.

Electro-magnetic. Sensors detect movement through an electro-magnetic field.

Infrared makes use of two systems:

Active. Beam emitters, similar to those used in burglar alarms, activated by an object breaking an infrared beam.

Passive. Thermal techniques used to detect changes in the heat pattern.

Television (TV), including low-light techniques.

Night Observation Devices. These devices employ one of three scientific principles, low light, image intensification or thermal imaging. They may be used to provide early warning of hostile movement close to defensive positions or they may be incorporated in longer range surveillance devices. They may also be used as gun sights or employed in conjunction with laser beams to determine with accuracy the range to targets so that the latter can be engaged with direct or indirect fire.

Airborne/Satellite Imagery and Reconnaissance

General. Air reconnaissance has progressed from the use of aircraft to RPVs and satellites. A permanent record may be obtained from photography, infrared sensors, including thermal imaging, and radar. TV (video) has a limited value in low-level conflict.

Satellites. Satellite photography, although degraded by cloud and mist, is now capable of producing good resolution pictures which can be transmitted to give real-time information. There will, of course, be delays between tasking a satellite system and receiving the information at a formation headquarters. Infrared photography can provide information at night, in thin mist and light rain. Satellites also have ELINT and COMINT functions.

Aircraft. Fixed-wing aircraft are used for long-range reconnaissance, usually operating at very high altitudes, and for short-range reconnaissance, normally of tactical objectives, at much lower levels. They carry cameras for vertical, oblique and panoramic photography, infrared line scan equipment and radar to supplement the direct visual observation of aircrew. The shortage of aircraft and the likely attrition rate will limit the effort available for reconnaissance missions.

Helicopters. In this role helicopter operations are divided into observation and reconnaissance tasks. Observation sorties are invariably designed to obtain information on enemy activity, such as watching an exposed flank or covering a gap in ground surveillance. A degree of continuity is usually implicit but sustained observation is extensive in sorties. Direction of fire is frequently combined with observation missions. Reconnaissance sorties are flown to seek out particular information. They may be tasked in support of armour, artillery, engineers or infantry to meet specific requirements. Reconnaissance missions are not necessarily concerned with enemy activity but they are invariably concentrated on a particular location, for example, a route or a bridge. The threat to helicopters from air defence missiles, guns and laser weapons can be minimised by operating with equipment which employs sideways looking devices and by the skilful use of terrain cover.

Drones and RPVs. While a drone can only be programmed to fly a pre-set flight pattern an RPV can be controlled from a ground station to fly any desired course. Whereas a drone is used primarily for surveillance and has only a limited target acquisition capability an RPV can be used equally well for both roles. Although there is little to choose between the two systems in radius of action, there is a marked difference in performance. A drone's night capability is confined to photography using flares and infrared, and its film cannot be recovered for processing until it lands. An RPV has a wider choice of systems, including thermal imagers which can transmit real-time information by day and by night, degraded only by heavy rain or fog. Drones and RPVs may be tasked in response to general information on enemy movement provided by other sources, including airborne radars.

Ground Observation and Reconnaissance

Observation. Observation based on the human eye, supplemented by the ear, may be limited in scope and range but is reinforced by the observer's ability to keep watch over a long period and interpret quickly what he sees and hears. The range of the eye and the discriminating intelligence of the brain can be extended by low-light level TV, image intensification and thermal imagers. Radar is used to detect movement.

Long-Range Reconnaissance. Long-range reconnaissance of installations in enemy rear areas, routes, beaches, helicopter and parachute landing areas, and the surveillance of enemy deployment, supply routes and other activity, may be carried out by special units such as the Special Boat Squadron, Royal Marines and the Special Air Service. These units employ a mixture of deployment methods including landing craft, submarines, aircraft and parachute.

Medium Reconnaissance. Medium reconnaissance is conducted by armoured reconnaissance regiments under the direct control of formation headquarters, usually corps or division. The range of operations will vary widely and may be conducted anywhere in the area of the formation within the limits imposed by the range of communications. While armoured reconnaissance units are both mobile and agile, and possess good communications, they have limitations in respect of armour and fire power. Their function is enhanced by reconnaissance helicopters allocated in direct support.

Close Reconnaissance. Close reconnaissance is the responsibility of the reconnaissance troops and platoons organic to armoured regiments and infantry battalions. Dismounted reconnaissance remains primarily an infantry responsibility although armoured reconnaissance regiments have some capability.

Combat Reconnaissance. Combat reconnaissance and surveillance are concerned with the collection of information by elements of the combat arms within battle groups while observing or engaging the enemy in close combat. This includes the continuous acquisition of information on terrain, obstacles and routes which may form the basis of engineer intelligence. Information may be gained by stealth, as much to prevent the enemy from guessing our intentions as to preserve the patrol, or by fighting for it. In the latter case it may be necessary to mount anything from a fighting patrol provided by a platoon to capture a prisoner to an attack by a formation to force the enemy to reveal his dispositions, defensive fire plan and counter-attack arrangements. The need to report combat information rapidly up the chain of command has already been mentioned in the previous section on intelligence.

Section 5 The Estimate Process

Background

Once the aim for an operation has been selected, the appropriate factors will be considered with the object of evaluating how they can support the achievement of that aim. This is known as the Estimate Process. As a situation changes, the mission and relevant factors are re-evaluated in a logical manner. In this sense, the Estimate can be looked on as a continuous cycle which can be returned to when needed. The formal Estimate is for use principally at formation level. While this description concentrates on the four stages of the process and sets out the sequence of factors to be considered to ensure uniformity, the detailed manner in which an Estimate is conducted should be determined by the local commander and staff.

As part of his Estimate the commander should consider what Intelligence, Surveillance, Target Acquisition and Reconnaissance (ISTAR) capabilities he requires. The operational context, the threat, limitations on sensor capabilities and constraints on usage or availability, will determine the precise ISTAR components for a particular operation. ISTAR links surveillance, reconnaissance and target acquisition systems and sensors to cue offensive strike assets, with particular emphasis on the timely passage of critical and targeting information. It encompasses the collection and management of information and intelligence to provide situational awareness for commanders and their staffs and to support the targeting process. Accurate, timely intelligence assessments of enemy capabilities and intentions are essential to enable commanders at all levels to focus combat power on exploiting enemy weaknesses and critical vulnerabilities – a concept known as 'recce pull'.

Consistent with the tenets of Mission Command a subordinate commander is directed by his superior as to what effect he is to achieve. At the operational level, the superior commander's intentions are expressed in a Statement of the

Commander's Intent which is normally refined in a Concept of Operations. At the tactical level, the superior commander's concept of operations should include both his intent and his design for operations. At all levels, stating the commander's intent allows subordinates to exercise initiative, but in a way which will be in accordance with the commander's aim. The Estimate Process, then, helps the subordinate commander at any level to decide how he will achieve the desired effect.

The Estimate

The Estimate has the following four stages:

Stage 1 – Mission Analysis. Mission Analysis is a logical process for extracting and deducing from a superior's orders the tasks necessary to fulfil a mission. It places in context what effect is to be achieved in the overall design for operations. A commander establishes what constraints apply, and determines, as the campaign, major operation, battle or engagement progresses, whether further decisions are required. As such it is a dynamic process which 'triggers', and then regulates, the remainder of the Estimate. It is continued thereafter as the situation and the mission are reviewed.

Stage 2 – Evaluation of Factors. The factors which affect the tasks are then considered. The following are essential: Enemy, Environment (including Ground and Weather), Friendly Forces (including Combat Service Support), Surprise and Security, and Time. Any further relevant factors are then considered. In Operations Other Than War, for example, political factors may be particularly important. Deductions will begin to reinforce some tasks; others may be eliminated because they are not vital to the mission. A list of tasks, which should be completed in order to fulfil the mission, will then emerge.

Stage 3 – Consideration of Courses of Action (COA). The next stage is to identify broad COA based on the identified tasks. For each of the COA, the advantages and disadvantages are considered in order to establish the combat power required and risks involved. The commander's decision then follows.

Stage 4 – The Commander's Decision. The decision has to be the logical result of the Estimate. With it the commander decides on (or develops) one of the possible COA, having taken into account the advantages and disadvan-tages of each COA in comparison with the likely COA of the enemy. The decision constitutes the basic directive for the completion of the planning and for all future actions. As such it represents the outline concept of operations and has to include the commander's intent (his design for battle).

Development and Review

Once the decision has been made, a plan is developed and directives or orders are produced. Subsequently, the situation is monitored. New information, as it becomes available, is used to re-evaluate the situation and, in turn, the tasks. If the situation changes radically, the commander should return to the Estimate, starting at the mission analysis stage, to test whether his mission, decision – or developed plan – are still valid. However, whilst this re-examination of the Estimate may occur at any stage of the decision-making process, commanders have to beware of over-loading either themselves or their staffs as a result of every unforeseen, or minor, change in the situation. A diagram describing the features of the Estimate Process is at Annex C to this Chapter.

Summary

This outline of the Estimate Process does not cover all eventualities, nor does it describe the procedures by which an Estimate is produced and the manner in which a commander's staff can assist in making an Estimate.

Section 6 Combat Forces

General

Combat forces are those forces which use fire and movement to engage the enemy with direct fire weapon systems, as distinguished from those forces which engage the enemy with indirect fires or otherwise provide combat support to manoeuvre forces. Combat forces are primarily armoured (armour and armoured/ mechanized infantry), non-armoured (infantry, airmobile infantry), reconnaissance (air and ground), and aviation (armed and attack helicopters).

Armoured Forces

Armoured forces include heavy (tank) and light armoured forces. Heavy armoured forces are primarily offensive in nature. The mobility, fire power, protection from enemy fire and shock effect make them an excellent weapon system for penetrating enemy defences, exploiting the success of offensive operations, deep strikes in the enemy's rear areas, and pursuing defeated forces. Armoured units can also blunt enemy attacks and launch counterattacks as part of defensive operations. Tanks can destroy enemy armoured vehicles, infantry units, anti-tank guided missile units, and under certain conditions effectively engage aircraft in flight.

Light armoured units can be used in a variety of environments. Tactical missions include providing security, reconnaissance, and anti armour fire power support to non-armoured or airmobile units. Light armoured units can conduct standard armoured operations including the destruction of enemy forces in co-ordination with other arms.

Armoured infantry units have the same mobility as armoured forces, but less fire power and protection. When equipped with infantry fighting vehicles, the armoured infantry can accompany tanks in mounted assaults, but commanders must be careful in determining if, when and where infantrymen must dismount to accomplish their mission. In the attack, armoured infantry can act as fixing forces. In the defence, they act as pivot points for manoeuvring tank-heavy forces. Additionally armoured infantry units equipped with long range anti-armour missiles can be used to provide over watching fire and assist in delay missions in combined arms formations. Armoured infantry and armoured units should act as a team to defeat enemy armoured forces in a variety of environments.

Non Armoured Forces

Non armoured forces include dismounted and airmobile (air-assault and airborne) infantry. Dismounted infantry units can operate in most terrain and weather and are capable of performing a number of tasks across the spectrum of conflict, especially for Operations Other Than War (OOTW). Because of their raid deployability they may be the dominant arm in rapidly developing operations. In such cases, they can take the initiative early, seize and hold ground, and mass fire to stop an enemy in restrictive terrain. Dismounted infantry operates primarily at night or during periods of limited visibility. They are especially useful for operations in difficult terrain and urban or built-up areas. They can infiltrate and can move rapidly to the enemy rear to accomplish special missions or in conjunction with armoured forces. Dismounted infantry units achieve decisive results through the employment of organic and supporting forces and weapons systems.

Airmobile forces have the greatest tactical and operational-level mobility. Their deployability and significant anti-armour capability, makes them particularly well-suited as an early deploying force in contingency operations against heavy forces. They train and fight as a team in combination with airmobile artillery. Attack and transport aviation are capable of penetrating deep into enemy territory to cut lines of communication (LOCs), seize airfields, destroy command and control installations, block reinforcing units or seize key terrain.

Airborne forces are capable of being deployed over great distances. These units can be projected to virtually any objective under most weather conditions. Commanders must consider that deployment at great distances may preclude airborne forces from being augmented with additional anti-armour weapons systems. Once on the ground their capabilities and lethality are similar to other infantry units.

Aviation

Following the introduction of the Attack Helicopter (AH), aviation will provide capabilities for combat (direct fire) surveillance, target acquisition and reconnaissance, combat support (direction of fire etc) as well as for limited combat service support.

The range, lethality, speed and survivability of AH will allow it to make significant contributions to deep, close and rear operations. With AH and Lynx, aviation will be able to find, fix, manoeuvre and strike an enemy in most weather conditions by day and night, unhampered by the limitations of ground movement.

Aviation is capable of gathering information (visual electro-optical and electronic) quickly over large areas. It will be able to react to this information and could concentrate rapidly to attack land and air targets with its own direct and indirect weapons, or in conjunction with other forces making use of electronic warfare, artillery, air, naval and special forces as appropriate.

Reconnaissance Forces

The basic tasks are reconnaissance, security and economy of force activity. Reconnaissance units should be capable of finding the enemy and developing the situation thereby providing the commander with reaction time and security. Such units are also capable of delaying an attacking enemy as well as assisting in any planned withdrawal.

Section 7 Combat Support (CS) Forces

General

Combat Support is defined as fire support and operational assistance provided to combat elements. It is composed of two distinct but complementary elements providing both lethal and non lethal support essential to the conduct of operations. Combat forces are, generally, not able to operate effectively without such support which has to be co-ordinated with, and integral to, the operational plan.

Fire Support

Fire support is the collective use of indirect fire weapons, armed fixed-wing aircraft and all available target acquisition assets. Fire support is therefore provided by artillery (including mortars and naval gunfire), air and aviation (reconnaissance helicopters). Likely tasks for fire support assets include the provision of firepower in support of deep, close and rear operations and ISTAR.

Artillery provides target acquisition and indirect fire across the whole battlefield in the following ways:

> *Field Artillery.* Field artillery provides close support to combat forces, counterfire, the suppression of enemy air defences (SEAD) and deep fire as required. This fire will suppress, neutralise, canalise or destroy enemy attack formations or defences; obscure the vision of the enemy or otherwise inhibit his ability to acquire and attack friendly targets. It can also destroy enemy targets deep in his rear with long range rocket or missile fire. Field artillery can be rapidly shifted, by day and night, in all types of weather, to mass fire at the critical time and place.

Mortars. Mortars are not normally held outside an infantry battalion and are considered to be their integral fire support. Their fire will nevertheless need to be integrated with the other fire support resources available to the battalion's fire support co-ordinator.

Naval Gunfire Support (NGS). Some land operations may be supported by sea based indirect fire systems. Field artillery will have the added responsibility of observing and controlling NGS. Specialist NGS co-ordinators may be deployed for this purpose.

The types of fire support provided by air forces and Army aviation has been covered under joint operations.

Long range patrolling activity provide real-time depth surveillance of the enemy and have the capability to provide target acquisition and fire direction in support of OAS, long range artillery and attack helicopters. They are also capable of limited offensive action and can be tasked for certain other special operations.

Targeting

Targeting is defined as the process of selecting targets and matching the appropriate response to them, taking account of operational requirements and capabilities. It is the mechanism for fusing ISTAR and STRIKE assets such as air, aviation, indirect fire and offensive EW, ensuring that they are properly co-ordinated and that the most appropriate weapon system is used to attack each target. Aviation is only incorporated when it is being employed on raids against a specific target. Like armour and infantry, aviation is not subject to the targeting process when it is conducting manoeuvre missions. It is, therefore, a tool for the efficient and effective management of resources and is fundamental in the speed of reaction towards the enemy. Targeting is a G3 operations responsibility and not simply a G2 intelligence gathering process. It has to be a co-ordinated part of the overall concept of operations.

Operational Assistance

Operational Assistance is any form of support to combat forces other than fire support or CSS. It can be provided by Air (Counter Air and Air Transport), Aviation (Utility and transport), Air Defence, Engineers and EW:

Counter Air Activity. Counter air operations are conducted at the operational level, in order to obtain an advantageous air situation in which to conduct land operations. Their results can be measured in terms of control of the air, which will clearly have a major impact on the conduct of operations at the tactical level.

Air Transport. At the tactical level air transport includes the use of aircraft for airborne operations, casualty evacuation and logistic support.

Aviation. Suitable roles for utility and transport helicopters include insertion of patrols, aerial command posts, casualty evacuation and search and rescue operations.

Air Defence. One of the most effective means of destroying the cohesion and freedom of action of forces involved in an operation is through attack from the air. AD considerations are consequently of vital importance to commanders at all levels. AD will normally be carried out by two complementary components; aircraft involved in the counter air campaign and surface to air systems. At the tactical level, a commander will be most concerned with the deployment and tasking of his integral surface to air systems for protection at various high levels, coverage of particular sites and a specific area and for gaining additional information about the enemy.

Airspace Control. It is essential for AD commanders at all levels to work closely with air and aviation in order for the AD of ground forces to be effective without causing fratricide. The purpose of airspace control is, therefore, to balance two conflicting requirements; the need to optimise AD protection and the need to allow aircraft freedom to operate with the minimum restrictions. This control may be achieved by using positive control, procedural control, or a combination of both.

Engineers. Formation and units at all levels require engineer support. The engineer commander should advise on the correct mix of engineer support to formations or units, as well as the engineer material to accomplish the mission. This allocation could be altered as priorities change and tasks progress. The command relationship between engineers and the formations or units they support will depend on the nature of the mission and needs to be clearly stated. Scarcity of engineer units may require other arms units to execute simple engineer tasks. The main roles of engineers are:

- Support to mobility.
- Support to countermobility.
- Support to survivability.
- General engineer support.

Electronic Warfare (EW). The electro-magnetic spectrum is the battlefield for EW. As with any military operation, the function of EW operations is to find, fix and attack the enemy whilst at the same time defending friendly forces against his attempts to do the same. EW is defined as 'military action involving the use of electro-magnetic energy to determine, exploit, reduce or prevent hostile use of the electro-magnetic spectrum and action to retain its effective use by friendly forces'.

Section 8 Combat Service Support (CSS) Forces

Administration and Logistics

While logistics encompasses the broad range of sustainment activity from production to consumption as well as medical support, CSS is concerned more directly with the operational and tactical support for combat forces. An outline of the purpose of CSS support and its application is given below.

The Aim of CSS

The purpose of CSS is to maintain a force with the necessary combat power for the duration required to achieve its objectives. It is the provision of supplies including their storage, handling and transportation, the maintenance and repair of materiel, medical care and treatment of casualties, personnel replacement, equipment replacement and the provision of necessary welfare services. Those responsible for CSS are tasked to ensure that combat forces are supplied with what they need to accomplish the mission. It is important that the supplies and facilities needed are provided in the right quantity, at the right time, at the right place and in a serviceable condition.

The temptation to ignore logistic constraints and to take a risk to pursue a course which is operationally desirable may end in disaster and the history of warfare is full of examples of ambitious plans failing because they were not backed with adequate logistic resources. This does not mean that risks should not be taken, but that the penalties for failure are greater if logistic support is not available. A commander should always take account of any logistic short-comings when carefully calculating the risk of a particular operation.

Logistic Principles

Foresight. The first, and often most time consuming preparations that have to be made for an operation are frequently administrative. The objective of the logistician is to ensure that the execution of the operational plan is free from delay or limitations caused by the lack of essentials that could have been foreseen. The commander will aid the logistic process by involving the chief logistic officer in his planning group from the outset. This will enable the staff to anticipate changes in demand. The chief logistic officer should inform the commander of the support implications of the operational proposals, and advise what is and is not logistically possible. The commander and his chief logistic officer achieve foresight by applying all the principles of mission command. Consequently, misunderstandings that could lead to a delay in accumulating resources or, conversely, prejudicing operational security by too premature an action, can be avoided.

Economy. The logistic concept of operations has to satisfy three conditions: to use or apply resources to achieve that which is required (effectiveness); to use as few resources as necessary (economy), and to get as much out of them as possible (efficiency). The tendency to over-insure has to be resisted, even though it leads to a belief that the logistic arrangements are excellent. In reality, over-provision means that supplies, transport, time, manpower and money will all have been wasted because materiel has been unnecessarily demanded, moved, stored, repaired, consumed or abandoned.

Simplicity. A simple plan is more likely to survive the stress of intensive operations or sudden shocks. Simplicity enables faults in plans, systems or organisations to be more easily identified and confers flexibility. Simplicity of planning and execution will be aided if the commander's intent is understood and clear directives issued. The involvement of too many control agencies and over complex inter-relationships is contrary to the principles of mission command and increases the risk of a breakdown in the logistic system. Paradoxically, overall simplicity may have to be derived from complex sub-systems.

Co-operation. The joint and probably combined nature of most military operations has implications for the logistic system. In the same way that the fighting echelons of allied forces will be expected to co-operate, so will the associated logistic support. There is an increasing shift toward tri-Service solutions and in-theatre inter-dependence. For example fuel, particularly aviation fuel, may be best provided on a joint basis. In a multinational context the principles for logistic co-operation in a NATO operation hold good for all joint or coalition operations. While nations retain ultimate responsibility for the sustainability of the forces they contribute, the pace and unpredictability of operations will require a cooperative intent to give and receive logistic support from the most appropriate source. Multinational arrangements should however not be regarded as prescriptive; they should only be agreed where it is economic, efficient or effective to do so. Co-operation is equally applicable to staff within headquarters and formations. It has its roots in mutual trust, a clear statement of intent and an understanding of the need for unity of effort.

Flexibility. The logistic organization needs to support operations in a variety of scenarios across the spectrum of conflict. Specialisation should be avoided as this tends to produce a lack of flexibility. Flexibility underpins responsiveness and creates the ability to change direction and vary tempo. This responsiveness will be derived from the physical attributes of speed, capacity and mobility, and the mental capacity of the staff to adjust, improvise and adapt. It will be assisted by the establishment of logistic reserves, but the potentially conflicting demand for economy must be balanced with the need for flexibility in order to provide an overall robust system. Flexibility demands a strong command support system, which maintain centralised control of resources whilst allowing decentralised execution of logistic operations.

Logistic Concepts

Five precepts follow from the above principles:

> Logistic units and assets have to be deployed and controlled in a way which best supports the operational plan.

Logistic units should be able to move their assets quickly to match changes in the operational situation.

Scarce and vital items should be carefully controlled so that they can be found and moved quickly in accordance with operational priorities.

Unserviceable equipment has to be recovered to a secure environment to be repaired quickly, to maintain the combat capability of the fighting and supporting arms.

Casualties should be evacuated quickly in order to return mobility to units and formations and contribute to sustaining the moral component.

Operational plans are dependent upon the timely support of the logistic services. The logistic staffs have to be involved from the outset. To enable logistic planning to match operational planning the logistic staffs need guaranteed access to secure communications and data processing facilities.

Command and Control

General. The effectiveness of any CSS system is dependent upon accurate and timely reporting, clearly defined procedures, adequate communications, good liaison and a clear understanding of the operational plan.

Responsibilities. The commander should always take into account, at an early stage of planning, the combat service support situation. The plan may later have to be adjusted to what is possible allowing for the amount of time required to adapt CSS to a changing tactical situation. Commanders normally delegate the detailed planning and execution of CSS plans to their staffs, but they must be made aware of critical areas that may affect operations and require their personal decisions. CSS staffs have to ensure that they remain knowledgeable and aware of the current operational situation as well as maintaining foresight for possible future operational needs. Both CSS and G3 staff need to exchange information on a regular basis to ensure that they remain up to date on the situation in the other's functional area.

Medical Support

There are two main differences between the CSS provided by the G4 staff and the G1 staff. In planning for logistic support and equipment support the G4 planning staff should be considering activity several days ahead to anticipate future combat requirements. The G1 medical planning staff have to concentrate their effort on the current operational situation to ensure that medical treatment is provided promptly by the appropriately qualified medical staff. This activity takes a higher priority than the medical planning for future operations.

Similarly while the main G4 logistic effort is put towards back loading of equipment and supplies to suitable areas for repair or reallocation, the G1 medical effort should be geared to moving suitable medical staff forwards to deal with medical contingencies. This includes their equipment and medical stores.

Section 9 The Use of Special Forces

Special Forces (SF)

A large number of forces such as the Commandos were raised during the Second World War to carry out reconnaissance and raiding tasks in various theatres of war. Of these, the Special Air Service, the Royal Marines Special Boat Service, the Long Range Desert Group and the Chindits were notably successful. The number of special forces presented certain problems, such as the co-ordination of operations and competition for suitable leaders, manpower and other resources. After the war, special raiding and reconnaissance were concentrated in two units, the Special Air Service and the Royal Marines Special Boat Squadron.

Today these forces together comprise the United Kingdom Special Forces (UKSF) centrally controlled by HQ DSF in the MOD. UK SF comprises groupings and assets such as ships, aircraft and helicopters from all three Services, the core being 22 SAS as a multi-purpose unit and the SBS as the maritime specialists. Together they represent a highly adaptable capability. The SF Group includes a reserve from the Territorial Army with a particular commitment to the ARRC on full mobilisation.

Characteristics

Because the special forces are highly skilled and operate in small groups they should not be misemployed on missions which can be undertaken by normal combat arm units. They should never be used on defensive tasks; their training, equipment and small numbers make them entirely unsuited for, and wastefully deployed on, defensive operations. The main characteristics are:

> *Response.* Regular SF are maintained at high states of readiness to respond quickly to crises. Designated servicemen are held at under 24 hours notice to move. Troops also maintain high levels of training under all climatic conditions. SF therefore require minimal predeployment training. Much equipment is also prepared and pre-packed in readiness for a rapid response.
>
> *Reach.* In both the physical and psychological sense, SF have the potential to reach deep. SF are capable of rapid and covert strategic projection to the area of operations. Once deployed, improved communications and tactical mobility increasingly allow SF to respond to retasking. In addition, SF have the psychological reach to threaten an enemy. The psychological impact of SF operating behind the lines or simply poised to deploy may be considerable and tie down enemy resources to guard against the threat.
>
> *Versatility.* Since the nature of future conflict is uncertain, SF have to be prepared to adapt to new circumstances and change direction quickly. This implies an ability to be competent in a range of differing tasks, to be versatile. The sound base of personal skills, the flexible attitude of mind and the cohesion of UKSF, create conditions that fosters evolution to meet changing needs.

Precision. SF offer a suitable military response for situations that require a tailored, precisely focused use of force. Precision encompasses both an intellectual and physical component. SF first display precision in identifying the enemy's key weaknesses, which may be concealed or protected. They can then attack those weaknesses with surgical precision, in order to limit casualties and reduce collateral damage. This is a highly cost-effective use of force, which could achieve significant effect for little effort.

Discretion. The disclosure of SF operations may carry considerable political difficulty or operational risk. Discretion is therefore vital. SF are capable of conducting covert operations thanks to a well developed security awareness and discreet operating methods. SF are also capable of limited clandestine operations to accomplish intelligence, counter intelligence and other similar activities sponsored or conducted in such a way as to assure secrecy or concealment.

Command and Control

There should be SF representation at every level where decisions are taken about SF employment. Command of SF has to be linked to commanders and staff at the strategic and operational levels, where SF are primarily employed. The broad scope and varying scale of SF operations mean that the question of command and control is a factor to be determined at the outset of every operation and an inherently flexible system is required. The strategic SF commander may exceptionally be required to command a discrete operation as a tactical commander. Similarly SF unit and sub-unit commanders routinely work at the operational level.

An SF headquarters will normally be located alongside the theatre headquarters so that its commander can act in the dual role of advising the theatre commander and his staff, and commanding his own troops. Operational control will only be delegated to another formation when an SF element is operating as part of a subordinate formation's plans or when the particular SF operation will directly affect that commander's plans. When SF operate in close proximity to other forces they will provide liaison officers to co-ordinate operations and exchange information. Where there is a risk of mutual interference or a danger of an accidental clash between special forces and other friendly troops the passage of information down to the lowest level is vital.

Factors for Employment

The factors governing the employment of SF have been derived from and confirmed by operational experience. They are listed in outline below:

SF are employed on high value tasks, (probably with operational implications).

Command is retained at the highest appropriate level.

Access to the best available intelligence.

Determination and Audacity.

ANNEX A TO CHAPTER 6

THE LEVELS OF WARFARE – THE GULF WAR 1991

The Grand Strategic Level

The application of national resources to achieve policy objectives. In the Gulf War this was represented by the political decision taken by the Government to implement a series of responses, including the use of military force, following the invasion of Kuwait by Iraq. The framework was set by the joint statements by President Bush and Prime Minister Thatcher at Camp David in the immediate aftermath of the invasion, declaring the defence of Saudi Arabia and the sovereignty of Kuwait as matters of 'national interest'. Subsequent decisions at this level related to the framing and passing of UN Resolution 678, which represented the grand strategic objective, mandating the use of force against Iraqi forces should they not accede to the international demand to withdraw from Kuwait, and the limitation imposed on the mission of Coalition forces to liberate Kuwait rather than to defeat Iraq. Nationally, the grand strategic level was represented by the 'War Cabinet' – which established UK policy during the crisis.

The Military Strategic Level

The application of military resources to achieve the military aspects of grand strategic objectives. In the Gulf War this was represented by the joint planning between the principal members of the US led Coalition to identify the campaign objectives; initially to deter further Iraqi aggression against Saudi Arabia, and thereafter implement a series of SCRs, and to decide the allocation of forces and resources required to meet those objectives. Within the UK the military strategic level was represented by the work of the Ministry of Defence in consultation with other government Departments. Examples of decisions at this level include forces and resources being allocated to the theatre, establishing the operational objectives, and the implementation of the financial, political and legal limitations imposed by the 'War Cabinet'.

The Operational Level

The level at which joint campaigns and major operations are constructed and directed in the fulfilment of a strategic directive. It is the level which provides the gearing between military strategic objectives and tactical activity in the theatre of operations. In the Gulf Conflict this was represented by the work of the Joint Coalition HQ, under the command of General Schwarzkopf. This HQ planned and directed joint coalition operations culminating in Operation Desert Storm. From a UK national perspective the operational level was represented by the designated National Joint HQ at HQ Strike Command at High Wycombe and in theatre by the UK Joint Force HQ under General de la Billière. The prime responsibilities of these HQs was to mount, sustain and support UK forces deployed on the ground, to monitor operations and report progress to the MOD. These HQs had the delegated authority to allocate forces and resources as necessary for subordinate tactical commanders to be able to achieve their missions, to set priorities for the provision of combat service support, and to direct the activities of those formations, ships and aircraft not delegated to Coalition command. Illustrations of operational decisions include: first, the well publicised maintenance of the US Marine Amphibious Force off the coast of Kuwait creating the capability for amphibious landings, causing the redirection of Iraqi resources as part of the wider deception plan; secondly, the decision to mount the ground offensive into Kuwait as a huge left flanking manoeuvre, rather than a frontal assault on Iraqi defensive positions, thereby unhinging the defence and helping to neutralise the Republican Guard formations.

The Tactical Level

This is the level at which battles and engagements within a sequence of major operations are planned and executed in order to achieve the operational objectives of a campaign. From a Coalition perspective the tactical level was represented by the various component commanders. From a national point of view the higher tactical level was represented by the Royal Navy Task Force, 1 (UK) Armoured Division and the Royal Air Force Group. An example of a decision relating to tactical operations was the aim of mounting set piece attacks at night to exploit the quantitative advantage enjoyed by Coalition forces in night fighting technology and equipment.

ANNEX B
TO
CHAPTER 6

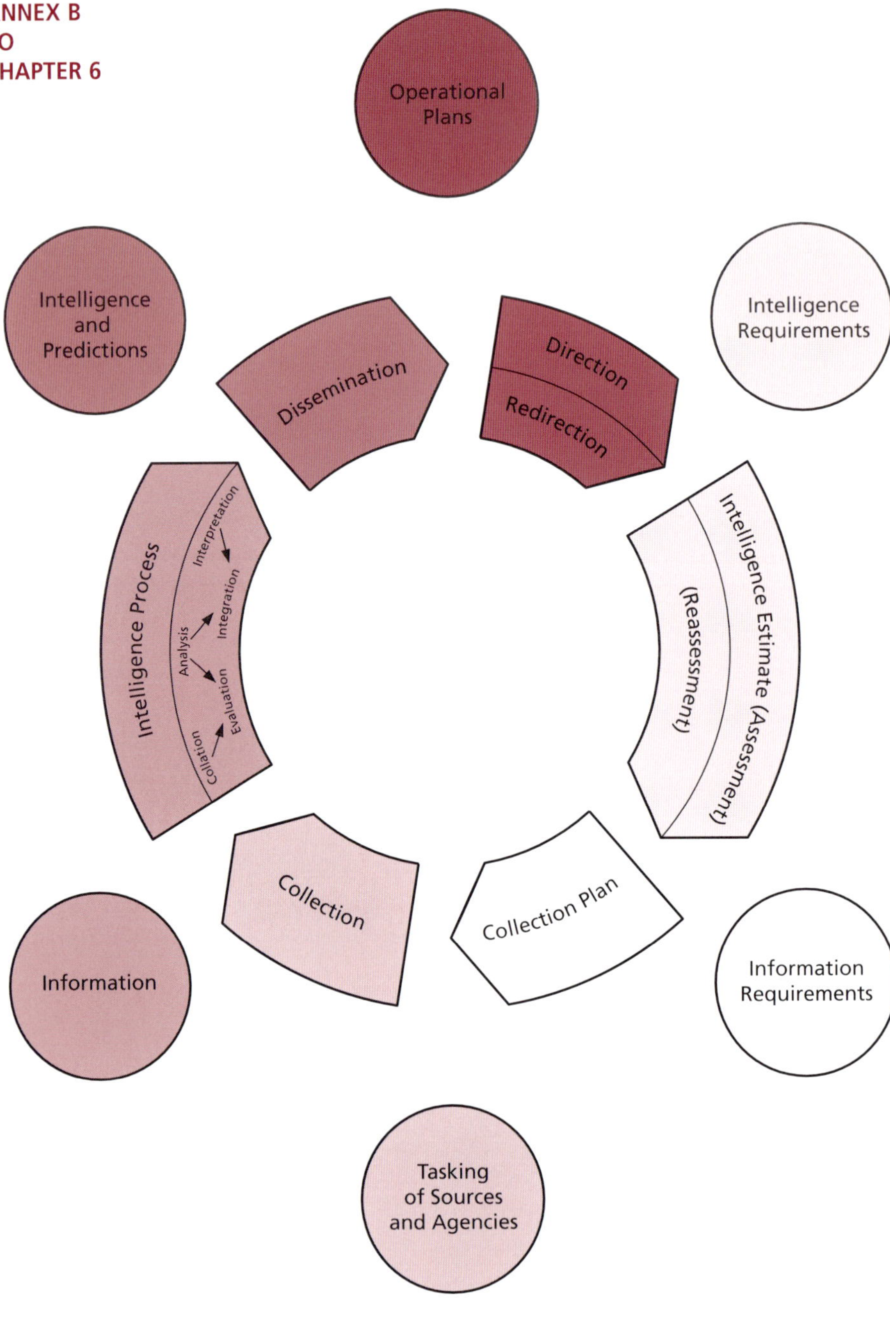

THE INTELLIGENCE CYCLE

ANNEX C TO CHAPTER 6

THE ESTIMATE PROCESS

GENERAL TASKS

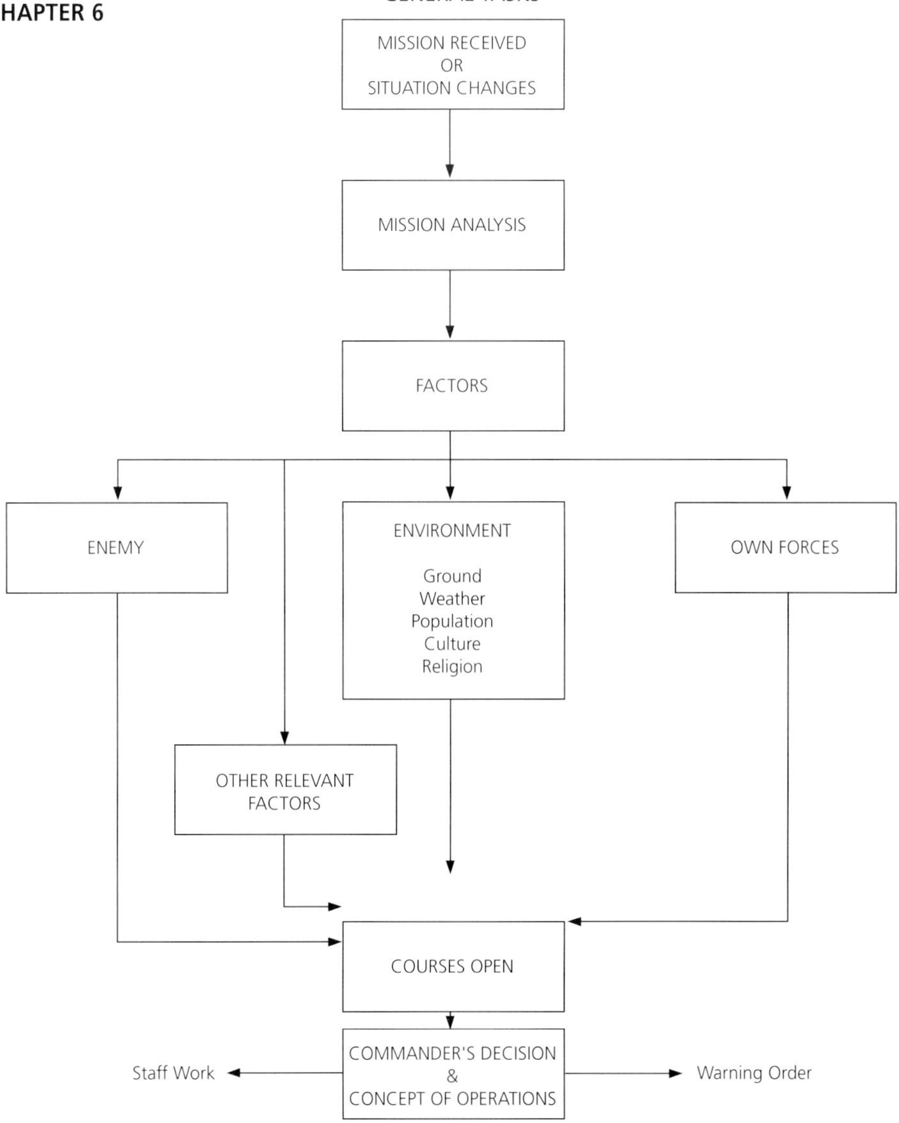

Notes:

1 This process applies to all staff branches

2 Information from outside agencies can be fed in at one time

3 The process is continuous

CHAPTER 7 COMMAND IN OPERATIONS

Section 1 Command and Control

"The sight of his long nose among us on a battle morning was worth ten thousand men any day of the week."

A PENISULA SOLDIER ON WELLINGTON[1]

The Function of Command and Control

Command and control are complementary. Command is the authority vested in an individual for the direction, co-ordination and control of military forces. It is the function of leadership to dominate, to persuade, to animate and to inspire confidence. It is concerned primarily with responsibility and decision-making. It is exercised most effectively face to face or over the radio, although written orders will invariably be required for the initiation of a plan at the higher level and often for the confirmation of verbal orders. Control embraces management and the technicalities of execution. As such it is largely the province of the staff to ensure that the details of a plan are carried out in accordance with the commander's intentions. Essential to the exercise of control are battle and standard operating procedures. Technology provides communications and computer facilities, and these are the means by which command and control can be exercised and information can be handled.

The commander's function varies with his level of responsibility. At the strategic level he will be concerned with the overall plan of campaign, allotting formations and co-ordinating the land/air battle with his component commanders. At the operational level he will be responsible for the design and co-ordination of the corps battles, for the broad plan of manoeuvre and the allocation of fire power and other resources to support them. At the tactical level lower formation and battlegroup commanders plan and fight the battle, co-ordinating the movement of forces in contact with the enemy with a detailed fire plan.

The function of command may be exercised through the issue of directives, instructions and orders to control and influence the battle in fulfilment of the commander's aim. It is generally preferable to allot a subordinate a mission and then to allow him as much freedom as possible in its execution. The subordinate exercising his initiative should always act within the spirit of his commander's directive and report what he is doing so that the commander may issue fresh orders if his action is inappropriate in a changing situation.

[1] Captain John Kincaid, as recorded by Thomas Gilby in his *Britain at Arms*, Eyre & Spottiswoode, 1953.

Explaining the Operational Plan. General Montgomery with a Corps and Division Commander, Sicily 1943.

Explaining the Strategic Plan. Mr Churchill in Normandy with Field Marshal Montgomery 1944.

Communications and Information Systems are essential to the function of command. Separated from them, a commander loses control of the battle. The speed, capacity, security and all-pervasive nature of modern communications both on and off the battlefield can support a wide range of information systems, tailored to meet the needs of a commander and his staff. These systems have the potential to enhance the commander's ability to control his forces and to increase the tempo of operations significantly. The electronic dissemination of orders, traces and overlays and the automatic collation of reports and returns can also reduce transmission times and improve situational awareness. However, in order to realise the full potential of modern technology, good organisation and battle procedures are more than ever necessary. The commander has to take his Command Support staff into his confidence early in the concept stage of an operation so that the communications and information systems needed to control the battle can be planned and established in good time. In particular, headquarters have to be sited not only to meet the requirements of subordinate and higher formations and concealment but also to allow access to the required communications systems; these may range from the civilian telecommunications infrastructure through strategic satellite systems to tactical trunk and combat radio networks.

The Commander and his Staff

The commander is solely responsible for the plan of battle and for inspiring and directing the men and women who execute it. Because of the complexities of command at formation level the commander will be assisted in the preparation of the plan by his principal staff officers and supporting arms commanders. This aspect is described further in Section 3 of this Chapter.

A good chief of staff is indispensable to the commander. Not only does he relieve the latter of the detail and the mechanics of control but he acts as his alter ego. There has to be a total rapport between the two so that they can discuss any matter with complete candour. The chief of staff will be responsible for the organisation and running of the headquarters. Although he wields great authority and his influence will be felt down the chain of command he exercises these powers on behalf of his commander and not in his own right.

The staff manages the machinery of command and control on behalf of the commander to help him co-ordinate the forces under his command and direct the battle. It is the task of the staff to collect and analyse the information and intelligence on which the commander bases his plans and decisions, to undertake the detailed planning for him and to transmit his instructions quickly and clearly to subordinate formations and units. The commander will decide to what extent he can delegate authority to his staff to implement the plan. He cannot, however, delegate his overall responsibility. To avoid overloading the commander and his principal staff officers, the staff should be encouraged to take minor decisions at the lowest possible level.

Section 2 The Commander

The Art of Command

'War does not belong in the realm of arts and sciences; rather it is part of man's social existence.' Although von Clausewitz was correct in classifying war as a social activity both art and science are employed in its prosecution. Science and technology may confer an advantage in weapons and machines but this alone will not win wars. Victory depends on good generalship, on how the commander applies technology on the battlefield, sound training and good morale. The conduct of war is an art, a skill requiring a combination of judgement to weigh up factors which can seldom be quantified precisely, insight to assess the value of information which may be inaccurate or misleading and flair to know when to be bold and when to be cautious. Generalship is the art of appreciating a situation, conceiving an original but workable plan, inspiring troops with confidence in it and with the will to win, and executing it in spite of the enemy's reactions.

Field Marshal Montgomery defined command as having 'the capacity and the will to rally men and women to a common purpose, and the character which inspires confidence'.[2] The art of command is a very personal matter and although no two commanders will work in the same way all commanders have certain attributes in common. An analysis of the careers of the great captains of the past indicates that a good commander should possess most of the following qualities. Apart from the first they are not in any order of importance.

Leadership	Professional Knowledge
Robustness	Imagination
Courage and Resolution	Judgement
Boldness	Decisiveness and Flexibility
Integrity	

Leadership

A commander has to be a leader. Leadership is a projection of personality and character. Field Marshal Slim described the attribute as, 'that mixture of example, persuasion and compulsion which makes men do what you want them to do'.[3] Field Marshal Montgomery placed less emphasis on persuasion and more on to dominate men and inspire confidence. There is no ideal pattern of leadership. The commander's temperament, the personality and capacity of his subordinates and the degree of dispersion of forces in a theatre are among the factors which influence the manner in which he exercises command, whether he maintains a tight control or allows his subordinates a measure of discretion. Leadership is essentially creative. It is the commander who determines the objective, who conceives the plan and who provides the will, motivation and energy to attain it. He should see and be seen by his troops and not let his staff get between him and his men. An interest in and a deep knowledge of humanity will help a commander assess the characteristics, aptitudes, shortcomings and state of training of his formations so that he can appreciate what they are capable of achieving in action and match formations to tasks in his battle plans. He has to give his command an identity, promote its self-esteem, inspire it with a sense of purpose and give it achievable aims to ensure success and to establish a tradition of victory.

[2] Field Marshal Montgomery, *The Memoirs*, Collins, 1958.
[3] Field Marshal Slim, 'The Officer' (lecture at West Point). In *Courage and Other Broadcasts, Marks of Greatness*, Cassell, 1957.

Robustness

A commander has to be robust if he is to stand up to the stress and uncertainty of war. Physical fitness is important because of the effect that a commander's health has on his mental attitude. Even more important is mental robustness. A certain toughness of mind is necessary to insulate a commander from the accidents and misfortunes of war. This does not imply a callous attitude to casualties. However, a commander must be able to control his emotions and conceal disappointment because discouragement spreads quickly downwards. He has to be able to throw off his cares and rest so that he will be in full possession of his faculties when a battle reaches its climax. Such detachment requires a conscious effort and mental discipline. Pressure generated by the international press and media organisations also can be a major source of concern to a commander and his staff which needs experience and careful handling by suitably trained officers. Public criticism can be especially dangerous to a commander's morale and this could have a similar depressing effect on those troops under his command.

Courage and Resolution

A commander has to have the moral courage and resolution to force through what he knows to be right in the face of weakness or strong, but misguided, opposition. Having made up his mind that the course which he contemplates is the correct one he must not be deterred by the obstacles and setbacks he will meet in its application. A constancy of purpose and resolution must inspire all his thoughts and actions. Physical courage may not be so essential a factor as it was in the days of close combat but it is still important in determining the degree of risk a commander will take to see the situation for himself. Sometimes, in a desperate crisis, a commander's presence amongst his troops in the forward area may have a calming and reassuring effect. When the Germans broke through in front of Ypres on the last day of October 1914, General Haig, commanding 1st British Corps, threw in his last reserve and, 'then, with his personal staff and escort, he rode slowly up the Menin road, through the stragglers, back into the shelled area, his face immobile and inscrutable – saying no word, yet by his presence and his calm, restoring hope to the disheartened and strength to the exhausted troops'.[4]

Boldness

Boldness and a healthy sense of aggression are essential qualities for a commander because a battle can only be won by seizing and keeping the initiative. In defence, carefully calculated counter attacks upset the enemy's plans and compel him to divert forces from his main effort. The object is to regain the initiative in order to restore the situation and compel the enemy commander to give up his aim. Boldness implies the willingness to take a calculated risk and the determination to win. 'Napoleon asked if a general was lucky. What he

[4] Brigadier General Charteris, *Field Marshal Earl Haig*, Cassell, 1929.

really meant was, "Was he bold?" A bold general may be lucky, but no general can be lucky unless he is bold.'[5] Implicit in the Emperor's question was whether a general's audacity and initiative created situations which could be exploited. Even with the most careful calculation of risks something must be left to chance. Only positive action can achieve success. Danton's words to inspire the French to meet the Prussian invasion in 1792, 'We must dare, and dare again, and dare forever', may have a melodramatic ring to the modem ear but they convey an essential truth.

Professional Knowledge

A commander has to be a master of his profession. His subordinates will have no confidence in him unless he is. He cannot be an expert in all the technicalities of modern war but he must have sufficient knowledge to be able to judge the soundness of the technical advice given him. He should know the capabilities, potentialities and limitations of his weapons, communications and surveillance systems. He must have an eye for terrain and know how to employ ground to the best advantage. He has to be a good organiser and administrator with a sound understanding of the mechanics of movement and supply. The importance of knowing the capabilities of his own troops has already been mentioned under leadership. Equally, he should study the characteristics, strengths and weaknesses of the enemy.

Imagination

Imagination is the quality which distinguishes the good commander from the mediocre and which turns a pedestrian plan into a brilliant stroke. It is the quality which enables a commander to surprise his opponent and outwit him. All the great captains of history have been innovators and possessed original minds. 'Alexander was imaginative, supremely undaunted and hence more likely to be lucky.'[6] William the Conqueror's ruse to lure the Saxons from their shield wall at Hastings, Marlborough's elaborate stratagem to persuade Villars to destroy the fort commanding the causeway across the Ne Plus Ultra Lines in 1711 and 'FORTITUDE', the brilliant deception plan to tie the German 15th Army to the Pas de Calais during the Normandy invasion, show how imagination has been the handmaiden of surprise and an essential attribute of the successful commander throughout the ages. Insight is an extension of imagination, the ability to read the mind of an opposing commander, to predict how he might react to certain circumstances, to exploit his weaknesses and parry his initiatives. Insight is not mere intuition; it is based on a careful study of the available intelligence on enemy commanders' personal characteristics and their past performance superimposed on a knowledge of the enemy's operational methods.

[5] General Wavell, *Generals and Generalship. The Good General,* Lees Knowles Lecture, 1939, Times Publishing Company, 1941.
[6] Robin Lane Fox, *Alexander the Great*, Allen Lane, 1973.

Judgement

Judgement is commonsense but required of a commander in an uncommon degree. To succeed he should be able to read each development in a tactical situation, interpret it correctly in the light of the evidence available and arrive at a well balanced decision. However, a commander seldom has a complete picture of the situation in battle and many of the factors affecting a commander's choice of action are not susceptible to precise calculation. Furthermore, a commander will be under stress and he may also be under political pressure. To weigh up the imponderables in a confusing situation a commander needs a clear brain to distinguish the essentials from a mass of irrelevant detail, to identify the fundamen-tal problems and to find practical solutions. Although the element of chance in war cannot be eliminated the risks may be reduced to the minimum by foresight and careful planning. Calculated boldness may create opportunities denied to more pedestrian commanders. Another aspect of judgement is the assessment of character, particularly of subordinates. The value he attaches to their reports and to their interpretations of a situation, and the nature of the missions he assigns to them, will depend on his opinion of their abilities and qualities.

Decisiveness and Flexibility

A commander will be advised by his superiors and subordinates and he will be briefed by his staff and supporting arms commanders before he has to make up his mind. He should not allow himself to be forced into making a hasty decision. On the other hand he must make his decisions in sufficient time for the staff to prepare the orders and pass them down through the chain of command to those who are to execute them. A commander should have confidence in his own judgement and should stick to his decisions unless the course of events should prove them to be wrong. Then he should have the moral courage to change them. A commander should also have the flexibility of mind which will enable him to react appropriately to changes in the situation. An unlooked for success in an unexpected quarter may offer a rich reward if the mind of the commander is flexible enough to perceive and exploit the opportunity. Conversely, he should avoid the stubborn pursuit of an unsuccessful course to disaster. The borderline between resolution and obstinacy is a fine one and its recognition is the hallmark of a good commander. Changes in plan may be necessary but they should not deflect a commander from his aim.

Integrity

The last word on leadership is the need for integrity. Moral courage, honesty and loyalty to subordinates and superiors are fundamental to good leadership. They create the bonds of mutual trust which weld together the links in the chain of command. In his dealings with his troops the commander must always be truthful. If he is not they will soon find out and their confidence in him will evaporate. In the field the needs for truth and security may not always be easy to reconcile. 'I did not always tell all the truth to the soldiers in the war', wrote

Field Marshal Montgomery, 'it would have compromised secrecy, and it was not necessary. I told them all they must know for the efficient carrying out of their tasks. But what I did tell them was always true and they knew it; that produced a mutual confidence between us.'[7]

Section 3 Relationship with Subordinates

The Selection of Subordinates

One of a commander's most important functions is the selection of his subordinates. The peacetime selection system aims to choose the most suitable officer for each post. In war, some leaders will become casualties. Inevitably, a few will fail. Field Marshal Montgomery estimated that he spent a third of his working hours in the consideration of personalities. He kept command appointments in his own hands down to the level of lieutenant colonel. The Field Marshal was at pains to explain that a good battalion commander does not necessarily make a good brigadier, nor a good divisional general a good corps commander.[8] Judging a man's ceiling in the higher ranks is, therefore, not easy. When an officer fails, possibly because he was promoted above his ceiling, he has to be removed. Field Marshal Slim made it a rule to undertake the unpleasant task himself. 'If I had to sack the brigadier, I didn't let the divisional commander do it, I did it ... He will not have a grouse so much against the divisional commander ... He will say that it is that "so and so" of an army commander, and that won't hurt you very much.'[9] The Field Marshal showed both moral courage and a concern to take a burden off his formation commanders' shoulders.

A higher commander should study the personalities and characteristics of his subordinate formation commanders. Some need a tight rein while others work best when given their heads. Some will be happy with a general directive while others will like more detail. Some will excel in a mobile, fluid battle; others are better in a set piece attack or a dogged defence. Matching talent to tasks is an important function of generalship. A commander has, therefore, to be a good judge of men so that he can put the right man in the right place at the right time.

Trust, Confidence and Understanding

Good senior commanders, once chosen, have to be trusted and supported. A subordinate is entitled to the help and backing of his immediate superior. A subordinate facing a difficult situation will need understanding and encouragement if he is not to lose confidence. Deciding whether, when and how to intervene in a subordinate's conduct of a battle calls for fine judgement. The risk of overall failure should be weighed against the consequences of unnecessary and irritating interference which may fetter a subordinate's initiative at a critical moment or impose an additional burden when he already has his

[7] Field Marshal Montgomery, *The Memoirs* (see note 2).
[8] Ibid.
[9] Field Marshal Slim, lecture on 'Leadership', delivered at the Staff College, 2 November 1967.

hands full. Field Marshal Carver observed that, 'if it is necessary for a commander to interfere constantly with a subordinate, one or the other should be relieved.'[10]

A commander should always think 'two down' when planning an operation. This does not mean that he will interfere with the junior commanders' plans at that level but by appreciating their problems he will the more readily understand what his immediate subordinates can and cannot achieve. In time a mutual confidence will grow up throughout the whole of the command structure. At each level commanders will understand how their subordinates are likely to react in various circumstances and will appreciate what their superiors will require of them in an emergency and anticipate their orders.

Advice from Subordinates

Subordinate commanders, certain staff officers and advisers have direct access to the commander. This personal contact serves to keep the commander informed and to ensure that advisers and staff are always fully aware of what is in their commander's mind. Consequently they will be able to take decisions without constant reference to him and so relieve the commander of much of his burden. Those who have frequent contact with the commander are:

> Commanders of armour, artillery, engineers, signals, infantry, aviation and the representative of the air force; of necessity this contact will often be through the principal staff officer.
>
> The chief of staff, the deputy chief of staff who is responsible for administration and the senior intelligence officer.

The heads of services also have the right of direct access to the commander, but unlike the arms commanders, they normally work through the staff.

Liaison

Liaison officers provide a means by which the commander can issue personal instructions to his subordinates without the necessity for long written orders and by which he can obtain first hand knowledge of the situation on his front and flanks. A liaison officer is not merely a mouthpiece but a person who can sum up a situation and give his commander an accurate picture of the progress of an operation, the state of mind of subordinate commanders and of the condition of their troops.

Liaison officers are chosen with some care for their powers of observation, experience, judgement, tact and integrity. They are the eyes and ears of their commander and, correctly used, they can provide valuable information for the commander across all levels of command.

[10] Field Marshal Carver, lecture at the Staff College, 27 October 1982.

Tools of command: Planning.

Tools of command: Briefing.

The Personal Touch

One of a commander's most important tasks is to support and sustain his subordinates. The only really satisfactory way to do this is by frequent personal contact. A commander should aim to uplift and invigorate his subordinates when he meets them. On important occasions, for example before a major attack, a commander can explain to his troops what is required of them and inspire them to make a great effort. It is most essential that a commander should prepare himself carefully before addressing his troops collectively. An ineffective or unnecessary appearance can do more harm than good.

Morale

One of the commander's most important tasks is to foster and sustain the morale of his troops. Since it is based on confidence, discipline and self-respect he will

Tools of command: Visiting.

Tools of command: Liaison.

aim to instil these qualities into his troops by realistic, arduous and imaginative training, by fostering regimental spirit and loyalty, and by insisting on intelligent man-management and efficient administration.

Success in battle is the quickest way to achieve high morale. Ideally, troops should not be called upon to undertake operations for which they are not trained and ready. If time and the situation allow, tasks should be graduated for fresh troops to build up their morale with a steady progression of inoculation to battlefield conditions.

The first major battles could make unprecedented demands on morale, stamina and professional skills. In peacetime the commander has to ensure that his troops are sufficiently well trained to meet a sudden challenge. In peace and in war a commander should take whatever opportunities arise to get to know and be known by his men. Then, when a special effort is called for, a few words from a trusted and familiar figure will inspire them with confidence and steel their resolve.

Three different examples concerning morale are given in Annex A.

Provision of Welfare Support

Important to the provision of adequate welfare support for operations is the consideration of such in the Commanders' Estimate. This Estimate has to be conducted by commanders and staffs at every level. It should consider such factors as: the length and intensity of likely operations: available infrastructure in the area of operations; the aspirations of the serviceman and indirectly his family; provision on other extant operations; and the level of support provided by any allies. All commanders should revisit continually their initial Estimate and recognise that as an operation develops a soldier's needs and expectations could well change.

Areas of likely requirements include:

Provision of mail, including airmail letters, welfare telephone facilities and newspapers.

How long and where (in theatre or home), increasing provision – or requirement – for evacuation.

Provision and maintenance of recreational facilities. Fitness equipment, TVs/ videos, NAAFI/EFI, library facilities and radio programmes.

Provision for wives and families. Family support, local newspaper visits.

Effective compassionate and casualty evacuation procedures ensuring that all troops and their families are briefed and understand the procedures.

Effective supervision of troops while off-duty, including the appropriate control of weapons and alcohol.

Provision of access to chaplaincy and Welfare Agency support.

Tools of command: Communications.

Commanders should ensure that all troops under their command are briefed on welfare provision. This briefing should, where appropriate, be extended to wives and families. This is particularly important where the full scope of arrangements for soldiers or their families cannot be met due to practical or operational imperatives.

Section 4 Command and Control Warfare (C2W)

Command and Control Warfare (C2W)

C2W is defined as the integrated use of all military capabilities including Operations Security (OPSEC), Psychological Operations (Psy Ops), Deception, Electronic Communications and Information Systems (CIS), to deny information to, influence, degrade or destroy an adversary's C2 capabilities, while protecting friendly C2 capabilities against similar actions. The five disciplines above can stand alone, but are at their most effective when integrated to form a unified C2W plan.

C2W is both offensive, seeking to attack the enemy's C2, and defensive, seeking to protect friendly C2 systems. C2W can degrade significantly an enemy's awareness, decision cycle, actions and reactions, thereby enhancing tempo and security of friendly forces. Its effectiveness is relative to the intended objectives,

The Five Pillars of C2W supported by Intelligence and CIS

methods employed and its integration within the overall concept of operations. It is therefore imperative that C2W is planned and controlled by the G3 Operations staff.

The components of the C2 process – the commander, his Command Support (staff, headquarters, communications and information systems) – are fundamental to the successful outcome of operations. Technological advances (not the least of which is widespread use of information technology and digitisation), have had a profound impact on C2, especially in terms of enhancing planning, passage of information, decision-making and tempo. External influences, such as media reporting, add to the requirement for precise and timely information and a rapid C2 process. Consequently, the battle for information, or denial of initiative, is an important factor in C2W planning. In this respect C2W complements manoeuvre and can be conducted in support of close, deep and rear operations. C2W can be employed in a variety of operations, tailored to achieve the desired effects on enemy C2 activity.

Within the UK the concept of Information Warfare (IW) is in its infancy, although elsewhere its concept and doctrine have been developed to a greater degree. (IW) is essentially the grand strategic (national level) application of C2W, and targets could include political, financial, commercial and public sector assets as well as military resources. 1W is beyond the scope of this publication and will not be considered further here.

The application of C2W is a command function. It is conducted at formation level and above, and can have applications across the spectrum of conflict. Although planned and directed at the strategic/operational rational level, tactical assets will be employed to support C2W. In certain circumstances it may be feasible to plan and conduct C2W at the tactical level.

Operational Security (OPSEC)

OPSEC is the process which gives a military operation or exercise appropriate security, using active or passive means, to deny the enemy knowledge of the dispositions, capabilities and intentions of friendly forces. OPSEC seeks to deny to the enemy sufficient information and intelligence to be able to identify in detail dispositions, capabilities and intentions of friendly forces. OPSEC is a force-wide process which addresses overall security for the whole campaign or operation in the light of the enemy's known or suspected ISTAR capabilities. It is not intended to provide blanket security: the enemy may know that friendly forces are in the area of operations, or that further operations are planned. The overall intention is to conceal from the enemy those indicators from which he could deduce vital elements of the plans, to:

Increase the element of surprise and reduce the enemy's capability to interfere with friendly operations.

Increase security and thus prevent the enemy obtaining information that would assist in his offensive planning process.

As part of the OPSEC process, the intelligence likely to be available to an enemy is continuously analysed, thus allowing friendly force plans to be reviewed in the light of probable enemy knowledge and activity.

Psychological Operations (Psy Ops)

Psy Ops aims to influence the attitudes and behaviour of enemy, friendly and neutral audiences in the furtherance of political and military objectives in peace and war. Contrary to widely held beliefs, Psy Ops is not a 'black art'; UK policy is to use factually based materiel and legitimacy to establish credibility in the minds of an audience. An example would be the use of provable facts to cause the target audience, in this case enemy soldiers, to question their leaders' motives, morals, abilities, or achievements, thus making them less willing to sacrifice themselves for a now discredited leadership. Psy Ops are designed to weaken the enemy's will, reinforce our own resolve and gain the sympathy and support of the uncommitted. Psy Ops may, therefore, be divisive to create apathy, dissension, uncertainty and panic in order to lower morale and possibly induce defection or surrender amongst the enemy, or they may be cohesive to foster goodwill, understanding, confidence and co-operation amongst friends and neutrals.

Psy Ops are essentially long-term undertakings. They are most unlikely to achieve quick results except in conjunction with some sudden and dramatic success, such as the German blitzkrieg campaigns in the early years of the Second World War. Nor can they take the place of military operations in winning a war, although they are a useful adjunct. In an adverse situation they are unlikely to make an impression on a victorious enemy but they may, mitigate the effects of a reverse on friendly forces and the general population. They are most effective in the exploitation of military successes to undermine the enemy's will to fight and induce an early capitulation.

Deception

Deception is defined as those measures designed to mislead the enemy by manipulation, distortion or falsification of evidence to induce him to react in a manner prejudicial to his interests. Unlike OPSEC, which seeks only to hide friendly dispositions, capabilities and intentions, deception presents a deliberately false picture to the enemy. The aim of deception is to cause the enemy to react by taking a specific course of action, which could include maintaining his status quo in a manner contrary to his interests; it is not an intellectual exercise seeking merely to confuse him. The aim of the deception plan has to stem directly from, and be supportive of, a commander's mission.

Successful deception achieves surprise and contributes to security; it multiplies the effect of force; it is a traditional recourse of the weak against the strong; it can reduce expenditure of time, effort, resources and casualties; and its psychological effects, for deceiver and deceived alike, can be far-reaching. It involves entering the mind of the enemy commander, an ability which is a hallmark of successful operational leadership. The feint, the selection of the less obvious line of advance, the diversion and raid are all the tools of deception and should be at the forefront of a commander's thinking.

There is a view that advances in technology are progressively making deception more difficult to achieve. This, however, is not necessarily the case: most modern ISTAR systems can still be fooled, albeit the methods of achieving this are more complex and technical than was the case in the past; and many potential enemies lack the full range of such technologies. The ultimate target of deception, the human mind, is just as susceptible to being deceived as in previous times and the increasing dependence of the human mind on automatic processing of ever greater volumes of battlefield information could make the target of deception more vulnerable to all manner of ruses.

Electronic Warfare (EW)

General. EW is military action taken to exploit the electro-magnetic (EM) spectrum; it encompasses the interception, identification, analysis and, where possible, the understanding of the enemy's EM emissions; the employment of EM energy, including directed energy, to reduce or prevent hostile use of the EM spectrum; and actions to ensure its effective use by friendly forces. EW is conducted within three main functional areas:

Electronic Warfare Support Measures (ESM).

Electronic Counter Measures (ECM).

Electronic Protective Measures (EPM).

ESM is that part of EW involving the action taken to search for, intercept and identify electro-magnetic emissions and locate their sources for the purpose of immediate threat recognition. It provides a source of information required for immediate decisions involving ECM, EPM and operational action.

ECM is the portion of EW involving the action taken to prevent or reduce an enemy's effective use of the EM spectrum through the use of EM energy. ECM has 3 sub-divisions:

Electronic Jamming.

Electronic Deception.

Electronic Neutralisation.

EPM involves those actions taken to ensure friendly effective use of the EM spectrum despite the enemy's hostile use of EM energy. EPM sub-divides into the following:

Active EPM. Detectable measures, such as altering equipment parameters to reduce emission power levels, to ensure effective friendly use of the EM spectrum.

Passive EPM. Undetectable measures, such as operating procedures and technical features of equipment, which are designed to ensure effective friendly use of the EM spectrum.

Summary. EW can support all aspects of C2W to varying degrees depending on the nature of the operation. Control of the EM spectrum is a significant factor in terms of enabling C2, CIS, ISTAR, manoeuvre and fire power. This necessitates a comprehensive EW capability and the ability to manage use of the EM spectrum to ensure dominance in the battle for its use.

Physical Destruction

The physical destruction, or at least the neutralisation, of enemy command centres and counter C2 assets is frequently an objective in C2W operations. Destruction, however, has to be co-ordinated with the demands of the other C2W components; it may be necessary to put certain command centres on a 'no strike' list to allow the passage of false indicators as part of the deception plan, or to give the necessary orders for the desired action resulting from that plan. Intelligence considerations will also play a part as the intelligence gained by EW from enemy transmissions may be vital to the commander's plan.

Equally, the effectiveness of physical destruction can be increased by co-ordination with the other elements of the overall C2W plan action; jamming communications elsewhere as part of the EW component can add to the confusion resulting from an attack, or a Psy Ops leaflet drop can be timed to exploit the morale effect of a successful attack. Destruction may be effective only for a relatively short period; given time and resources they will recover. It is important, therefore, to consider the timing of destruction as an instrument of C2W in order to deny the enemy the opportunity to replace or substitute what has been destroyed before its loss becomes critical. Destruction can be achieved through the use of all means; attack helicopters, indirect fire, SF, direct attack by elements of the main forces and air attack.

The Application of C2W at Tactical Level

C2W Awareness. C2W is primarily exercised at the strategic and operational level; it demands careful planning and control and integrated staff direction at these levels of combat and will be authorised at the highest appropriate level. Nevertheless, it may be made more effective as an instrument if tactical commanders are aware of the broad outlines of any C2W plan, commensurate with the overall need for security.

Practical Measures. Troops may be required to carry out particular operations, procedures or drills to support the overall C2W operation. The roles of surveillance, counter surveillance and security play a large part in the overall conduct of C2W both for gaining information and protecting and securing information from the enemy.

Section 5 Media Operations

Background

Technology has transformed the nature of society, international business and affected the way in which military operations are conducted. In particular, the rapid passage of information through global communications has a marked and increasing effect on public perception and opinion. It has magnified the impact of military operations on civilians. Those in the media have themselves become more significant and powerful. The impact of the media has changed the ability of all parties to a conflict to influence the attitudes and perceptions of specific target audiences. The media, particularly in non-democratic countries, often have their own agenda. Even a 'neutral' report can be slanted by editing, and commanders have to consider every 'angle' from which an incident can be reported. Local and apparently insignificant tactical events can quickly become of strategic significance particularly in military operations that fall short of general war.

Media operations are the principal activity in any 'information campaign'. Media reporting may well be influential in engaging the initial international involvement in a particular theatre of operations and may influence, for good or ill, public support for subsequent military operations there. International press interest, high at the outset, may well wane as a campaign becomes more protracted. The likely results of media reporting have to be calculated as part of any campaign plan. Media Ops staff then pass the message through the 'filter' of the media but have no control over the 'spin' that is put on reporting. Media Ops could be said to constitute a form of 'indirect information operations'

Relations with the Media

If military achievements and reverses are to receive the appropriate and sympathetic publicity they deserve, a commander and his staff have to establish good relations with the media. Normal business will be conducted by the Public Information staff at regular meetings when the spokesman should have a complete brief, including the answers to all likely questions and guidance on how to handle those which affect security or the public interest. Although fostering support for the war effort, a government responsibility and the way in which public information is handled in the field plays a significant part in stimulating morale at home and so, indirectly, motivating the soldier.

Digital cameras and lightweight satellite communications give media operators the ability to report on incidents often before military commanders are even aware of them. As a result, a commander can no longer control media reporting to the outside world. Some theatres of operations allow reporters to operate almost anywhere. Accreditation does provide the military commander with a degree of influence over a reporter's access to information. Accredited journalists are officially informed, not controlled, but as a result normally have a responsibility to exercise a degree of self-censorship which is created by mutual trust and an appreciation of common interests. Such trust results from regular briefings about military activity and the progress for any operations.

Links with the Media: The Gulf War 1991.

Links with the Media: Bosnia 1996.

Links with the Media: Kosovo 1999.

The Staff Function of Media Operations

From the first sign of the possible involvement of British forces on operations, there will be media interest. Media Ops is an essential part of contingency planning and has to be an integral part of the work of operational contingency planning teams. A commander should include Media Ops staff on his planning team and, subsequently, on all major deployments to ensure that the media line is consistent with his military intentions.

Media Ops is a G3 staff function although it is also the business of commanders at all levels. They have to be prepared to give interviews, hold press conferences and provide briefings. Experience has shown that a media adviser drawn from the ranks of the international media working direct to a commander has been of significant benefit. At lower formation levels a commander should be advised by the G3 Media Ops staff. The staff assesses the potential effect of media activity on operations and respond to it by providing further direction through the chain of command. Journalists can be given access to factual and timely information and subsequently the G3 Media Ops staff can evaluate the effects of that information from a wide range of sources in order to maintain the initiative. There is undoubted value in having officers at all levels of command who can discuss military matters across a wide range of topics coherently with representatives of the press and media.

CHAPTER 8 TRAINING FOR OPERATIONS

Training is, and will remain fundamental to the three inter-related components of fighting power. Properly conducted, it serves as a powerful reminder of the realities of soldiering and develops the true potential of individuals, units and formations.[1]

Section 1 Aims and Objectives

The Aim of Training

The Army has to be prepared to undertake a wide variety of tasks to fulfil their commitments to defence policy, as indicated in Chapter 1. Such tasks call for high standards of co-operation between arms, with the other two Services, with allies and sometimes with the police forces. The Territorial Army, and individual Regular and Territorial Reservists, also have to be trained for their mobilisation roles and other wartime tasks.

The ultimate aim of all training is to ensure military success. Training provides the means to practise, develop and validate, within constraints, the practical application of a common doctrine. Equally importantly, it provides the basis for schooling commanders and staffs in the exercise of command and control respectively. Training should be stimulating, rewarding, and inspire subordinates to achieve greater heights. A valuable by-product of good training is the fostering of teamwork and the generation of the confidence by soldiers in their commanders, their organisations and in their doctrine, a necessary prerequisite for achieving high morale before troops are committed to operations.

Military training develops individuals, groups and formations so that they can contribute fully to that success. The training should reflect the ethos and doctrine to which the Army subscribes. The product of military training should be highly skilled, confident and well-motivated individuals, units and formations, which are effectively commanded, cohesive, tactically and technically proficient, imbued with high morale, and a will to win.

The Importance of Training

In some walks of life training can be a minor activity to which relatively little time is allocated. In the Army, the core business of fighting wars, or keeping the peace, occupies usually only a small fraction of total time. The main pre-occupation is with preparing for the possibility of real operations.

[1] Extracted from the Foreword to ADP Vol 4, *Training*, by the then CGS General Sir Charles Guthrie, 1996.

It is axiomatic that training should be the Army's most important activity when it is not committed to operations. Commanders should reflect the importance of training in the quality of the servicemen and the resources which they allocate to it. When the time comes for operations, it may be too late to remedy deficiencies in training.

Training is fundamental to the three inter-related components of fighting power. It is an element of the conceptual component, in that training should be conducted in accordance with doctrine and develop an ability in officers and soldiers to cope with stress and uncertainty. It should provide a means, through the collation and dissemination of lessons learned, by which the Army can learn from experience. In addition, training, and thus readiness, contribute directly to the physical component of fighting power. Though training is not specifically represented as an element of the moral component, it has an important part to play in the development of confidence, motivation and leadership throughout the Army.

Training Principles

There are ten principles of training. Commanders are responsible for the training of their own men and should be given as much latitude as possible in the overall training of their units. Formation commanders, who are responsible for the overall operational efficiency of their commands, issue directives stipulating what has to be achieved by a given date. They provide advice, help and co-ordination with the minimum of interference and then check that the aims of their directives are being achieved by watching unit training and setting test exercises.

While the appropriate decentralisation of responsibility is a feature of training, some instruction has to be conducted on a centralised basis to make the best use of instructors for specialist, technical and leadership training. The benefit to the formation or unit as a whole should outweigh the disruption caused by removing the instructors from their normal duties.

Training Commanders

Leadership training is undertaken at all levels, at Army Schools, through NCO cadres, officers' days and TEWTs within units, and at formation study periods where particular aspects of each phase of war are examined and discussed. It is the commander's responsibility to see that his subordinates are fully trained in all the skills and techniques needed to deploy forces of all arms, make battle appreciations, issue orders and control their commands in action.

[2] Osipov, *Alexander Suvorov*, Hutchinson, 1944.

Re-supply.

Parachute insertion.

Live firing.

Firing practice.

Tactical Training

"Hard on the training ground, easy on the battlefield."

SUVOROV[2]

Training should be interesting and progressive. Once the basic features of any tactical procedure have been taught and practised they should be developed under increasingly difficult conditions. A unit should be trained to operate as well by night as by day. Training provides the opportunity for commanders and men to learn from their mistakes.

Officers and men have to be physically fit to stand the rigours of war. Attention has to be paid to the psychological aspect of training. Although no exercise can generate the blend of fear and courage, caution and gallant recklessness which inhibits and inspires the soldier on the battlefield, training should be as realistic as possible. At the culmination of the training cycle exercises should last long enough to test the will-power and endurance of tired leaders and soldiers. Fear of the unknown is injurious to morale. Commanders should tell their men what to expect in battle and they should prepare them to face operations in all environments including an NBC environment. Battle inoculation exercises may serve to accustom soldiers to operating in the noise, smoke and confusion of war. Arduous and adventurous training have their place in fostering resourcefulness and resolve, developing team spirit and in giving men confidence in their ability to cope with demanding situations.

Commanders should ensure that the potential difficulties of practising specialised forms of training, eg intelligence and logistics, do not deter them from exercising these vital skills. Training should continue in a theatre of operations whenever the opportunity offers. Each campaign will produce fresh lessons and initiate the development of new techniques and skills.

Bridge building.

Watermanship.

A unit's performance will reflect the standards achieved during training in peacetime. Although men and units will rise to an occasion and perform acts of great gallantry in action no unit will be able to repair the neglect of peacetime training standards on the battlefield. Effective and realistic training is expensive but money spent on costly items such as ammunition, the exercise of large forces and compensation for damage on requisitioned land to optimise the operational and tactical efficiency of our formations and units, is money well spent.

Categories of Training

Military training can be placed in a number of categories: These are:

- Individual.
- Team.
- Collective.
- Specific to Operation.
- Command.

Collective teaming for Cold Weather Operations.

In practice there is, or should be, considerable overlap, and in some cases integration between categories. Training should be regarded as a cohesive whole. There is, however, a temptation to focus only on one category at a time and to disregard the others. The emphasis may be on a particular category of training, but it should not be to the exclusion of others. There is also a danger inherent in adopting too rigid a cyclic approach, and in separating responsibilities for the different categories of training.

Individual Training

The purpose of individual training (including recruit training) is to produce a self-confident and disciplined soldier who is physically fit, well motivated, and equipped with the basic skills and fighting qualities needed to survive on the battlefield

Movement and Manoeuvre.

Crossing difficult terrain.

Rapid insertion.

Re-deployment.

and to operate as a member of a team or crew. Individual training has two elements, that of skills training and more generalised training that contributes to personal development. This may be more knowledge-based and include education. Skills training may be equipment-related or aimed at personal or physical aptitude. Some skills are considered as core or mandatory, which all should possess. These, and the standards required, are governed by Individual Training Directives (ITDs). The number of core skills, and the standards to be achieved in each, should be reviewed regularly.

Skills of all kinds deteriorate, especially if not used regularly, the extent of the deterioration depending on the individual and the particular skill. This can usually be overcome by incorporating these skills into other categories of training. The frequency of skills practice in order to sustain acceptable operational standards should be governed by balancing deterioration, operational efficiency, time and cost, rather than by any particular fixed time frame. The annual or bi-annual testing of skills in accordance with ITDs is separate from this process.

Individual training of a more general nature is aimed at developing the potential of the individual to fulfil his or her role as a commander or as a soldier in a team or unit. It is a long term investment. Such training may be carried out both on an individual and a group basis, on formal courses or informally, and be voluntary or prescribed.

Team Training

Team or crew training provides an immediate context for most individual skills training. It is when, for example, the specialist and complementary skills of the individual members of the gun detachment or tank crew are brought together. The output is team skills and proficiency which no individual alone can achieve. The team or crew is the basic unit in all low-level operations. Hence, training at this level should be revisited regularly, and particularly when there has been a change in team composition.

Collective Training

Collective training involves the training of two or more crews or detachments, sub-units, units and formations in the conduct of tactical operations. There is in theory no limit to the size of formation which may engage in collective training. There are three types of collective training:

> *Special to Arm Training.* Special to Arm training is collective training on a single Arm or functional basis. It provides the immediate context for team or crew training.
>
> *Combined Arms Training.* Combined Arms training is the collective training of several arms together such as infantry, armour, artillery and aviation. Such training will normally be at sub-unit level. It provides the immediate context for Special to Arm collective training.

Joint and Multinational Training. Joint and multinational training will normally take place at unit level and above, and involve two or more Services or nations.

Specific Training for Operations

Since the Army is for general war-fighting skills, and one which tends to be expeditionary in nature, there may be a requirement for some additional training for specific operations to reflect the particular circumstances of that deployment. Such training may take place before deployment or once the force has been deployed, or both. It should:

Ensure that those being committed to the operation are prepared fully, both mentally and physically, for the conditions which they might encounter.

Be completely relevant and reflect the most recent military experience.

Specific training for operations often has to encompass the whole range of training categories. Few units are likely to be permanently at an operational readiness, and most will require reinforcement and training prior to operations.

Command Training

The effective training of commanders and staff is the basis of operational success and has to be given a high priority. The potential to command is innate, but it needs to be developed, and may require specific training if the individual is to perform effectively, especially within the context of the Army's doctrine. That doctrine requires a style of command which promotes decentralised command, freedom and speed of action, and initiative. Mission Command meets this requirement and is a central part of the Army's doctrine. It is designed to promote a robust system of command to achieve unity of effort at all levels.

The attributes required of commanders, and by the command philosophy, should be inculcated at the earliest stages of an officer's or a soldier's career. Arms Schools and Colleges have an important role in developing these attributes in commanders from the most junior to the most senior during courses and training. The process should be continuous throughout an Individual's career, and superiors have to play their part in developing their subordinates' qualities as commanders through training and coaching. Coaching is an informal process requiring particular skills which also have to be developed before most individuals can feel sufficiently confident to enable them to accept fully this further command responsibility. Training commanders to think and act two levels higher is an important and necessary part of gaining overall experience of command.

Command training: Wargaming.

Command is often viewed only in individual terms, whereas in reality and particularly in war, effective command is achieved by team effort. The effect of a sound and reliable staff will be to free the commander from detail and enable him to concentrate on decision-making and exercising leadership. Staff training should be considered as inextricably linked with command training. The ability to build the command team and create the right climate are essential ingredients of command. The command team, which may change frequently, requires its own collective training and development if it is to realise its potential. This may be a separate exercise, or incorporated into other training. Technology offers a great deal in support of effective command team training.

Training Progression

Training should develop logically from individual training through team training to progressively more sophisticated and challenging collective training. This may be followed by operationally specific training prior to or after deployment to an operational theatre. Within each of these categories there will be initial training during which skills are learned, refresher training to maintain troops at a certain level of capability, and continuation training to develop further those skills in which a degree of competence has already been achieved. To achieve a progression in training standards, units and formations should be competent in special to arm skills before combined arms training is undertaken and competent in single Service operations before undertaking joint or multinational training. The training strategy is designed to ensure that, where possible, units and formations at the highest states of operational readiness have been through this process before being placed at readiness.

Learning from Experience

In peacetime the Army's experience of fighting will inevitably be more limited. To compensate for this, emphasis should be placed on learning from the experience of others. The study of military history will broaden and deepen understanding of doctrine, and assist a future commander in his study of his potential adversary. Military history will not, however, provide universal remedies. It can only offer accounts of problems, particular solutions, and the reasons for historical successes and failures.

In addition to learning from history, experience can be gained from current operational experience, both British and foreign, and from a wide variety of training. A Lessons Learned system should provide a means by which observations from After Action Reviews (AARs), Post Exercise Reports (PXR), operational reports and other sources can be collated to establish whether changes may be required in doctrine and training. Such lessons should be disseminated widely and in a timely fashion. On operations there will be even greater need to learn rapidly from experience and implement changes without delay.

Section 2 Simulation Training

Introduction

Simulation training is now a regular and routine part of any form of military training. It has been apparent for many years that the complexity and cost of newly acquired weapons systems would make it more difficult to train properly using suitable ranges, live ammunition and other realistic conditions. The growth of simulation by use of electronic means to replicate near-real operating conditions in the appropriate environment has enabled many of these training requirements to be achieved at much lower cost and without disruption to other activities.

The Role of Simulation

Simulation is defined as the technique of providing a working representation of a real system, process, task or operational condition. Simulators can range from simple, inexpensive, devices to complex and costly all arms trainers. Simulation is a tool which can be used to enhance training and it should be fully integrated into any training programme so that it can be applied at the appropriate time in the correct quantity.

Simulation has many advantages. It can allow certain types of training to be carried out that would be too costly or dangerous in peacetime and can increase throughput which allows more frequent repetitions of training. It can provide objective feedback and assessment of training. However it also has disadvantages, particularly where the training is carried out in a wholly synthetic environment. Because of this, field and live fire training are still needed in order for soldiers to have the proper confidence in themselves and their equipment in all conditions both day and night.

Priority for the use of simulation should be given to areas of high cost training, where there is a lack of realism or effectiveness and where it is unacceptably constrained by range or training area availability. Simulation should only be considered where it can be shown that it will enhance the quality or quantity of training to proper effect or it can be shown to be more economical than current methods.

The Army has developed a strategy for the introduction and use of simulator and synthetic training. This strategy forms a major component part of the Army Training Strategy and begins to address the training and simulation requirements some ten to fifteen years ahead.

Simulation systems have already been introduced into service to cover the following training categories.

Individual/Team Training. Early examples are the Small Arms Trainer and the CHALLENGER 2 training systems.

Collective Training. Examples are the Tactical Engagement Simulation and the Combined Arms Tactical Trainer.

Command and Staff Training. Examples are the Brigade and Battlegroup Trainers and the Higher Formation Trainer.

Joint and International. Plans are in hand to combine the separate Service requirements to provide a joint training capability probably at one or two central locations. The problems of providing controllers and staff to operate the simulation process could be overcome with suitable computer networks to allow controllers, and players, to operate from their own base locations, (as already practised in America).

Section 3 Enemy Force Scenarios for Use in Training

Background

There is no doubt that simulation will continue to enhance and improve the ability to train and it will play a growing role in the future at all levels. It has to be understood that whatever the degree of sophistication that is reached in simulated training it can never replace live training. Nor can it be used exclusively to test and evaluate the achievement of particular standards of training. There are, and will continue to be, problems associated with the compatibility of data, the number of simulator systems, their location and availability and the need to brief controllers and their staffs.

GENFORCE

The British Army has, since the Cold War ended, become a doctrine-based army in which units and formations stand ready for all types of military operations almost anywhere in the world against differing types of enemy forces. This new feature complicates training in that there are few norms against which to set any training standards. In effect there is little or no substantial tactical information about any potential enemy forces. Thus scenarios and background situations for use in training could vary widely and perhaps lead to confusion in the evaluation of suitable training standards. To offset this a standard layout of enemy forces has been devised for use in all training processes and simulation exercises and these are recorded in an appropriate handbook for use by all those planning and conducting exercises.

Section 4 Training Publications

All Arms Training Publications

Historically, official training publications have been controlled by the appropriate training branch of the General Staff, but have not, until recently, been incorporated into the overall all-arms doctrinal publications. Pamphlets for training have either been published as separate documents such as the 'Training for War' series of pamphlets or incorporated within particular pamphlets such as in 'The Land Battle' series of pamphlets. It has now been recognised that training is an important part of all arms doctrine and this is reflected in the updated series of publications in the Army Field Manual.

Directives and Collective Tasks

In conjunction with the changes outlined above, ten Individual Training Directives have been promulgated and published which itemise the policy, direction and co-ordination of the standards of individual training worldwide. Similarly, a compendium for Collective Training has been issued in five volumes which incorporates collective training tasks for units and sub-units including CSS units. This is intended to be a check list for unit and formation commanders to use when writing their own training programmes. It also provides an indication of the time taken to carry out the prescribed training and the resources necessary to complete the task. Outline costings are also indicated.

Handbooks/Aides-Mémoire/Training Notes

In addition to these publications there are other All Arms Handbooks, *Aides-Mémoire* and Doctrinal Notes that will assist commanders and staffs in ensuring that operational and training points are borne in mind when planning future training. Similarly the periodical *Army Doctrine and Training News* published on a wide scale twice a year provides further articles about improving and developing training.

ANNEX A

THE EXPERIENCE OF HISTORY

EXAMPLES TO HIGHLIGHT THE PRINCIPLES OF WAR

Historical examples to illustrate the Principles of War are contained in this Annex. The examples chosen are taken from the Second World War onwards, and cover several different armies and situations to demonstrate the international applicability of the principles even though techniques and tactics may vary Success in the future will however not be gained by a slavish imitation of the past. Rather the experience of history should serve to illuminate the present and inspire future commanders to conceive original ways of applying the principles to defeat an enemy. With the exception of the first principle, undue emphasis should not be accorded to the order in which the others are placed.

In some of the examples the convention of showing opposing forces in blue and red has been modified. On maps illustrating recent campaigns in which the United Kingdom took no part the use of red, the colour associated with the enemy, is pejorative and might give unintended offence. However, red is an appropriate colour for the British army from the days when soldiers wore scarlet or madder red, and also for the Soviet army, formerly the Red Army, which uses the colour to mark its own troop positions.

The ten examples are as follows:

APPENDIX 1 SELECTION AND MAINTENANCE OF THE AIM

GENERAL TAL'S BREAKTHROUGH AT RAFA, 1967

Israeli War Aims

In May 1967, following an airbattle over the Golan Heights, President Nasser asked the United Nations to withdraw its Emergency Force from Sinai. He reinforced his troops in the Peninsula to six divisions, moved about 40 fighters on to the Sinai airfields, concluded defence arrangements with Jordan, Syria and Iraq and closed the Straits of Tiran to Israeli shipping. When three Egyptian divisions were concentrated on the Israeli frontier the Israeli Defence Force (IDF) was mobilised. Whereas Egypt could menace the Negev with her Regular Army indefinitely, Israel could not remain mobilised long without damage to her economy. Concerned that an Arab military combination might move against her on three sides, the Israeli Government determined on a pre-emptive war.

As Egypt possessed the largest armed forces amongst her Arab neighbours and presented the most serious and immediate threat Israel decided to deal with her first. If the other Arab states remained quiet, no action would be taken against them. If not, Jordan would be attacked next to relieve the pressure on Jerusalem and the waist of Israel. Syria, which threatened no vital point immediately, would be dealt with last. To forestall a concentric attack and to beat the 'diplomatic clock' in the Security Council speed was essential.

Initially, the Egyptians had only two infantry divisions on the Sinai border, 20 Palestinian in the Gaza Strip and 7 Infantry Division on a frontage of 140 miles between the sea at Rafa and Kuntilla. The 7th was shuffled sideways to the coast to allow the 2nd to take over its right in the Agheila Um Katif area. The 3rd and 6th were deployed in depth behind the 7th and 2nd respectively and 4 Armoured Division was kept well back in the Bir Gifgafa area.

One of the latter's brigades was detached to the Quraya Pass area for an offensive in the Negev to link up with the Jordanians at Beersheba. The Egyptians under General Mortagi were deployed for defence in great depth with the option of a small scale offensive. Their divisions were too far apart for mutual support and their logistic system was in disarray.

Eshkol's Israeli Cabinet, stiffened by the appointment of General Moshe Dayan as Defence Minister during the crisis, took the decision to fight on the evening of 3 June, the day Iraq joined Nasser's Arab Pact. Any possibility of strategic surprise had evaporated during the three weeks of tension. The next day, the unclassified items on the previous night's Cabinet agenda were published together with a disarming press statement by Moshe Dayan that diplomacy must now be given a chance. Pictures of reservists relaxing on Israel's beaches were given a good deal of publicity. This was enough to give the Israelis tactical surprise on the following day.

Air superiority was the key to success in the war as a whole. A combination of brilliant planning, surprise and execution knocked out the Egyptian Air Force on its airfields in 2 hours 50 minutes on the morning of 5 June. When Jordan and Syria entered the war later in the day their air forces were dealt with in two strikes lasting just 25 minutes each. From the Army's point of view freedom from enemy air attack conferred immense advantages but, initially, it would have to rely on limited air support from the slow Fouga Magister trainers until the high performance Mirages, Mysteres and Ouragons could be released from the airfield strikes.

Sinai. Israel's Aims and Plans

The plan for the Sinai campaign was the work of the Chief of the General Staff, Yitzhak Rabin, and GOC Southern Command, Yeshayahu Gavish. The aim was the destruction of Mortagi's forces. Sharm-esh Sheikh, controlling the Straits of Tiran and the east bank of the Suez Canal, would then fall into Israel's lap. The plan was to be executed in three phases.

First, two ugdas[1] were to break through the Egyptian crust defences at Rafa and Abu-Agheila to open the two main routes into Sinai while a deception operation distracted enemy attention towards Kuntilla. A third ugda was to infiltrate an armoured brigade along the Wadi Hareidin, a supposedly impassable route some 10 to 15 miles south of the coast road, which had been secretly reconnoitred[2] to prevent reinforcements being sent against Tal's Ugda on the coast and to win the armoured battle which would ensue when the Egyptian 4 Armoured Division counter-attacked. The ugda's second brigade remained in reserve. In the second phase the three main passes through the Western Hills (Khatmia, Giddi and Mitla) would be seized behind the Egyptians so that their forces could be destroyed in the third phase. The Gaza Strip and other sectors of the front were watched by reserve infantry brigades. This account concentrates on the breakthrough of Tal's Ugda at Rafa.

General Israel Tal was the tank expert in the OF. Starting his military career as a carrier platoon sergeant in the British Army in the Second World War he became a machine-gun officer in the Haganah and only transferred to the Armour Corps when the OF appreciated the importance of the tank during the 1956 campaign. After three years at university he became Chief of the Armour Corps in 1964, at the same time holding the shadow appointment of an ugda commander on mobilisation. He brought a coherent system of tactical doctrine to the IDF based largely on Liddell Hart's theories and Guderian's experience, besides overhauling training in the Armour Corps and creating an elite officer cadre. A professional to his finger tips, a disciplinarian, an exacting trainer, and yet a sensitive man, he was a born leader who pondered deeply on how armour should be used in

[1] In 1967, the IDF did not have permanently established divisions. Brigades were formed into ugdas (groups) for each operation.
[2] During the temporary occupation of Sinai after the 1956 War, two Israeli officers carried out a covert reconnaissance in Arab dress wearing sandals to avoid leaving tell-tale boot marks.

battle. After the war he was to design the IDF's first indigenous tank, the Merkeva, incorporating many original features.

General Tal's Plan

Facing Tal's Ugda was a brigade of 20 Palestinian Division in Khan Yunis and two brigades of 7 Egyptian Infantry Division astride the coast road at Rafa Junction. A further brigade was disposed in depth, split between El Arish and a defile on the road near Jeradi railway station, eight miles short of the town. In all, the position was 35 miles deep. Unaware of the recent changes in the Egyptian deployment, Israeli intelligence thought that Rafa Junction was occupied by only one brigade. The battalion at the Jeradi defile was a surprise.

Tal's aim was to break through this formidable 'crust' as quickly as possible and at all costs, so that his armour, and that of Yiska Shadmi's Brigade moving down the Wadi Hareidin, could deploy clear of the defences in time to beat off 4 Egyptian Armoured Division's expected counter-attack in the open. The attack had to succeed at the first attempt. There would be no opportunity to regroup and mount a second attack after a battle of attrition, as at El Alamein. Tal had three brigades: the crack 7 Romani Armoured Brigade, commanded by a stern martinet, Colonel Shmuel Gonen, another armoured brigade under Colonel Menachim and a scratch brigade under a parachute officer, Colonel Raphoul Eytan. The first two were conventional armoured brigades, each of two armoured battalions, a mechanised infantry battalion and a reconnaissance company. Colonel Eytan's Brigade consisted of an armoured battalion and a parachute battalion hurriedly married to its APCs a week before the war. The Ugda had plenty of armour but lacked sufficient infantry and artillery. Short of funds, the Israelis gave priority to their Air Force and relied on it for close support.

The obvious place to attack was the 'Opening of Rafa', a narrowing tract of good going between the sand dunes on the coast and the sand sea to the south at the hinge between the Egyptian border and the Gaza Strip. The Egyptians had blocked the approach with wire and mines and had registered artillery DFs. Tal knew that the Egyptians had not registered their camps and towns in the Gaza Strip and reasoned that they would not have mined the coast road and railway supplying them. His plan was to concentrate behind a low ridge amongst the cultivation four miles south of the Gaza Strip. 7 Armoured Brigade would break into Khan Yunis, brushing aside the Palestinians occupying the town, and using the road and railway as axes of advance, would take Rafa Junction from the north and drive on to El Arish. Raphoul Eytan's Brigade would cross the frontier south of the hinge to pinch out Rafa Junction from the south. Menachim's Brigade would drive along a track through the sand sea five miles south of the coast road to link up with a drop by 80 Parachute Brigade on El Arish airfield. Tal had enough artillery to engage the Egyptian defences with covering fire but not enough for counter-bombardment. To silence the Egyptian guns he would have to rely initially on the Fouga Magisters.

General Tal and Colonel Gonen.

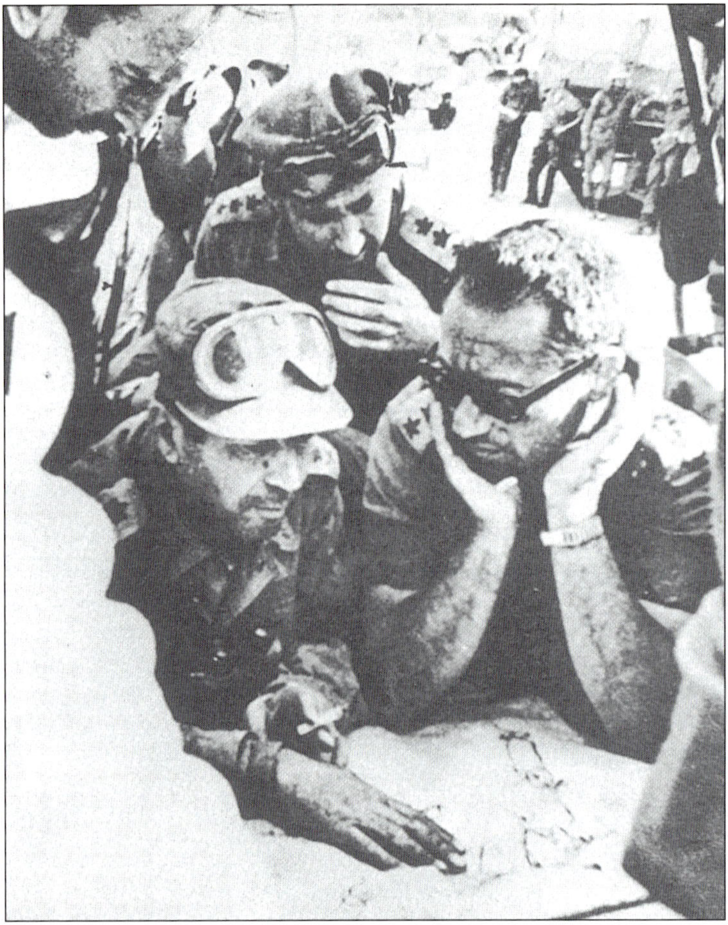

The Break-in Battle

At 0845 on 5 June 7 Armoured Brigade's reconnaissance company led the way across the border in single file to minimise the mine threat. As it entered the narrow lanes on the outskirts of Khan Yunis it ran into trouble and its burning jeeps and half tracks blocked the route. To their surprise the Israelis discovered that the town was occupied by a brigade instead of a battalion. Colonel Gonen decided on a two-prong attack. The Patton battalion was sent round to the right and half the Centurion battalion straight on. The other half remained in reserve under the brigade's deputy commander. The mechanised battalion had been sent to occupy Kerem Shalom in case the Egyptians launched a counter-attack on the hinge.

The attack started badly because only half the tank commanders in the Patton battalion heard their CO's orders over the radio. Too much reliance was placed on visual contact and flag signals. Luckily Khan Yunis railway station had been

Patton tank in action, near Rafa Junction.

General Tal.

nominated as the battalion RV in the preliminary orders and so the CO was able to rally his unit and regain control. The sudden irruption of 60 tanks into the town firing their guns unnerved the Palestinian infantry, who emerged from their defences with their hands up. However, there was no mechanised infantry to take them prisoner so that when the tanks left the town and the shock wore off the Palestinians returned to their positions. Ashamed of themselves, they offered a spirited resistance to a follow-up infantry brigade for three more days.

The Brigade advanced towards Rafa Junction, the Pattons on the railway track, the Centurions on the main road and the reconnaissance company in the lead once more. The Egyptians allowed the latter to come within 100 yards of the Junction before ambushing it to reveal a second brigade where only a battalion had been expected. Gonen ordered another two-prong attack, the Centurions along the road, the Pattons to the west of it. The Patton commander split his battalion, sending half under his second-in-command along the edge of the dunes to the north to swing in from the west while he attacked frontally with the remainder. Simultaneously, the Egyptians counter-attacked from the south-west with a T54 tank battalion. It drove straight into the jaws of the Israeli pincer movement and was repulsed with the loss of nine tanks.

With the defeat of their armour the Egyptian infantry went to ground. 7 Armoured Brigade moved on, the Centurions along the road and the Pattons on the railway to overrun the Egyptian Division's gun area and headquarters, killing the GOC.

Set-Back at the Jeradi Defile

At about 1300 the two tank battalions rallied under the Brigade Commander at Sheikh Zuweid. An hour later, to maintain the momentum of the advance, Gonen committed his reserve of two Centurion companies and the reconnaissance company under his deputy commander westwards to El Arish. At the Jeradi defile, where the road winds down a short steep sand dune into a wadi, the Egyptian battalion group was asleep and the Centurions drove on to El Arish without casualties. The reconnaissance company, following in its wake, was not so lucky. It lost two more vehicles and was forced to remain on the near bank. At El Arish the Centurions met the rest of the Egyptian reserve brigade, knocked out three T34s and retired into a palm grove to await the arrival of reinforcements.

Immediately south of the road Eytan's Brigade was in difficulty. With inadequate inter-arm training the tanks fanned out and drove off leaving the paratroop battalion in its APCs behind. The latter, with only one company of tanks remaining, was counter-attacked by a JS 3 battalion. Tal halted the advance on El Arish temporarily to divert Gonen's Patton battalion, his mechansed battalion, which was still holding the hinge at Kerem Shalom, and Menachim's mechanised battalion from the southern axis. During the time it took to extricate these units the Fouga Magisters had dealt with the JS 3s and Eytan had fought his way north to Rafa Junction. The diverted units were returned to their brigades, except for Gonen's mechanised battalion, which was set to work with a company of Pattons to clear the Egyptian brigade north of Rafa Junction while Eytan's

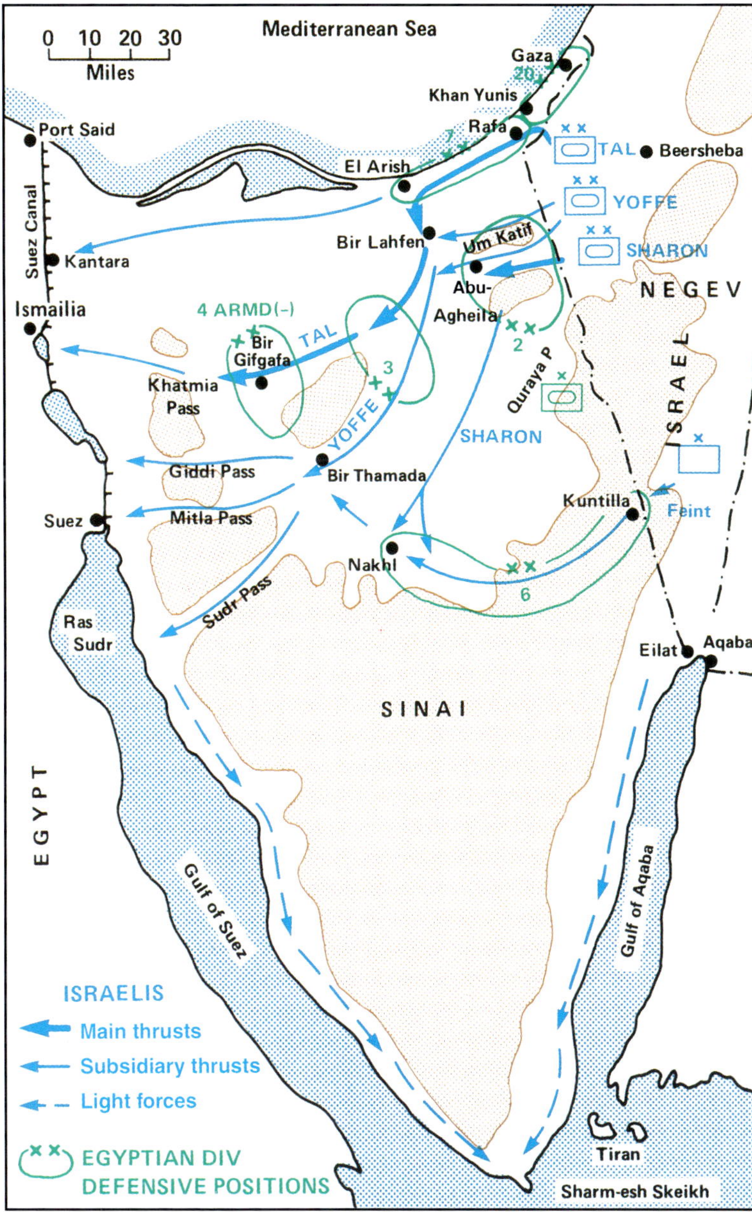

Egyptian Defences – Israeli thrust lines. The Six Day War 1967

Brigade mopped up the area to the south. Menachim's Brigade was making slow progress through the soft sand to the south when news arrived that the parachute brigade he was to relieve at El Arish airfield had been diverted to Jerusalem. Jordan had entered the war.

Tal established his headquarters at Rafa Junction and ordered Gonen to resume the advance on El Arish with the Patton battalion, leaving the two remaining Centurion companies in divisional reserve. Joining the reconnaissance company at the Jeradi defile, Gonen found a well prepared position. The wadi was mined and covered by machine-guns, anti-tank guns and tanks. The palm grove to the north was too thick for armour and the ground to the south was open soft sand. Tal ordered Menachim's Britade to take the defile from the south but the sand was too soft and the attempt had to be abandoned.

When the Patton battalion arrived at the defile at 1700 Gonen ordered it to mount a frontal attack straight down the road and a flank attack over the open sand to the south. The frontal attack was repulsed and the flank attack bogged down in soft sand. The CO was killed and all three company commanders were wounded. The second-in-command rallied the battalion on the road out of sight of the Egyptians for another attempt at 1800. Calling for air support and an artillery concentration the tanks closed down and rushed the position with the loss of only one tank. However, the Brigade command post, the remnants of the reconnaissance company and the Brigade 'A' Echelon trying to follow on were held up when the Egyptians recovered from their initial shock. The new Patton battalion commander offered to clear the defile from back to front to open the route but Gonen ordered him on to El Arish to relieve the Centurions. The battle was still in the 'advance at all costs' phase.

The situation was serious. It was getting dark. The Ugda was spread over 30 miles. One and a half tank battalions of Gonen's Brigade were at El Arish. The Brigade Commander and the remains of the reconnaissance company were on the east bank of the Jeradi. The Brigade's two remaining Centurion companies were in divisional reserve and the mechanized battalion group was clearing the area north of Rafa. Eytan's Brigade was clearing the area south of the Junction and Menachim's Brigade was stuck in the sand to the south. If the Egyptian 4 Armoured Division should arrive in time for a counter-attack next morning Tal's Ugda might never break out of the frontier defences. Tal ordered Menachim's Brigade to make one more effort to reach the Jeradi but by 1930 his tanks had stuck in the sand, were short of fuel and had lost touch with their infantry in the dark. This attempt was also abandoned.

Maintaining the Aim

The attack had lost momentum. The Ugda's only uncommitted reserves were the two Centurion companies. A lesser man might have given up or at least waited for daylight. But the whole campaign depended on a rapid breakthrough and Tal was as determined as ever to maintain the aim. He decided to take a risk at Rafa Junction where Gonen's mechanised battalion and a Patton company were clearing the area to secure it for the Divisional Administrative Area. He released the battalion group to Gonen and added a Centurion company to it.

The problem was how to rally the mechanised battalion group, spread over seven square kilometres, in the dark. Fortunately its CO was another remarkable man. Mordecai Avigat was quiet and unassuming but resourceful and enterprising. He radioed his company commanders, telling them to return to their APCs and drive to the main road. Motoring along the road he picked up each company in turn and led the complete unit to Tal at the Junction. The delighted general kissed the CO on both cheeks! The whole Ugda artillery was placed at the CO's disposal, including an illumination shoot. The Centurion company was sent on ahead to join Gonen at the Jeradi who deployed it to gain a foothold in the defile and to prevent the Egyptians from moving reinforcements from one side of the road to the other.

Putting the Patton company at the head of his mechanised battalion the CO led the column through the press of vehicles jamming the road west of the Junction. The drivers of the administrative vehicles were reluctant to risk the mines and soft sand off the tarmac and had to be forced out of the way. On arrival at the Jeradi the CO closed the column up, called for covering fire from the artillery and Centurions, and an illumination shoot to light the route. Then he led the group at full speed down the road. He had arranged an RV at Jeradi Station, a small shack and the only landmark recognisable in the dark, at the end of the defile. There he halted the battalion, placing the Pattons and one mechanised company as a road block facing west. With his other two companies formed up on either side of the road facing east he fought his way backwards to clear the position. It took four hours to mop up the mile of trenches back to the entrance on a 200 yard frontage. At dawn the infantry and tanks continued mopping up away from the road. The battalion was left to secure the defile while the rest of the Brigade and the echelons passed through.

Meanwhile the deputy brigade commander, who had broken through to El Arish with one and a half armoured battalions the day before, had blocked all the routes leading out of the town during the night to seal off the Egyptian garrison.

The next morning, 7 Armoured Brigade concentrated at El Arish, where it turned south to fight its way through the last Egyptian defences at Bir Lahfan. The position was fortified in depth and the approaches were constricted by a wadi and sand dunes. When the Brigade attacked this time the tank crews made use of their long range marksmanship and such manoeuvring as the ground permitted. It took the whole morning of 6 June to chip away the position but by midday the Brigade had broken through to link up with Yiska Shadmi's armoured brigade moving down the Wadi Hareidin to cut the El Arish–Gebel Libni road south of Bir Lahfan. Together, the two brigades defeated a counter-attack by elements of 4 Egyptian Armoured Brigade. The 'advance at all costs' phase was over.

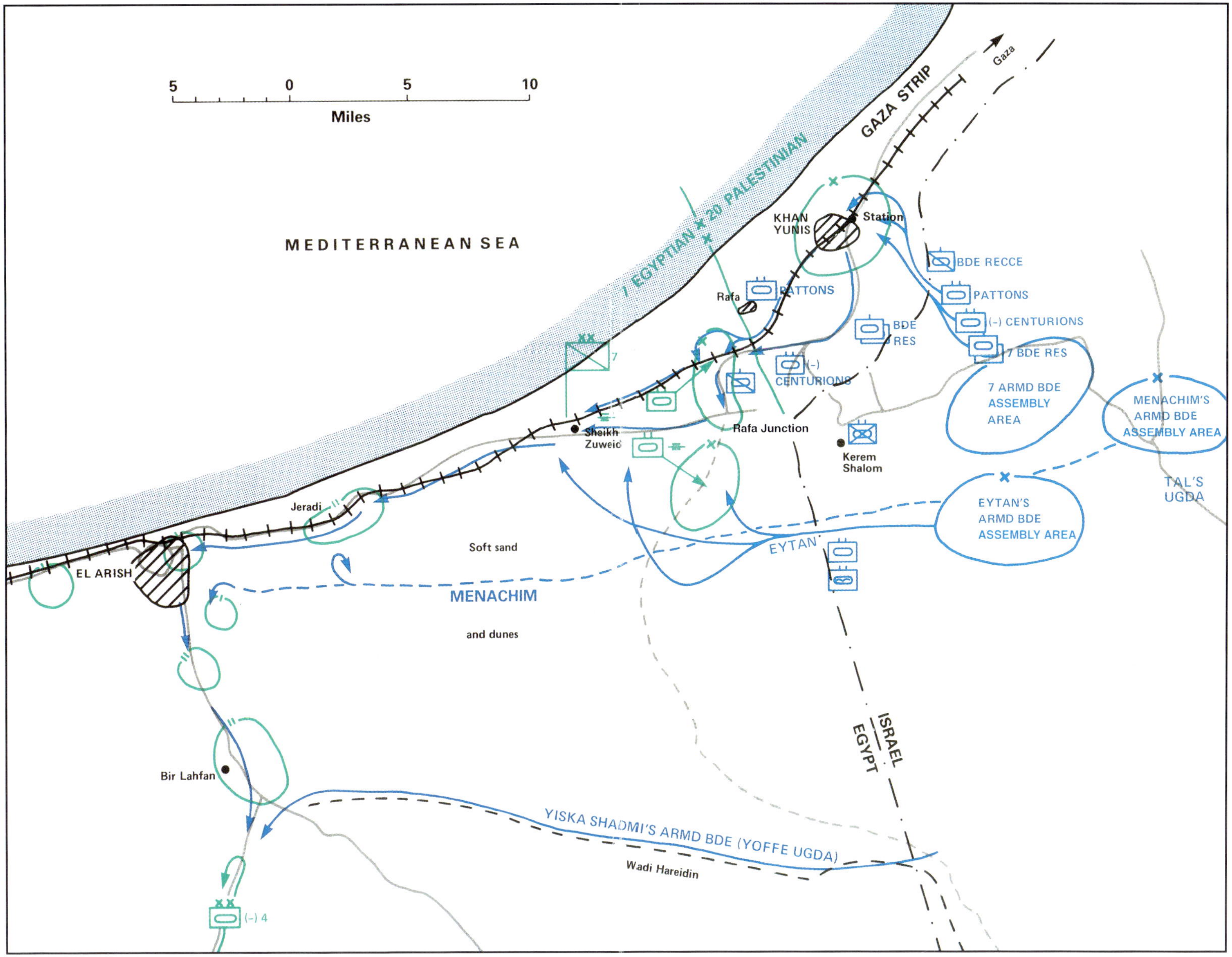

Breakthrough of Tal's Ugda at Rafa-el-Arish 5-6 June 1967

Aim Achieved

Tal had achieved his aim by sheer perseverance. The Egyptian defences had turned out to be far stronger than anticipated. One brigade had become hopelessly bogged down in the soft sand on the southern flank. The parachute drop at El Arish was cancelled. A second brigade, with insufficient time to convert paratroops to mechanized infantrymen and train with tanks, had fought resolutely but had been hard pressed to clear the area south of Rafa Junction. The third brigade had driven through a defended town, cleared the area north of the Junction and pushed some tanks through to El Arish. Twice the Egyptians had cut the axis at the Jeradi defile. With single-minded determination more tanks had been sent through to El Arish, despite the risks, and a desperate operation to clear the defile had succeeded in the dark. The Brigade had concentrated at El Arish for a further breakthrough battle at Bir Lahfan. When the last defences of the frontier 'crust' had been breached the Brigade took part in the repulse of the Egyptian armoured reserve. Mistakes there were in plenty, especially in all arms co-operation, but as an example of the successful and determined pursuit of an aim Tal's leadership and 7 Romani Armoured Brigade's performance have few equals.

Bibliography

Allon, Major General Y, *The Making of Israel's Army*, Vallentine, Mitchell in association with Weidenfeld and Nicolson, 1970.

Bacon, Wing Commander G McA, and Lieutenant Colonel J A Sellers, *The Six Day War, NDC Report on Visit to Israel*, 1972.

Bagnall, Brigadier NT MC, *The Israeli Experience. A Study in Quality.* Defence Fellowship, Balliol College, Oxford, 1972–73.

Bar-On, Colonel Mordechai, *Israel Defence Forces. The Six Day War, IDF and Ministry of Defence, Tel Aviv*, 1968.

Barker, A J, *Arab-Israeli Wars*, Ian Allan, 1980.

Carver, Field Marshal Lord, *The Apostles of Mobility*, Weidenfeld and Nicolson, 1979.

Churchill, Randolph S and Winston S, *The Six Day War*, Heinemann and Penguin, 1967.

Dayan, Moshe, *Diary of the Sinai Campaign*, Weidenfeld and Nicolson, 1966.

Dayan, Moshe, *The Story of My Life*, Weidenfeld and Nicolson, 1976.

Depuy, Colonel T N, USA, *Elusive Victory, The Arab-Israeli Wars 1947–1974*, Macdonald and Jane's, 1978.

Henriques, Robert, *100 Hours to Suez*, Collins, 1957.

Herzog, Major General Chaim, *The Arab-Israeli Wars*, Arms and Armour Press, 1982.

Hogg, Ian V, *Israeli War Machine*, Hamlyn, 1983.

Kimche, David and Dan Bawly, *The Sandstorm. The Arab-Israeli war of 1967: Prelude and Aftermath*, Secker and Warburg, 1968.

Luttwak, Edward and Dan Horowitz, *The Israeli Army*, Harper and Row, New York, 1975.

Messenger, Charles, *The Art of Blitzkrieg*, Ian Allan, 1976.
O'Ballance, Edgar, *The Third Arab-Israeli War*, Faber and Faber, 1972.
Perrett, Bryan, *A History of Blitzkrieg*, Hale, 1983.
Pimlott, John, editor, *The Middle East Conflicts from 1945 to the Present*, Orbis, 1983.
Prittie, Terence, *Eshkol of Israel, The Man and the Nation*, Museum Press, 1969.
Rabin, Yitzhak, *The Rabin Memoirs*, Weidenfeld and Nicolson, 1979.
Rothenburg, Gunther, *The Anatomy of the Israeli Army*, Batsford, 1979.
Teveth, Shabtai, *The Tanks of Tammuz*, Weidenfeld and Nicolson, 1968.
Teveth, Shabtai, *Moshe Dayan, The Soldier, The Man, The Legend*, Weidenfeld and Nicolson, 1972.
Wallach, Colonel Dr J L, 'The Israeli Armoured Corps in the Six Day War', *Armor,* LXXVII, No 3, May–June, 1968.
Weller, Jac, 'The Breakthrough of Rala, June 1967', *The Army Quarterly,* LXXXX0 (sic), No 2, July 1968.
Young, Peter, *The Israeli Campaign 1967*, William Kimber, 1967.

APPENDIX 2

MAINTENANCE OF MORALE

THE SENIOR COMMANDER

Introduction

The make-up of good morale is primarily leadership. Three separate and very differing accounts of leadership follow. In the first, General Slim seeks to revive the flagging spirits of the 14th Army that had retreated from Burma, considered itself forgotten and operating on limited resources in a most inhospitable environment. The second depicts leadership and bravery of the highest order in a remote location with little initial prospect of support. This was achieved by a young officer and a small group of men against almost overwhelming odds. The third is a clear example of quick decisive leadership and good morale at the start of a very hazardous operation.

The selection of these three examples of leadership is necessarily arbitrary and by no means exhaustive. Many others could easily have been chosen but together they indicate a few of the different aspects of leadership that make up the composition of good morale.

General Slim and the Burma Campaign 1942–45

The retreat from Burma in the first few months of 1942 and the disasters in the Arakan had brought the morale of 14th Army to a low ebb. It was a heterogeneous force of British, Indian, Gurkha, Burmese and African troops, men with very different cultural and religious backgrounds. When Slim was appointed to the command of 14th Army in October 1943 one of the first tasks he set himself was the restoration of its morale. He described morale as '... a state of mind. It is that intangible force which will move a whole group of men to give their last ounce to achieve something, without counting the cost to themselves; that makes them feel they are part of something greater than themselves. If they are to feel that, their morale must, if it is to endure – and the essence of morale is that it should endure – have certain foundations. These foundations are spiritual, intellectual, and material, and that is the order of their importance. Spiritual first, because only spiritual foundations can stand real strain. Next intellectual, because men are swayed by reason as well as feeling. Material last – important, but last – because the very highest kinds of morale are often met when material conditions are lowest.'

Although he appreciated the importance of religion as a foundation of morale, the ability of Islam, Hinduism and Sikhism to inspire bravery and a contempt for death, and the power of Christianity to promote an enduring courage, he thought of the spiritual element more in terms of belief in a cause. For men to be prepared to die for a cause it had to be vital. At stake in 1943 was the future freedom of

India and the liberation of occupied territories. Although part of the British Empire, the Indians had far better prospects under the British than the Japanese. But something more was needed than the defence of a just cause – an active, aggressive fighting spirit to attack and destroy the Japanese Army as the embodiment of evil.

Slim made a practice of visiting units to speak to the officers and men, usually from the bonnet of his jeep. He found that if he kept the bulk of his talk to the material things which interested them, food, pay, leave, beer, mails and the progress of operations, it was safe to end on a higher note, the spiritual foundations. He had not only to find out what appealed to the British and Gurkha soldiers, with whom he was familiar, but the Indians of all religions and classes, some of whom had not been recruited into the Army before and whose self-esteem and confidence needed appreciation and promotion. The arrival of African divisions added a new dimension in applied psychology

The fighting formations of 4, 15 and 33 Corps were less of a problem than the administrative units along the lines of communication. Slim made a special effort to visit the logistic units to make the office clerks and storemen, the telephone operators and fitters, feel that they were important and that what they did and the way they did it really mattered. He paid particular attention to the reinforcement system. He found the transit camps full of dispirited men living a boring life in unnecessarily poor conditions. Some men spent five months in the chain of camps before they arrived in a unit as a battle casualty replacement. The camp commandants and staffs, with some notable exceptions, were officers and NCOs whom their regiments had rejected. Slim found an energetic and experienced colonel to take overall charge of the whole organisation. Fighting units were pressured into releasing some of their best officers as commandants. Each transit camp was allotted to a division in the line. The camp flew its divisional flag and the reinforcements wore its badge. The division provided the camp's officers and instructors. Because the future success of the division depended upon making the replacements feel part of it and on training them for the special conditions they would meet, there was every incentive for the parent formation to allocate good officers and NCOs. Further back in India, two training divisions were formed to provide practical jungle training for soldiers who had completed basic training. Each regiment in the Indian Army had a battalion in one of the divisions. When a batch of reinforcements left, it was sent to a transit company run by the same regiment in one of the forward transit camps in the divisional area which the regiment served. From basic training to active service a man was made to feel part of his old family, the regiment, and carefully inducted into his new family, the division. The benefits to the morale of 14th Army were immeasurable.

On the intellectual level the main problem was to dispel the legend of Japanese invincibility. There was the obvious basis for the legend, the Japanese Army's careful preparation for jungle warfare and its method of leaving the tracks to encircle defensive positions. Stories of Japanese prowess grew in the telling as some of the defeated soldiers excused themselves with exaggerated stories of overwhelming

General Slim visiting a unit.

Lieutenant General Sir William Slim, GOCinC 14th Army, Monywa, 1945.

odds and superior tactics. Those along the lines of communication magnified the stories to hair-raising proportions. Confidence that the Japanese could be outwitted, outfought and beaten at their own jungle game was encouraged by news of the Australian victory at Miine Bay (New Guinea) in September 1942.

Realising that the recent defeat in the Arakan was caused by launching inadequately trained troops into over-ambitious, large scale operations, Slim decided to build up 14th Army's confidence starting at the lowest level. At first the emphasis was on patrolling, the basis of all minor tactics. With careful training and rehearsal, superior skills and intelligence began to tell. Nine patrols out often were successful. Next, a series of well prepared offensive operations was staged, using battalions against Japanese platoons and brigades against companies. So the intellectual foundations of morale were created. The Japanese could be defeated; the superman myth was destroyed.

The material foundations of morale remained to be laid. Slim's energies were bent to making his men feel that they belonged to a worthwhile and efficient organisation. As the lines of communication were improved, rations became more varied and the unpalatable and unpopular soya link ceased to be the staple diet. Mail arrived quicker and a welfare service was put in hand. Frank Owen, a brilliant young Fleet Street editor, was sent out to organise a theatre newspaper, 'Seac'. At unit level information rooms were established when units were out of the line. Keeping men informed of what was happening Slim regarded as essential to maintaining morale.

The medical services were reorganised to treat the sick, particularly malarial cases, in the forward area. Previously men who contracted malaria were sent back to hospitals in India. The journey by road, rail and boat did nothing to improve their condition. Once back in India a sickness casualty took anything up to five months to return to Burma. Malingerers would omit to take anti-malarial precautions to contract the disease as an easy way out. The Malaria Forward Treatment Units stopped the wastage and deterred the fainthearted. Nurses were brought further forward than usual; diseases like mite typhus, for which there was no proved cure, responded more to the quality of the nursing than to medicine. Aeromedical evacuation saved many lives which would otherwise have been lost. Quick surgery and treatment were a major factor in sustaining the morale of the individual. Air supply and casualty evacuation gave the men of the encircled 4 Corps at Imphal in 1944 the assurance that they were not isolated. It added to their determination to stick it out and let the Japanese destroy themselves against their defences. Senior officer replacements from India were not automatically put into command appointments. First, they had to become familiar with the jungle conditions and prove to their seniors, their subordinates and themselves that they could handle the responsibility

14th Army knew that it was at the bottom of the priority list because victory had to be assured in Europe first. But, in unfamiliar surroundings, the Army triumphed. Rangoon fell three days before the end of the war in Europe. Morale had been one of the most important factors, if not the most important, in 14th Army's success and the mainspring of that morale was Slim.

The Battle of Mirbat July, 1972

On 18 July 1972, the British Army Training Team at Mirbat (Oman) – a meagre group of ten SAS soldiers, despite its grandiloquent title – was looking forward to the following morning, a Wednesday. On that day, the men, drawn from the Regiment's B Squadron, would fly out of the desolate, barbed-wire enclave they had occupied for more than three months and return to England. They were glad to be going home. Even by Omani standards, Mirbat was not much of a place – a huddle of flat-topped houses and a couple of ancient, mud-walled forts flanked on two sides by the sea, 40 miles from the provincial capital, Salalah. Children and insects were numerous, but not much else. More than most wars, this one was a long, grinding spell of boredom punctuated by brief spurts of action. In Mirbat even the 'action' was frustrating: the whistle of incoming mortar bombs or anti-tank missiles fired by an unseen enemy. On 28 May, six mortar bombs had hit the town. On 6 June, another six. Two days later, three 75mm shells, and that was about all until 18 July.

The training team had kept busy and alert, training local forces, repairing vehicles and dispensing rudimentary medical care to human beings and camels in the quest for goodwill, while keeping their undisciplined allies in check through a prudent control of the ration stock. Their departure date was well into the monsoon season. It was time when visibility towards the hostile mountain three miles inland was dangerously limited. The season favoured the Marxist guerrillas of the Dhofar Liberation front, biding their time in limestone caves on the mountain, in another important way. It usually made flying all but impossible. In a tight situation, as both sides well understood, the British team might depend upon air supply for ammunition, reinforcement and casualty evacuation, as well as supportive aerial bombardment. On the eve of their departure it seemed that no such problems existed. As the soldiers turned into their sleeping bags for their last night in the 'Batthouse', they could hear the wind screeching in from the Indian Ocean and buffeting past them to rage against the mountain. But that night the guerrillas were also on the move, launching a silent attack on the town to begin the most ambitious frontal assault of their ten-year war against the Sultan and his British advisers. More than 250 of their best warriors had been assembled for this battle, armed with Kalashnikov AK-47 automatic rifles, light, heavy and medium machine-guns, mortars of various calibres up to 82mm, two 75mm recoilless anti-tank rifles and an 84mm Carl Gustav. As well as ammunition for these weapons, each man carried a profusion of hand-grenades. The guerrilla column marched south towards the town and the sea, and then broke into carefully organised combat groups, each of about ten men, which spread out in a wide arc around the town. Another group made a circular trek east to the beach and then back again along the coast to penetrate the town from that side. Before dawn, the garrison was isolated with no way of escape.

Inside the wire, in addition to the SAS team, was a group of about 30 Askaris from northern Oman, 500 miles away, armed with accurate but slow-firing .303-inch rifles. They served the Sultan's representative, the Wali, as town gatekeepers, searching all who came and went for messages and supplies, including food, that might be going to the enemy on the hill. The Askaris occupied a fort near the water's edge, known as the Wali's Fort. Living in the town itself, armed with FN automatic rifles and light machine-guns, was the local 'firqa'. Normally its strength was about 60, but at least 20 of them were somewhere on the mountains on a reconnaissance patrol. The remaining 40 were in bed with their wives. Finally, there was another force of about 25 men of the Dhofar Gendarmerie, armed with FN rifles and a single light machine-gun, in a second fort just inside the wire. In front of the fort was the dug-out position for a venerable 25-pounder artillery piece of Second World War vintage. The DG Fort dominated the town and Mirbat's only airstrip. It was a vital position. Apart from the artillery piece, the heaviest weapons available to the SAS, at their nearby Batthouse, were a single .50-inch Browning and an 81 mm mortar.

About 800 yards outside the wire, on a hill to the north of the town, another eight Gendarmes were on picquet duty. Predictably, it was their position, known as Jebal Ali, that first came under attack. Completely surrounded, it was to have been suppressed in a silent attack, but, as the guerillas crept up on the position just before 5.30 am, the Gendarmes spotted them and a single high-velocity shot rang out. In the fight that followed, four of the Gendarmes were killed; the other four escaped. It was the start of a battle as remarkable as that fought at Rorke's Drift during the Zulu War.

Guerrilla mortarmen, realising that surprise had been lost, immediately began raining bombs on the DG Fort, the Batthouse, and the town itself. Inside the house, Captain M J A ('Mike') Kealy, aged 23, rolled out of his sleeping bag, slipped on a pair of 'flip-flop' sandals, seized his automatic rifle and ran to the rooftop to see what was happening. What he saw was unlike any enemy attack of the war, and Kealy thought it possible that the firing was an appalling confusion caused by false identification of the friendly firqa patrol on its return. In the half-light of a grey dawn he could see groups of armed men running across open ground in front of the Batthouse, pausing to fire at the DG Fort away to his right. Men were also swarming over the picquet position on Jebal Ali: clearly it was already in enemy hands. Kealy ordered the team's only mortar, pre-laid to fire over the picquet to cover just such a situation, to open fire with high explosive and white phosphorus smoke to obscure the enemy's vision. Another of his soldiers, Trooper W., opened up with the Browning, raking the area between the two forts, while others, firing from the roof of the Batthouse, picked off targets with careful precision with FN automatic rifles and a light machine-gun.

Kealy was by now profoundly disturbed. A frontal assault of this sort on a government garrison must mean that the guerrillas had assembled an unusually large force and that they probably knew the real fighting strength of the defenders (effectively, about 50 men). He handed control briefly to one of his NCOs, Corporal B., while he drafted an urgent signal to the provincial headquarters of

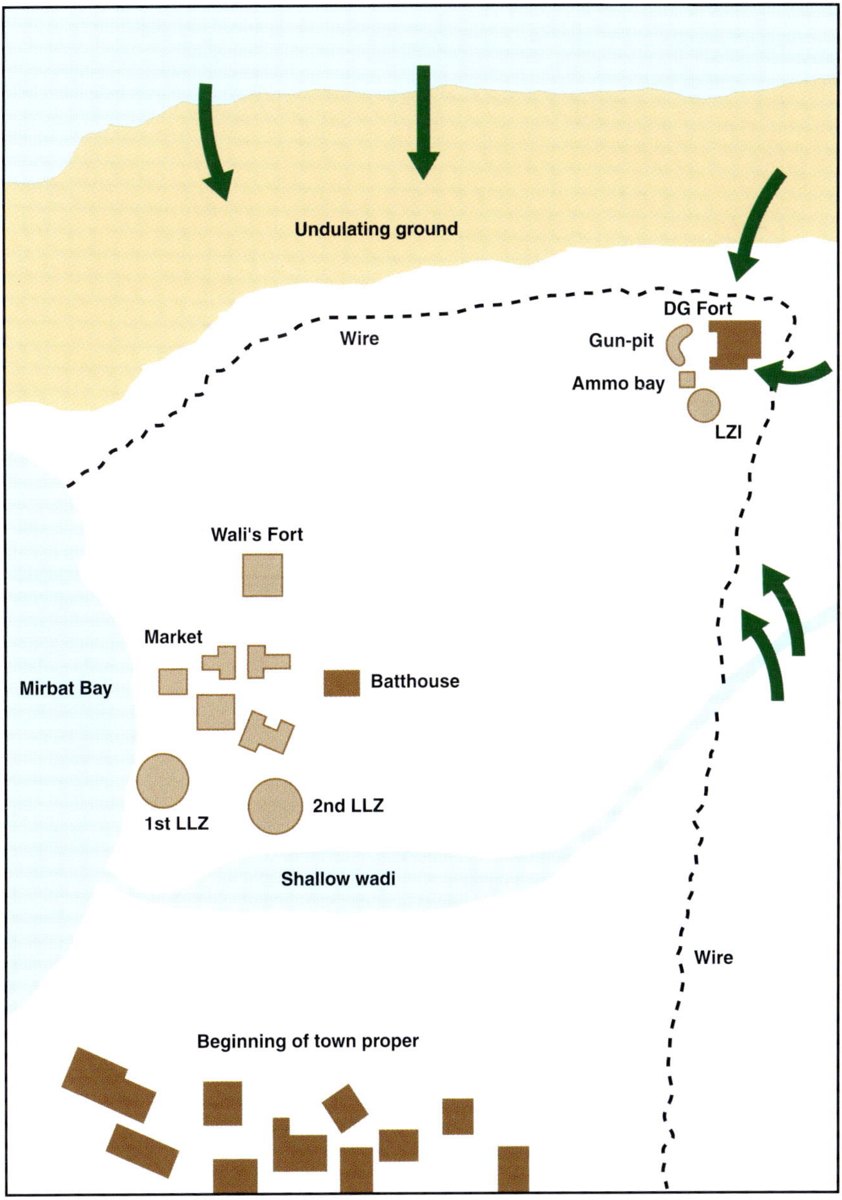

Mirbat – The Layout of the Battle Area

Satalah. The message safely away, Kealy prepared for a long, hard day by changing from flip-flops into desert boots.

By now, a well co-ordinated assault was underway, guerrilla combat groups moved as though presenting an infantry demonstration of fire and movement back home in Britain, one group advancing under covering fire until it could find dead ground from which to cover those who followed. From the overrun Jebal Ali, above the town, came accurate, considered bursts of heavy machine-gun fire, and mortar bombs were landing all round the DG Fort and the Batthouse. Even more sinister, stray enemy rounds were whistling in from the southern, seaward side of the town, 'overs' which told Kealy and his men that they were surrounded. The battle now raging round them was a three-cornered affair in which the Askaris were firing from the Wali's Fort near the water's edge on guerrillas advancing towards the DG Fort and gun position; the SAS mortar team under Corporal B. was identifying its targets from the flash of enemy mortars; and the DG Fort was hitting back with everything including the artillery piece. The 25-pounder was manned by an Omani gunner, Walid Khamis, and two Fijian SAS men, Corporal Labalaba and Trooper Ti., who had run to the fort at the start of the fight. The noise was stunning.

None of this deterred the guerillas despite the casualties they were suffering. As one group was cut down another replaced it, until they advanced to within a few yards of the perimeter wire. Once there they open fired on the DG Fort with Soviet R1PG-7 rockets and the Carl Gustav. At a range of only thirty metres the Carl Gustav's 84mm armour-piercing rounds had a devastating effect on the fort's ancient masonry: its tower crumbled in a plume of smoke and dust. Throughout the confusion, Corporal B. calmly indicated targets for the SAS mortar, the Browning and light machine-guns, using lines of tracer to emphasise his fire orders. He also picked off leading guerrillas with his own rifle. This fire power, such as it was, now turned on the leading group of guerrillas at the wire, manning the Carl Gustav, as it attempted to rush the fort less than a hundred yards away.

Kealy meanwhile was trying to maintain radio contact with the gun crew in its pit in front of the DG Fort and the Wali's men in their fort. Messages from the gun crew were laconic, giving little sign of a situation that was turning from bad to desperate. On the radio, Labalaba's voice, which had been indicating possible mortar targets to the Batthouse crew, announced, 'Enemy now very close, I've been chinned but I'm all right'. It was now about 7 am. Within the Batthouse it was almost impossible to hear anything but a steady roar or battle as rounds from the Carl Gustav hissed across the roof to explode just behind the building. Kealy had already asked for strike aircraft at Salalah to stand by, but in these conditions, with cloud almost at ground level, it seemed a remote hope that the Air Force could do much. Now, in the light of Labalaba's message, Kealy summoned a helicopter to attempt a casualty evacuation.

Both sides had been firing intensively at one another for about an hour. The guerrillas, although they had breached the wire, had not yet taken the DG Fort.

The action at the DG Fort, Mirbat.

Both sides needed to pause to see to their casualties and bring up more ammunition. In the lull that resulted, the firing became spasmodic – so much so that children gathered on the roof of a building behind the Batthouse to watch the action.

Kealy, concerned about the absence of any return fire from the Gendarmerie Fort and its nearby gun position, as well as continued radio silence, now took a brave decision. He would go to the fort himself. This meant crossing about four hundred yards of almost open ground under enemy fire. It was also possible that by now the fort had been overrun. Others in the training team volunteered to share the risk, but he took just one man, his medical orderly, Trooper T P A Tobin to aid the casualties. Simultaneously, Lance-Corporal C. slipped away from the Batthouse, through the town to a helicopter landing-pad near the beach, to guide the machine in as a preliminary to clearing the casualties. Kealy and his medical orderly were en route to the DG Fort when the 'casevac' helicopter clattered in over the sea. On the landing site, the lance-corporal threw a green smoke grenade to indicate that all was clear. But, as the aircraft made its final approach, the guerrillas, reinforced and rearmed in dead ground around the DG Fort, started shooting with renewed ferocity. One of the first targets was the helicopter. Another was the man trying to guide it in. The lance-corporal stayed long enough to throw a red grenade to warn off the helicopter, and then dived for cover. The helicopter whined back into the cloud, its cabin pockmarked by machine-gun bullets.

When the battle erupted afresh, Kealy and his medical orderly were still 350 yards from the fort. From the Batthouse their comrades laid down a covering barrage from the Browning and light machine-guns, as the two men bobbed and weaved their way forward through the smoke, one pausing to fire while the other advanced. Luck was with them and they at least reached the gun position. As Kealy and Trooper Tobin slithered into the gun-pit and peered through the smoke, they found an appalling situation. Walid Khamis, the Oman Artillery gunner, lay on his back seriously wounded. Above the gun-pit on the parapet of the DG Fort, a dead soldier sprawled across his machine-gun. Another dead Gendarme was in the pit itself. Both the SAS Fijians were still fighting. One of them, Trooper Ti., was propped against the wall of the bunker, bleeding from serious head and shoulder wounds, still firing his rifle at the guerrillas. The other, Corporal Labalaba, wore a shell dressing on his face to staunch the blood from his chin wound. He was loading and firing the 25-pounder unaided. The gun itself, its shield riddled with bullet holes, had been depressed through 45 degrees to be sighted down the barrel and fired at point-blank range.

Labalaba reloaded the gun yet again as the medical orderly set to work to dress Trooper Ti.'s wounds. From the ammunition bunker, Kealy snapped a terse radio message to the Batthouse calling for an air strike. Before he had completed it, Labalaba was shot dead, and soon afterwards Trooper Tobin had his jaw shot away. (Later in the battle, the same man was to be wounded in the back and hand by a grenade). The bunker was now being defended by two men, Kealy and the wounded Fijian Trooper Ti. By now, the guerrillas were only thirty yards away, moving on the gun-pit and ammunition bunker from left and right. Both gun position and the fort behind it were being hammered by small-arms fire and shuddering blows from the 84mm Carl Gustav. Kealy, from the right of the bunker wall, picked off first one guerrilla who was about to shoot Trooper Ti., then another who clambered out of a ditch towards their position. Trooper Ti., still propped up, fired carefully aimed shots at enemy coming from the left. From somewhere too close for comfort, a light machine-gun fired at the two men, and Kealy felt a bullet pass through his hair. Now came the enemy grenades, which burst near, but not near enough to achieve their intention. One, lobbed right into the gun-pit itself, landed among the dead and dying, but failed to explode. From his position on the left of the bunker the obstinate, brave Trooper Ti. asked Kealy for more ammunition.

A hopeless position was retrieved at that moment by the arrival of two Strikemaster jets of the Sultan's Air Force, hurtling over the scene just above ground level and under a cloud base of only 150 feet. From the radio in the ammunition bunker, Kealy passed targets to the Batthouse: 500-pound bombs on a ditch where the guerrillas had gathered in force and 7.62mm machine-gun fire along the wire only 60 yards from both fort and gun-pit. As the guerrillas retreated, Kealy hastily draped an air identification panel over the body in the bunker to identify his own position to the jets. Even before the first air strike was over, Kealy was also issuing orders to his mortar position at the Batthouse, a few hundred yards away. The man, Lance -Corporal H., found that the proposed targets were now so close that he could not elevate the barrel sufficiently by orthodox means. His solution was to pull the barrel up to his chest, lifting the supporting bipod off the ground, and to grip the weapon with his legs before dropping bombs down the barrel.

The battle around the bunker had now been going on for ninety minutes. From the Batthouse, Corporal B. directed the second wave of Strikemasters. One of these hit guerrilla machine-guns on Jebal Ali, overlooking the town, while the other made several attacks on the enemy hiding in dead ground near the fort and the wire perimeter. 'There are hundreds of them down there!' an astonished pilot reported. One of the aircraft, seriously damaged by heavy machine-gun fire at close range, cut out of the battle and limped back to Salalah.

While the pressure was off his position, Kealy gave water to the wounded and re-dressed their injuries, then went to fetch the DG Land Rover inside the fort for use as an ambulance to the heli-pad. He found the vehicle unusable, its tyres and petrol tank holed by machine-gun fire.

If the air strikes had taken the heat off the fort for the time being, it was clear that nothing less than substantial reinforcements could save the situation completely. That they were on their way was due to a fortunate coincidence. Before B Squadron (to which Kealy belonged) could leave the territory, it had to hand over to its successor in Oman. This group, from G Squadron, had arrived in Salalah the previous day. When Kealy's first messages alerted the base, the men of G Squadron were dressed and armed to check their weapons on the firing range. Instead they flew by helicopter, almost at sea level, direct to Mirbat beach. Their arrival at 9.15 am almost coincided with the second air strike around the fort. A party of 18 from the first helicopter lift advanced inland in two groups, wiping out a ridge position held by five guerrillas. The new SAS group was spotted by guerrillas near the DG Fort, who fired at it before starting to withdraw. The tide had turned at last.

From the beach, a second wave of SAS reinforcements, operating in three-man teams, engaged in brief, vicious battles with three guerrilla positions on the southern, seaward side of the town. In another incident the SAS party covering the helicopter landing zone waited in concealment as three guerrillas came closer. They were only five yards away when an SAS officer stood up and ordered them to drop their weapons and surrender. They did so, instantly. It was almost 10.30 before the most seriously wounded – the medical orderly, Trooper Tobin, whose jaw had, been blown away, the obstinate and thrice-wounded Fijian Trooper Ti., and the Omani gunner, Walid Khamis – could be removed by helicopter. The Fijian insisted on walking into the aircraft. By then, Lance-Corporal H., the man who had held the mortar between his legs, had moved from the Batthouse to the gun-pit to aid the wounded in the closing stages of the battle. By clearing Trooper Tobin's windpipe of blood, it seemed that he had saved the man's life; but Tobin was to die of his wounds later. The next group of wounded to be flown out included some of the enemy who had been taken to the Batthouse during the first lull in the battle. By lunchtime it was clear that the position was under control again.

Kealy, whose judgement throughout the battle had been impeccable, now decided to see what could be done to save the original firqa patrol still in the mountains. He took a group of men outside the wire and up to the Jebal Ali area, which had been the first position to come under attack that day. But by now there was no way of knowing whether the patrol had encountered the retreating guerrilla force and if so, where. The firqa limped back later in the day with four men dead and three wounded.

SAS casualties were two dead – Corporal Labalaba and Trooper Tobin – and two seriously wounded; the Gendarmes lost one man killed, one wounded; and the Oman Artillery, one dead. The retreating guerrillas left about thirty bodies and about ten wounded, taken prisoner, but their sources later admitted that the toll was much higher. Factional feuds provoked by the defeat at Mirbat caused further casualties. Others died of their wounds and these, added to the list of surviving wounded and taken prisoner, left fewer than half of the guerrillas'original elite force unscathed.

When the war ended four years later, one authority concluded: 'The rebel forces never recovered from this defeat and were never able to deploy sufficient forces to mount a similar attack elsewhere'. Back in Britain, the battle received no publicity. Gallantry awards made public four years later included a DSO for Kealy, a DCM for Trooper Tobin, a MM for Corporal B. and, posthumously, a Mention in Despatches for Corporal Labalaba. In February 1979, Kealy, now a major, died of exposure while taking part in an SAS exercise in bitter conditions on the Brecon Beacons in Wales.

The extract is taken from *Who Dares Wins – The Story of the Special Air Service 1950–1980* by Tony Geraghty, published by Arms and Armour Press.

MAKING OPERATIONAL DECISIONS

The Aerial Photograph Incident. Burma 1944

For the Second Chindit Operation, General Wingate had devised a three-brigade plan whose outline was as follows: 77 Brigade was to be flown in to the Kaukkwe valley north-east of Katha where they would establish a stronghold, a block on the Indaw-Myitkyina railway, and a block on the Bahmo-Lashio road; 111 Brigade was to be flown in to the country south of Pinlebu from where they would establish a stronghold and attack communications to Wuntho and in the Mu valley; in the meantime 16 Brigade would march overland from Ledo, and after seizing Lonkin, would go on south to establish a stronghold north of Indaw from where they would attack the Bonchaung gorge, the Meza bridge and seize the Indaw airfield. The plan was to establish in the centre of Japanese communications three strongholds near enough for mutual support, and strong enough for constant and strategically damaging raids. With garrison troops assured, the Chindits had come into their own again, so it seemed. The expedition was coded named Operation THURS-DAY.

General Wingate with Colonel Cochrane.

Examining the aerial photograph, Lalaghat airfield, 5 March 1944.

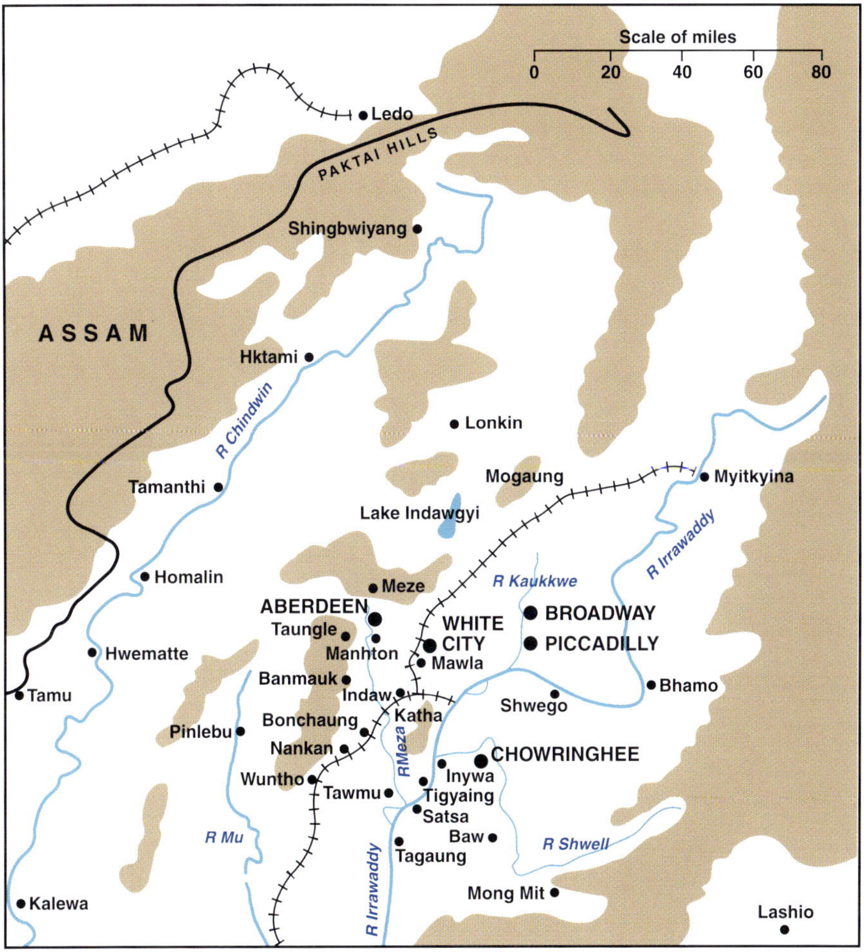

Area of the Second Chindit Expedition Burma 1944

16 Brigade left Ledo in North Burma on 3rd February 1944 to march towards the Chindwin River which was crossed on the 28th and then on to their stronghold area north of Indaw.

Brigadier Tulloch the Chief of Staff at Chindit HQ takes up the narrative:

"The prelude to Operation Thursday opened on 4th March, when Colonel Cochrane's bomber and fighter squadrons carried out a strike against Anisakan airfield. There they destroyed twenty-six aircraft which had been brought forward to support the Japanese offensive against Imphal, and damaged several others. On 8th March, Cochrane had an even greater success, his squadrons catching a large concentration of enemy aircraft on the ground at Onbaik and Shwebo, and destroying thirty completely and damaging others. These raids, together with those carried out by the RAF, were to have a major impact on events to come.

On Sunday, 5th March 1944, all preparations for the fly-in were complete. At Lalaghat airstrip near Sfichar eighty gliders were stretched out in pairs in two long lines, while Dakota tug-aircraft were dispersed along the sides of the runway, each one ready to move out and connect up with its pair of gliders, starting at 5.00pm that evening.

Time seemed to go very slowly, despite the activity and the continual arrival of senior officers to watch the operation. General Slim flew in followed by Lieutenant General Stratemeyer, the American Commander of Eastern Air Command who controlled all Allied air forces in Burma, Air Marshal Baldwin who commanded 3rd Tactical Air Force, and Air Vice-Marshal Williams and General Old of Air Transport command. The lunch produced for this distinguished company was a poor one, but we had no establishment of cooks at this temporary headquarters at Lalaghat.

In the afternoon an air of complete calm and relaxation pervaded the airfield, a tribute, I thought, to the faith all ranks had in Wingate. Quietly the troops moved forward to the gliders and settled down to rest under the shadow of their wings and there seemed no reason for any hitch. After our long months of training we were ready down to the last detail and poised for action. Then at 4.30 pm came a nasty jolt. One of Colonel Cochrane's light aircraft was seen approaching the airfield and, after a hurried landing, the pilot ran across to Colonel Cochrane and thrust something into his hand. This proved to be a collection of photographs of two of the landing zones PICCADILLY and BROADWAY taken from a B-25 just a few hours previously. PICCADILLY was seen to be blocked by a carefully arranged pattern of teak trunks, spread out over the proposed landing area. A similar photograph of BROADWAY showed it to be clear of obstructions.

"Here indeed was a dramatic curtain raiser to our operations. Standing next to Wingate, 1 heard him demand who had disobeyed his orders that no one should fly near the proposed landing grounds for a week before operations. Cochrane replied that he took full responsibility: he had ordered a Major Russhon to take the photographs at the last minute with a hand camera. Wingate then apologised for his outburst and thanked Cochrane for having taken this action."

Wingate's biography Christopher Sykes, then takes up the narrative:

"Air Marshal Baldwin then came up and examined the photographs with Wingate, Calvert, Cochran and Alison. Someone took a photograph of the group of worried men. A decision had to be taken quickly, and the decision could only be between whether to risk the possibility of an opposed landing which would mean certain disaster, and whether to call off the operation altogether and thus almost inevitably bring an end to the whole second Chindit venture.

It was one of those moments when everyone knew the other's thought and looked desperately for a new one.No new thought presented itself. The evidence of the photograph almost proved Japanese alertness, and there seemed nothing for it but to postpone the operation. Wingate strenuously objected to postponement, but for once he could find no argument to sustain his objection, and the photograph at which they looked continually had a horrible eloquence of its own.

After further discussion about a previous operation whereby photographs of jungle airstrips with aircraft had been published in the British and American press, it was thought that perhaps the Japanese had blocked PICCADILLY as a routine precaution. Everyone seized on this point and, at Wingate's suggestion, it was decided that the fly-in should be attempted at BROADWAY and 111 Brigade's trans-Irrawaddy landing ground, CHOWRINGHEE. Wingate then went to inform General Slim. He listened to the proposal, turned to Wingate and said that he would give the order if Wingate was fully prepared to take the risk. Wingate said that he himself was prepared, but before giving a definite answer he must consult Calvert again. Slim agreed to this.

Wingate then went back to Calvert, and said: 'Well, Mike, it looks as though the Japanese have tumbled to our plans. I leave the decision as to whether we go on with it to you. Do you want to go on?' Calvert said: 'Definitely yes."

Brigadier Tulloch later recorded that:

"This was indeed a shattering experience for Wingate, coming just a few minutes before the results of all his planning were due for their final test. As he knew full well, many people honestly considered his fly-in not only hazardous but impossible to achieve, even under normal conditions, and now he had to face the possibility of an opposed landing. I am convinced, however, that what made the decision harder than ever to take was the fact that, while committing his troops to unknown hazards, he was not going himself. However, in my view the decision had been made in his own mind, even before he moved over to speak to General Slim who was standing nearby.

I admired Slim tremendously on that occasion. He had, of course, a poker face – useful for any commander – which enabled him to appear completely unruffled, indeed almost unconcerned. Yet the final decision to go on with the operation rested squarely on his shoulders, and in the event of disaster he would carry a major share of the blame. Watching him closely at this moment of crisis, I gained the impression, which has always remained, that he had the utmost confidence both in Wingate and in the success of the operation.

Beneath his impassive mask, Slim must have been doing some deep thinking on his own account. If he postponed the operation – which virtually meant cancelling it because of the moon conditions – he would no doubt please GHQ India and perhaps Mountbatten too. On the other hand he had just left Stilwell to whom he had given a firm promise that the Japanese line of communications to their XVIII Division would be cut. There was no chance of discussion with other commanders. He had to decide one way or the other within minutes. In the event he allowed the operation to go ahead, and the manner in which he did so earned the respect of all concerned. Air Marshal Baldwin (who bore the final responsibility for all air operations and therefore for the fly-in) also agreed."

At the end of this twenty minutes of conference and decision, Wingate rebriefed the officers of 77 Brigade, and Cochrane rebriefed his pilots. The American colonel showed himself a master of the art of leadership, particularly in time of crisis. He sprang on to the bonnet of a jeep and began by saying, 'Say, fellas, we've got a better place to go to.' The first Dakota took off at twelve minutes past six, only seventy-two minutes behind schedule."

Bibliography

General Slim and the Burma Campaign

Evans, Geoffrey, *Slim as Military Commander*, Batsford, 1969.
Lewin, Ronald, *Slim The Standard Bearer*, Leo Cooper, 1976.
Slim, Field Marshal, Sir William, *Defeat into Victory*, Cassell, 1956.
Slim, Field Marshal, Sir William, *Courage and Other Broadcasts*, Cassell, 1957.

The Battle of Mirbat

Jeapes, Major General, *SAS Secret War*, Harper Collins 1996.
Geraghty, Tony, *Who Dares Wins-The Story of the Special Air Service 1950–1980,* (Arms and Armour Press) Cassell plc

The Aerial Photograph Incident

Tulloch, Major General, *Wingate, In Peace and War.* Macdonald & Company (Publishers) Ltd, 1972.

APPENDIX 3 OFFENSIVE ACTION
FALKLAND ISLANDS, 1982

Encouraged by a decision to withdraw the ice patrol ship *Endurance*, the denial of full British citizenship to the Falklanders in 1981 and their own flag-raising incident on South Georgia in March 1982, the Argentinians invaded the Falklands on 2 April, achieving a strategic surprise. The British Cabinet immediately broke off diplomatic relations with Galtieri's government, announced economic sanctions, called for a UN Security Council resolution demanding Argentina's withdrawal and backed up its diplomacy with the assembly of a task force.

Argentina probably took the final decision to invade on about 26 March. It was anticipated that the landing of Argentinian marines on South Georgia on the 23rd would precipitate a British reaction. Preparations in Argentinian naval ports, Hercules overflights of Port Stanley and the diversion of two missile corvettes alerted the British Government to the possibility of a serious threat on the 28th. The decision to despatch three submarines to the South Atlantic was taken the following day. At a conference that afternoon to assess the situation the First Sea Lord, Admiral Sir Henry Leach, decided that only a major task force, employing all the resources available, could operate in the South Atlantic in the face of the Argentinian air and naval threat.

The Argentinians possessed a substantial navy. The *Veintecinco de Mayo* carried twelve Skyhawks, at least six of its ships carried the Exocet missile and of her four submarines two were modern and difficult to detect. A combined air force and fleet air arm of about 160 combat aircraft,[1] including five Super Etendards armed with the Exocet, provided a formidable opposition to the 20 Sea Harriers embarked in *Hermes* and *Invincible*. As the Royal Navy lacked a long-range airborne early warning capability, an amphibious assault within 500 miles of Argentinian air bases was a major risk. It was estimated that the Argentinian Governor of the so-called Malvinas, General Menendez, had 10,000 troops on the islands. The Antarctic winter was approaching and operations would have to be conducted in gales, high seas, driving rain and snow. The decision to sail the Task Force on 5 April and to follow it up with an amphibious assault force to fight a campaign 8,000 miles from the United Kingdom base was a bold one.

The amphibious assault force was based on 3 Commando Brigade reinforced by the 3rd, and later the 2nd, Battalions of The Parachute Regiment and supported by two medium reconnaissance troops of the Blues and Royals, 29 Commando Regiment, RA and a reinforced air defence battery. SBS and SAS squadrons were added for reconnaissance, beach survey and raiding. The bulk of the troops sailed in the 45,000 ton cruise liner *Canberra* with the vehicles and stores embarked in *Fearless* and six LSTs. The whole operation was controlled from Admiral Sir

[1] At the time the Argentinians were thought to possess up to 247 combat aircraft.

John Fieldhouse's Fleet Headquarters at Northwood.The Falkland Islands Task Force was formed around Rear Admiral Woodward's First Flotilla, which had been exercising in the Atlantic off Gibraltar. Ships requiring refit were sent home and replaced by others which sailed on 5 and 6 April with *Hermes* and *Invincible*. Initially, the land force commander was Brigadier Thompson, Commander 3 Commando Brigade. When, later, it was decided to send 5 Infantry Brigade to form a small division, Major General Moore succeeded him.

On 12 April the first of the submarines, *Spartan*, arrived off the Falklands to enforce a 200 mile Maritime Exclusion Zone. In mid-April the Task Force assembled at Ascension Island where stores, spares and equipment flown out from the United Kingdom had turned the island into an advanced base, roughly 4,000 miles from the United Kingdom and the Falklands. Three Type 42 destroyers and two frigates were sent south, in radio and radar silence, to a holding position some 1,000 miles equidistant from the Falklands, South Georgia and Buenos Aires where their presence could be revealed at the right moment. A destroyer and a frigate, accompanied by a RFA tanker with a commando company, a SAS squadron and a SBS party embarked, had already sailed to join *Endurance* to retake South Georgia. Both operations were to demonstrate an earnestness of intent to back up the negotiations which were taking place at the United Nations and through the American Secretary of State's shuttle diplomacy.

On 17 April Admiral Fieldhouse and Major General Moore arrived at Ascension to review the situation. Three alternatives were considered:

> A preliminary landing on South Georgia in brigade strength to make sure of success and to provide a dress rehearsal for the Falklands.
>
> The seizure of West Falkland where the Argentinians were weakest, to build an airstrip and develop a base for the recapture of East Falkland.
>
> The capture of the flat plain of Lafonia in the south of East Falkland.

Admiral Fieldhouse preferred to move against Port Stanley with all possible speed to secure a decision while the landing force was in good shape and before the severest of the winter weather closed in. South Georgia was politically significant but strategically irrelevant; it could be left to the force already despatched there. West Falkland would involve a further landing with more delays to take Port Stanley. The southern half of East Falkland would have entailed a long approach march with the possibility of a serious delay at the Goose Green isthmus and perhaps the need to make another landing. The approach was also exposed to air attack because the bare Lafonia plain provided no cover. It was clear that 3 Commando Brigade could only secure a bridgehead and that more forces would be required. The aim was modified from 'repossession of the Falklands' to planning 'for a landing with a view to repossessing the Falklands'. As a consequence, 5 Infantry Brigade, which had been warned for service in the South Atlantic, was despatched from Southampton in *Queen Elizabeth II* on 12 May. The Brigade had already lost the 2nd and 3rd Battalions of the Parachute Regiment [2] and had absorbed 2nd Battalion Scots Guards and 1st Battalion

[2] Hereinafter known by their familiar abbreviations, 2 PARA and 3 PARA.

Fleet Headquarters. Admiral Sir John Fieldhouse, with his staff.

3 Commando Brigade. Brigadier Thompson and his staff.

Welsh Guards in their place to join 1/7th Battalion Gurkha Rifles. However, the Brigade had only one field battery in support and lacked many of the normal supporting arms and services. Furthermore the Brigade had only been formed in January and much of April was spent training in Wales in conditions as close as possible to the Falklands.

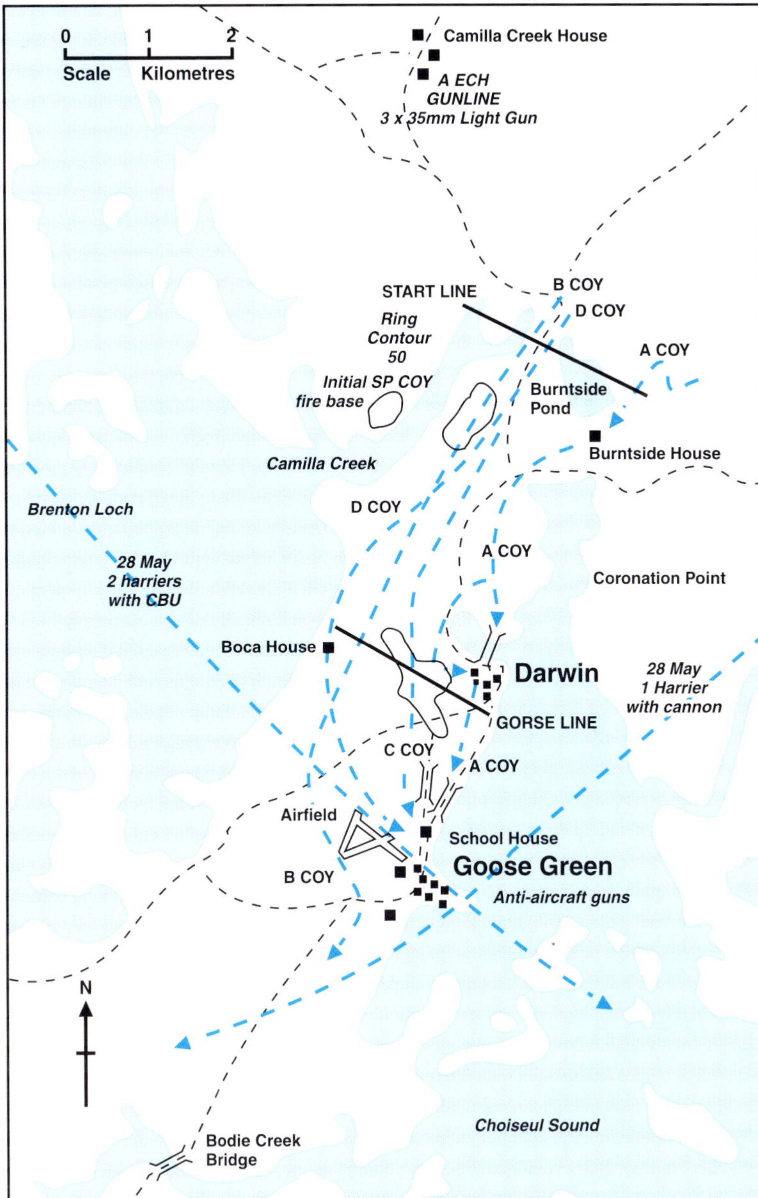

2 PARA's Battle for Darwin and Goose Green

Shipping under attack in San Carlos Water.

South Georgia was reoccupied on 25 April. The day before, Woodward's Task Force rendezvoused with the squadron sent ahead into the South Atlantic and, proceeding south, entered the Maritime Exclusion Zone with its two carriers and eleven other ships to enforce a Total Exclusion Zone (TEZ). On the same morning a lone Vulcan hit Port Stanley airstrip with one bomb in a mission from Ascension involving seventeen air-to-air refuellings. While Harriers attacked Goose Green and Port Stanley's airstrip, radar and anti-aircraft defences, a destroyer and two frigates closed with Port Stanley to bombard Argentinian positions. The first phase of offensive action to reinforce diplomatic pressure and to tempt the Argentine Navy into an engagement had begun. The Argentine Air Force counterattacked the bombardment squadrons immediately, losing two Mirages to combat air patrols and a third to their own shore defences for only superficial damage to the ships. The battle between the Argentine Air Force and the Royal Navy was to continue for a month and a half.

On 2 May the cruiser *General Belgrano* was sunk on the south-west approaches to the Falklands outside the TEZ to remove the threat from the Argentine Navy's second most powerful unit. Two days later *Sheffield* was sunk by an Exocet missile and the first Sea Harrier was shot down over Goose Green. On 7 May the TEZ was extended to within 12 miles of the Argentine coast to give the Task Force as much sea room as possible to deal with hostile ships and submarines. However, no more Argentinian ships were sighted at sea after the sinking of the *General Belgrano*.

Offensive action for defensive purposes had paid off. The Task Force steered a north-south track pattern well to the east of the Falklands, sending in Harriers to attack targets ashore and coastal craft by day while closing in to the coast to bombard shore targets at night to maintain offensive pressure. The bombardments served to disturb the Argentinians' rest and confuse them as to the choice of the landing area. However, the airfields on the Argentinian mainland were out

3 PARA landing at San Carlos.

2 PARA 'O' Group at Camilla Creek, before Goose Green.

RFA Sir Galahad *hit at Fitzroy. 2 PARA patrol in the foreground.*

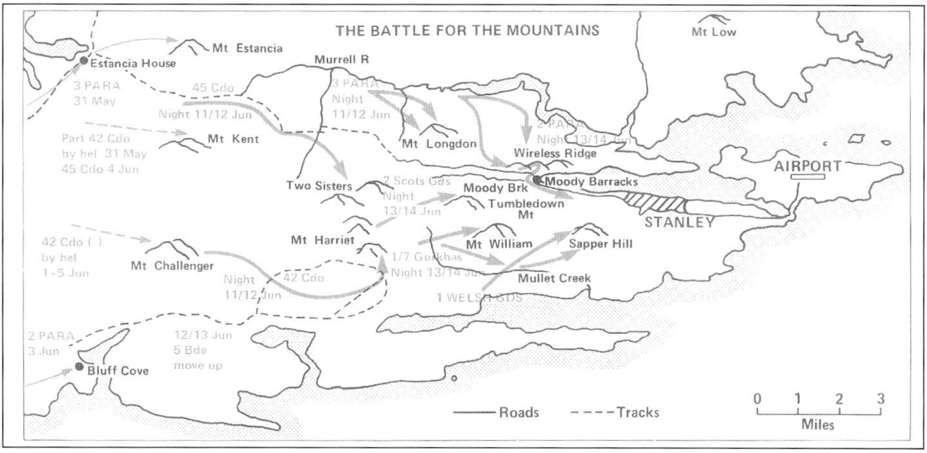

The Battle for the Mountains.

of reach, politically and militarily, and so it was impossible to gain air superiority over the Falklands and the surrounding waters.

On 8 May the War Cabinet took the most important decision of the war. The amphibious assault force was ordered south from Ascension even though it would have to operate in the teeth of Argentinian air power. In default of a sudden Argentinian change of heart the landing would take place between 18 and 21 May.

From early May SAS and SBS parties were slipped ashore by night in helicopters and inflatable craft to reconnoitre the dispositions and strengths of the Argentinian forces. Six SBS teams concentrated on possible landing sites and seven SAS patrols, three round Port Stanley, one near Darwin, one above Bluff Cove and three on West Falkland, observed the areas in which air reconnaissance had revealed the major Argentinian concentrations.

The Argentinians' main forces, a strong brigade of six marine and infantry battalions, an artillery battalion and an armoured car squadron, were dug in on the hills round Port Stanley, which General Menendez had to hold. Elements of two battalions and a troop of guns held Goose Green and a small brigade of two battalions held West Falkland. Just over a dozen transport and attack helicopters were based on Port Stanley to give a small reserve some mobility.

An opposed landing was ruled out as the assault shipping was too vulnerable and there was insufficient fire support. The choice of beaches narrowed down to Berkeley Bay, Volunteer Bay and Bluff Cove near Port Stanley or Cow Bay and San Carlos Water on the north-west corner of East Falkland. The risks of failure close to the main Argentinian position and the need for a sheltered anchorage which would give some protection from high seas and air attack determined the selection of San Carlos Bay. The chosen landing place was separated from the ultimate objective by 50 miles of moorland, peat and bog but it was anticipated that the heavy lift Chinook helicopters embarked in *Atlantic Conveyor* and the assault ships' LCUs and LCVPs would be able to assist in the movement of men, weapons, ammunition and stores.

As a preliminary, a SAS squadron, guided in by a patrol put ashore earlier, landed by helicopter to destroy ten Pucara and Turbo-Mentor light ground attack aircraft and a transport. The sheer daring of the attack, which destroyed an immediate threat to the landing area, raised the morale of the entire force.

In anticipation of a political decision to reoccupy the Falklands the final orders for Operation 'SUTTON' were given by Brigadier Thompson on board *Fearless* 900 miles off Port Stanley on 13 May. On the 18th negotiations through the UN Secretary General broke down and on the following day the War Cabinet authorised the landing. Miraculously the South Atlantic calmed down sufficiently to allow the LCUs to conduct a complicated cross-decking operation to distribute some of the units aboard *Canberra* to other ships to avoid a disaster should the liner be hit. The forecast for 20 May was thick weather so, while the carrier group, reinforced to a strength of 35 Harriers from the *Atlantic Conveyor* and *Ascension*, steered its north-south course 100 miles to the east of the Falklands, the assault group, including *Fearless*, *Intrepid*, *Canberra*, *Norland* and supported by seven frigates, closed on Port Stanley to hide the true objective in case of discovery. Just over the horizon the group altered course to the west to make the final approach to San Carlos Water in the dark. Naval bombardments at Fanning Head, Berkeley Sound and on West Falkland distracted the Argentinians' attention. The SAS made a noisy diversion at Darwin while a SBS party dealt with an Argentinian outpost on Fanning Head overlooking the entrance to San Carlos Water.

3 Commando Brigade started going ashore just before 0400 on 21 May and established a bridgehead on the hills overlooking the inlet. Complete surprise had been achieved. Once the hills were reported clear, *Canberra*, *Norland* and all their boldness and good planning had secured a beach-head. When General Menendez received the first report from the area he assumed it was a diversion. An Argentinian naval Aeromacchi sent to reconnoitre the Water discovered the assault group at about 1000 hours. Shortly afterwards the Argentine Air Force made the first of a constant succession of attacks on the assault group in San Carlos Bay, the escorts on anti-submarine duty outside in Falkland Sound and shipping in the vicinity of the islands. In the next four days the Royal Navy suffered the bulk of its losses, *Ardent* in Falkland Sound, *Antelope* in San Carlos Water and, on 25 May, *Coventry* off Pebble Island plus the *Atlantic Conveyor* to the north of Teal Inlet. The latter went down with three Chinooks and ten Wessex helicopters together with the tentage which would have provided shelter for the force in the Antarctic winter. The loss of the helicopters was a serious blow to the force's mobility. The defence was handicapped by lack of long-range early warning radar and deficiencies in the Sea Dart, Sea Wolf, Sea Cat and Rapier systems. Nevertheless, the Argentinians successes cost them a third of their fighter-ground attack force to the Harriers and ground defences. 25 May was the turning point after which the Argentinians made only brief hit-and-run raids on the Fleet.

Following the establishment of the beach-head it was decided to eliminate the Argentinian force at Darwin and Goose Green to secure the southern flank before the advance on Darwin. After a false start occasioned by bad weather, which prevented the helicopter lift of supporting artillery, 2 PARA's attack finally went in before dawn on 28 May. A consequence of the loss of the helicopters was the lack of fire support. Only three field guns could be moved and the Battalion's 81mm mortar ammunition ran out in the middle of the morning. The Battalion had laid up, out of sight and sheltered, in a farmhouse the day before. An Argentine patrol was ambushed before it could give warning of the Battalion's approach and the patrol leader volunteered the information that the Goose Green garrison had been substantially reinforced. Breaking into the position under cover of darkness the Battalion advanced with very few casualties until dawn. Then, at daybreak the advantage swung to the defenders. With grim determination the Battalion pressed on against increasingly effective opposition, led by Lieutenant Colonel 'H' Jones with conspicuous bravery until he was killed. It took another 24 hours of dogged fighting to finally clear the position but 450 men had defeated four times their number in an offensive action which demonstrated remarkable courage and tactical skill.

Meanwhile 3 PARA and 45 Commando had set out on the direct route for Port Stanley, reaching Estancia House at the east end of Teal Inlet on the night of 31 May. They were within sight of Mount Kent, which the SAS had been patrolling since the beginning of the month. The peak was secured by a party of 42 Commando, flown in by helicopter at last light on the 31st. 3 Commando Brigade now held the high ground overlooking the approach route up which the rest of the Brigade would have to 'yomp'. Patrolling started on the northern axis to Port Stanley.

5 Infantry Brigade had transferred from *Queen Elizabeth II* to *Canberra* and *Norland* at South Georgia on 28 May. On 1 June the Brigade started coming ashore at San Carlos. Major General Moore arrived to assume command of the two Brigades, now totalling 9,000 men and soon after he decided to commit the new Brigade to the southern axis. When a call over the Island telephone network revealed that Fitzroy was unoccupied 2 PARA was lifted, a company at a time, in the surviving Chinook, to occupy it on 1 June. Moore decided to use the bulk of the helicopters to assemble 3 Commando Brigade and its supplies forward at Mount Kent. As 5 Brigade had neither helicopters nor Volvo tracked vehicles, it was decided to risk a move to Fitzroy by sea. The air attack on *Sir Galahad* on 8 June caused 97 casualties and immobilised 1st Battalion Welsh Guards until it could be reinforced by two companies from 40 Commando at San Carlos.

Yet the disaster did not delay the final offensive scheduled for 11 June. With the destruction of so many helicopters and the need to restrict reinforcement by sea to night time it had taken a fortnight after Goose Green to concentrate the assault troops, the guns, ammunition and supplies in the Mount Kent area. The time was usefully employed in patrolling to locate the Argentine defences and minefields. Mount Challenger to the south of Mount Kent was occupied in early June. The merits of advancing on a narrow front in the south to capture Mounts

Harriet and Tumbledown, and outflank Twin Sisters and Mount Longdon, were weighed against an advance on a broad front to open up more than one route for resupply and casualty evacuation which would also forestall possible counter-attacks and to ensure mutual support. The importance of maintaining the momentum of the advance to keep the Argentinians off balance and to finish the campaign quickly in the appalling weather were major considerations. Fresh units were to be passed through quickly to keep up the momentum.

The plan was for 3 Commando Brigade to open the offensive on Mount Longdon, Two Sisters and Mount Harriet on the night of 11/12 June. The following night 5 Brigade would pass through to take Mounts Tumbledown and William. Then 3 Commando Brigade would move through again the next night, maintaining the pressure by continuous offensive action until the Argentinian position collapsed. The enemy had used their time to good purpose, wiring, mining and fortifying the hillsides in depth. The strain was telling on the Fleet and only four frigates were available for naval gunfire support.

3 Commando Brigade's attack went in with effective support from the guns ashore and afloat. On the right, 42 Commando turned the southern flank of Mount Harriet along a previously reconnoitred route leading into the rear of the Argentine position. The enemy only discovered their presence when the assault companies were within 100 yards of the summit. With light anti-tank weapons and grenades the bunkers were taken one by one. In the centre 45 Commando had some difficulty in breaking through the crust but, once through, managed to maintain the momentum of the offensive in the face of accurate Argentinian DFs to capture Twin Sisters in two and a half hours. On the left, 3 PARA cleared Mount Longdon in the costliest attack of the war. The Argentinians made the best use of their night sights against the assaulting companies and their supporting Milans. Delays in the approach march and in fighting through the objectives prevented any exploitation before dawn.

Lack of helicopters for troop lift and shortage of time for reconnaissance precluded an assault the following night by 5 Brigade on the second defence line. On the night of 13 June 2nd Bn, Scots Guards took Mount Tumbledown in the centre in a bitterly contested six hour struggle against the 5th Marines, Menendez' best troops. It was positive leadership at company and platoon commander level which kept the momentum of the attack going. On the left the SAS launched a diversionary attack from the Royal Marines Rigid Raider Squadron's boats on the east end of Wireless Ridge to distract attention from 2 PARA's attack on the western end. Although the diversionary attack ran into serious trouble losing all its boats in a hail of fire, 2 PARA's attack was a most professional affair. As surprise had been lost the attack was 'noisy' from the start. Two field batteries and a frigate provided devastatingly accurate artillery support and a specially organised sustained fire machine-gun platoon gave covering fire from the start line. The Blues and Royals' CVR(T)s with their 76mms and Rarden cannon, using improved night sights, gave invaluable support. 35 men were taken off the least essential tasks and formed into a platoon of porters to bring up reserve ammunition and carry back the wounded. This improvisation alone did much to keep the attack going and Wireless Ridge was cleared before dawn.

Suddenly, Argentinian morale cracked. Five of their mountain strong points had fallen and OPs could look down on Port Stanley. Everywhere the Argentinians were running. 1/7 Gurkhas and 1st Welsh Guards were opposed only by spasmodic shelling as they moved forward to occupy Mount William and Sapper Hill. That evening, 14 June, Menendez surrendered and 11,313 prisoners and all their equipment fell into our hands.

One of the prisoners made an illuminating remark – 'When we heard that you were on Mount Kent, we knew that we could not win.' Menendez did nothing to prevent it. In contrast to the aggressiveness shown by the Argentine Air Force, the only offensive action their ground forces took was the virtually unopposed landing on the island. Thereafter they remained on the defensive and did not counter-attack and so they lost the initiative to a smaller force which was embued with the spirit of offensive action. The decision to attempt a landing in the face of superior air power was a major risk but one accepted in full realisation of the implications. In the air, at sea and finally on the ground, the Task Force kept up the offensive. Logistic constraints, especially the loss of the *Atlantic Conveyor*'s helicopters, and the bleak weather enforced pauses but, whenever the opportunity offered, the momentum of the offensive was maintained. The campaign demonstrated that only offensive action can wrest the initiative from the enemy to bring victory.

Bibliography

Ethell, Jeffrey and Alfred Price, *Air War South Atlantic*, Sidgwick and Jackson, 1983.

Fox, Robert, *Eyewitness Falklands*, Methuen, 1982.

Frost, Major General John, *2 PARA Falklands. The Battalion at War*, Buchan and Enright, 1983.

Gueritz, Rear Admiral E F, 'The Falklands, Joint Warfare Justified', in *RUSIDS,* Vol. 127, Sep 1982.

Hastings, Max and Simon Jenkins, *The Battle for the Falklands*, Michael Joseph, 1983.

McManners, Hugh, *Falklands Commando*, William Kimber, 1984.

Preston, Antony, *Sea Combat off the Falklands*, Collins, 1982.

Watson, Bruce W and Peter M Dunn, editors, *Military Lessons of the Falkland Islands War. Views from the United States*, Arms and Armour Press, 1984.

APPENDIX 4

SURPRISE
THE INCHON LANDINGS, 1950

On 25 June 1950 the Communist state of North Korea invaded the Republic of South Korea, quickly occupying Seoul, the capital, and overrunning much of the country. Only at the beginning of August did the South Korean Army, reinforced by three American divisions, a regimental combat team and a marine brigade to form the 8th Army, stabilise the situation along the Naktong River to secure a defensive line round the port of Pusan. For the rest of August and early September the North Koreans applied continuous pressure on the western and northern sides of the perimeter. Lieutenant General Walker, the Commander, fought a brilliant defensive battle, transferring his meagre reserves from one threatened point to another and constantly counter-attacking to eliminate potentially dangerous bridgeheads. The survival of the perimeter was only possible through the intervention of American shore and carrier based air power.

The Russians and the Chinese had built up the North Korean Army into a formidable fighting force of ten infantry divisions, an armoured brigade which was raised to the status of a division a few days after the invasion, and two independent regiments. In addition, there was a Border Guard of 18,600 fanatical Communists which was trained for warlike operations. The North Korean Navy was insignificant but a small Air Force could put about 110 combat aircraft into action. The South Korean Army was no match for this aggression. Half of its eight divisions were very lightly equipped and the other half had no tanks, heavy mortars or effective anti-tank weapons. It had little artillery while spares and ammunition stocks were low. During the retreat from Seoul the bridges over the Han River were blown prematurely and the Army lost much of its vehicles and heavy equipment. The Air Force had only light liaison aircraft and the pilots to fly its first consignment of fighters had not been trained. The Navy had only coastal patrol boats.

In the absence of the Soviet Union, the Security Council called on the members of the United Nations to go to South Korea's aid on 29 July. Altogether, sixteen nations responded with combat units and four more with medical contingents. The first British brigade arrived at the end of August and a carrier, two cruisers and some destroyers were provided from the Far East Fleet. Three American divisions came from the army of occupation in Japan, leaving only one division, in the islands. Further reinforcements would have to come from the United States.

General of the Army MacArthur, CinC Far East and Supreme Commander Allied Powers (in Japan) became CinC United Nations Command on 7 July. His problem was how to reverse the situation in South Korea. A break-out from the Pusan bridgehead and an advance to the 38th parallel would require considerable reinforcements. A frontal offensive through the mountains would be expensive in casualties and very time-consuming. One of the more brilliant strategists of the Second World War, he had established his reputation by a series of amphibious operations in the South-West Pacific which constantly outflanked the Japanese and isolated large numbers of their forces. When he visited the Korean front on the fifth day of the war, before American troops were even committed, he formed the idea of an amphibious assault at Inchon. His aim was to occupy Seoul to cut the main road and rail communications to the south at the waist of Korea. Because there were no adequate roads to the east, except for the coastal road on the other side of the mountains, the North Korean Army would be cut off. In combination with a counter-offensive from the Pusan perimeter it would be destroyed. His first idea, Operation BLUEHEARTS to put 1 Cavalry Division from Japan ashore on 22 July was not feasible. All the formations which could be scraped together from Japan, and a Marine brigade from San Diego, had to be committed to the perimeter to avert a disaster. The amphibious shipping could not be concentrated in time.

On 10 July, the day that BLUEHEARTS was cancelled, the Commander of the Pacific Fleet Marine Forces offered MacArthur the whole of 1 Marine Division, provided the Joint Chiefs of Staff in Washington agreed. The Division could be ready for action in Korea in mid-September. Its 5th Regiment was already nominated for duty in the perimeter. The Pentagon released another Regiment immediately but delayed until 10 August before releasing the final Regiment. At least one other division would be required to secure Seoul and block the main escape routes. The only available formation was 7 Infantry Division in Japan but this had been bled to provide reinforcements both for the American formations already in the perimeter and cadres of officers and NCOs to stiffen the South Korean divisions.

A planning staff and a corps headquarters were required for the assault, renamed CHROMITE. Rather than use the Commander and staff of the Pacific Fleet Marine Force MacArthur appointed Major General Almond, his own Chief of Staff, to command the newly formed 10 Corps and provided him with a staff from the Joint Strategic Plans and Operations Group. The reasons MacArthur gave were that, once ashore, the force was required to fight a fast-moving land battle and that a predominantly Army staff was required. By appointing his own Chief of Staff, MacArthur could also be sure of maintaining a close control of the planning which involved Admiral Struble, the Commander of the 7th Fleet. This Fleet would provide the covering forces, the close escorts, the bombardment forces, the air support and the amphibious lift. The latter, 1 Amphibious Group, was commanded by Rear Admiral Doyle in USS *Mount McKinley*. A veteran of Second World War seaborne assaults, he was an enthusiast for amphibious operations at a time when many thought that the nuclear weapon had made such a concept obsolete. The US Navy could only find 17 of the 47 LSTs required. The remainder were provided by MacArthur's civilian administration from wartime LSTs allotted to the Japanese inter-island ferry service. Mostly manned by ex-Imperial Japanese Navy personnel one, at least, was commanded by an ex-battleship captain.

General of the Army, MacArthur.

All turned on what was possible in terms of an amphibious landing. Although Inchon was the most favourable place strategically, from an operational point of view it presented almost insurmountable difficulties. The approach to Inchon was up the Flying Fish and Salee River Channels where the corridor of islands and rocks exaggerates the effects of the high tides of the Yellow Sea. The tidal range at Inchon is 32 feet and tidal rips in the narrow channels make navigation difficult. There are no conventional beaches and at low tide the sea retreats to leave miles of oozing mud flats, too soft to land men and vehicles. Inchon is a harbour of projecting moles, breakwaters and sea walls. Landing craft could only disembark troops at the sea walls and could only remain there for a short period on either side of high water. An especially high tide was needed to prevent the landing craft from grounding by the stem short of the walls. To make the approach in darkness but to have sufficient light for the final run-in, a high tide was needed at dawn. Such a combination of spring tides and dawn occurs only about once a month. Only on 15 September and 11 October would these conditions obtain. The latter date might have been too late to save the Pusan perimeter and the

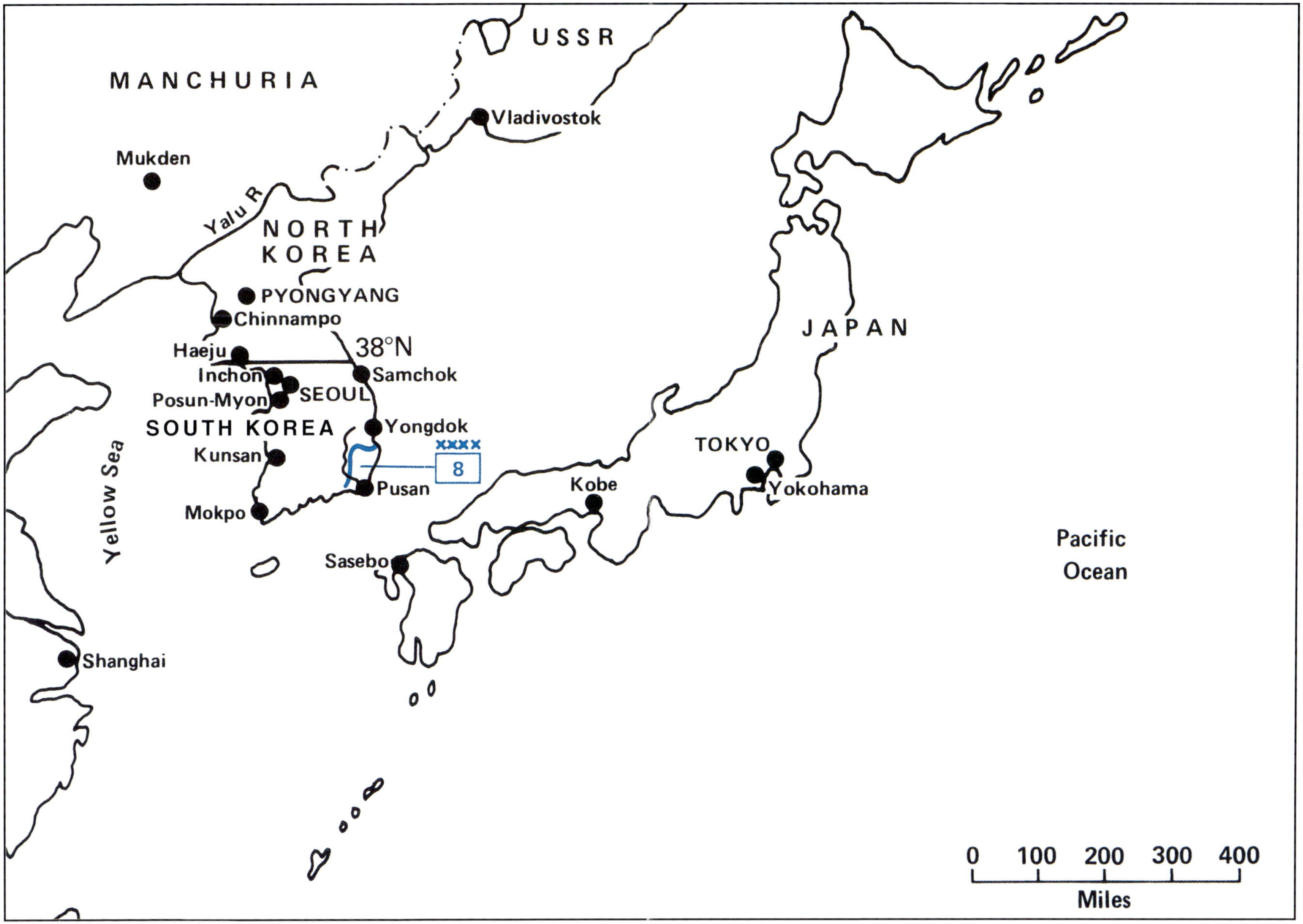

Korea – The Theatre of War 1950

former would have been running it very fine. The channels were easy to mine and it was known that the Russians had supplied their Communist allies with a large quantity of mines. To add to these problems the harbour is dominated by the hill on Wolmi Do Island, the hills in the town itself and those in the surrounding area.

A conference was held on 23 August at MacArthur's Headquarters in Tokyo to review planning progress. Besides MacArthur's main subordinates, the Army and Air members of the Joint Chiefs of Staff attended. All the objections to the plan were aired and suggestions were put forward for alternative landing sites, at Kunsan, where the assault force would be nearer the Pusan perimeter if anything went wrong, at Pusung-Myon near Osan to the south of Inchon and at Chinnampo, the port of the Northern capital Pyongyang. Kunsan was too far from the Seoul – Pusan road to threaten the North Koreans' communications. Posung-Myon was too ill served by roads. Chinnampo was much too far to the north and alternative routes would remain open to the North Koreans even if the main road there was cut. Only at Inchon could the road be cut within reasonable distance of the bridgehead.

MacArthur defended his plan passionately, 'The very arguments you have made as to the impracticabilities involved will tend to ensure for me the element of surprise. For the enemy commander will reason that no one would be so brash as to make such an attempt.' MacArthur recalled Wolfe's surprise landing at the inadequately guarded Anse du Foulon to take the Heights of Abraham and Quebec in 1759, another risky and seemingly impossible enterprise. In contrast, he emphasised nothing in war is more futile than short envelopment. He concluded his 45 minute appreciation with, 'I realize that Inchon is a 5,000 to 1 gamble but I am used to taking such odds ...'. Then, dropping his voice so that his listeners had to strain to hear him, 'We shall land at Inchon and I shall crush them!'

The tasks of the ground forces were:

> 3 Battalion Landing Team from 5 Marine RCT was to capture the island of Wolmi Do which overlooked Inchon at high tide 45 minutes after dawn (GREEN Beach).
>
> At the next high tide in the early evening the rest of 5 Marine RCT was to land on the sea wall at Inchon RED Beach to the north and 1 Marine RCT was to land on BLUE Beach to the south of the town. The two RCTs were to capture the port in a pincer movement.
>
> 1 Marine Division was then to advance on Seoul, capturing Kimpo airport on the way.
>
> 7 Infantry Division was to follow to protect the right flank and link up with 8 Army advancing from the south at Osan. The Division would also provide a reserve to help capture Seoul if necessary.

Even so, the achievement of surprise would be difficult. The security so essential to such an operation was hard to maintain in Japan where there was a large Communist Party, a Russian diplomatic mission and an inquisitive press corps. Preparations could not be hidden at Yokoharna, 7 Infantry Division's port of embarkation, at Kobe, the amphibious force base, or at Sasebo, the Fleet base. News correspondents in Tokyo had got wind of the situation and had dubbed it Operation COMMON KNOWLEDGE. From 5 September, when the air interdiction and preparatory phase began, air attacks were spread along the west coast for 150 miles to the north of Inchon to 100 miles south of the port. Only 40% of the effort was directed at the Inchon – Seoul area, the remaining 60% being divided equally between north and south. On the east coast two diversions were mounted near Yongdok by Korean marines and on 12 September 8th Army attempted to put 800 guerrillas behind the North Korean lines at Samchok without telling CinC 7th Fleet. The landing ship broached and five days of fighting and air strikes were required to bring the survivors off. On the west coast a party from 41 Commando, RM and a US special operations company were landed from the frigate HMS *Whitesand Bay* on the night 12th/13th at Kunsan. South Korean marines raided Mokpo. Further north the South Korean Navy made a number of minor raids near Inchon in early September and later on near Haeju further north. The aim of the raids near Inchon was to promote a double bluff. The raid on Haeju made the disconcerting discovery that Russian magnetic mines were being supplied to the North Koreans. Fortunately the consignment sent to Inchon was missing its cable harnesses.

These raids and the reconnaissance to provide vital information on the Inchon area ran dangerous security risks. The South Korean Navy landed a small force on Yonghung Do, a small island 14 miles south of Inchon, to establish a patrol base for an enterprising US Naval Lieutenant. Enlisting loyal Koreans, he sent them into Inchon, Seoul and Kimpo airport to establish the size of the North Korean forces, check on the beach defences and the beaches themselves. From this and other sources it was estimated that there were 500 North Koreans on Wolmi Do, another 1,500 at Inchon and 500 at Kimpo airport. Clark rowed into the harbour at night to establish the height of the sea walls and the consistency of the mud. He also landed on the small island of Palmi Do at the junction of the Flying Fish and Salee River Channels to ascertain whether the lighthouse, extinguished by the North Koreans, could be relit to guide the invasion force on the final approach. He obtained the information, reported the lighthouse to be serviceable and confirmed by observation that the Japanese tide charts were more accurate than the US Navy's. He also took part in a number of sampan battles to drive off North Korean attempts to evict him with local forces.

There were a number of hitches in so extensive an operation launched at short notice. 5 Marine Regiment had to be recovered from the Pusan bridgehead for the assault. Because 1 Marine Division's third regiment, the 7th, had been released by the Joint Chiefs of Staff too late to arrive by D Day the 1 ROK Marine Brigade also had to be pulled out of the bridgehead to take its place. A savage North Korean offensive opened on the perimeter on 2 September and General Walker was reluctant to release the 5th Marines. Eventually a compromise was

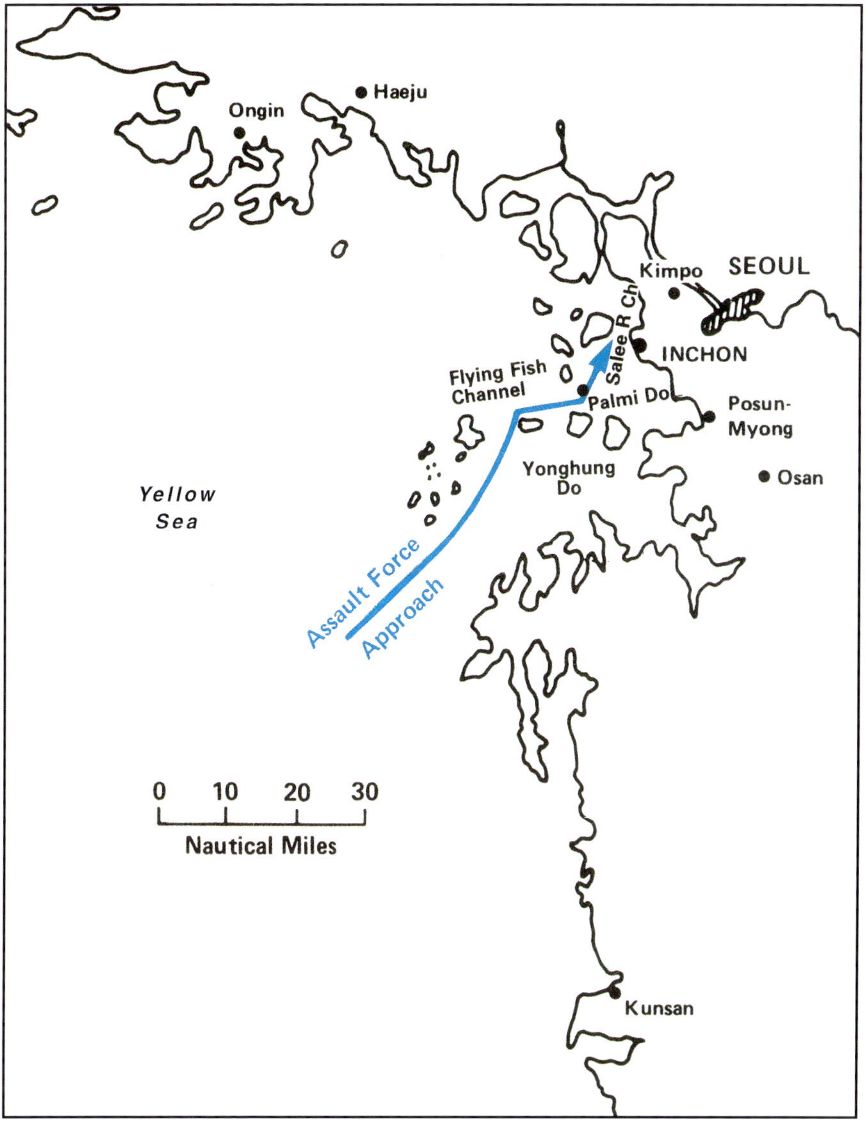

The Inchon Approaches

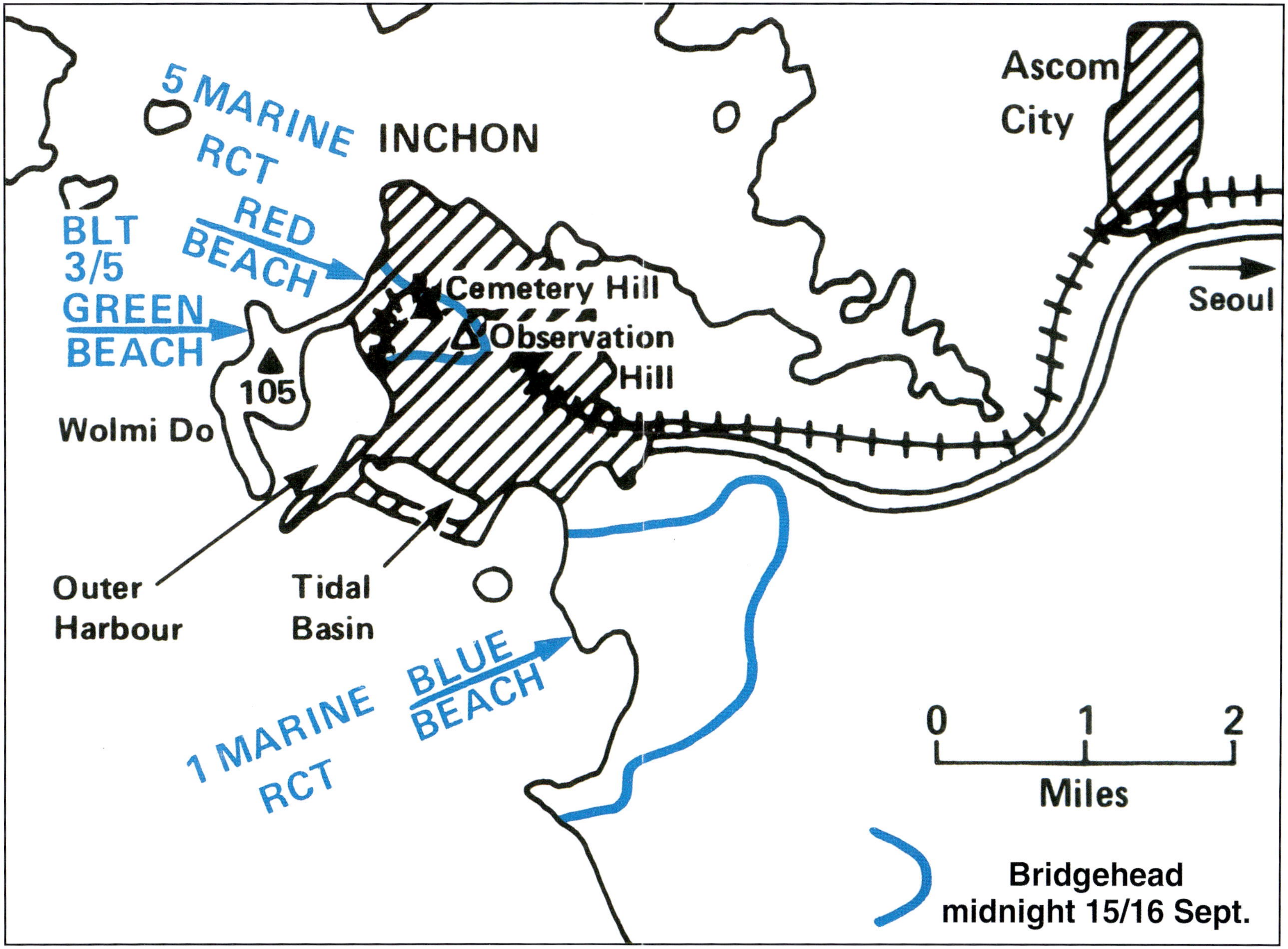

Inchon Landing 15 September 1950

The assault on RED Beach.

LSTs unloading supplies on RED Beach.

reached. A regimental combat team of 7 Infantry Division was embarked and held as an afloat reserve in Pusan harbour. When the 5th Marines were withdrawn for embarkation at Pusan they were briefed in an open field over a public address system for a descent on Kunsan.

The complicated pattern of ship movements for the assault began on 5 September with the sailing of the slow Pontoon Movement Group from Yokohama. September is the typhoon season in the East China Sea and typhoon Kezia was forecast to hit Kobe on the 12th. Amphibious Group 1 had to embark hurriedly and put to sea a day before schedule into mountainous seas. At Sasebo the flagship of the Amphibious Group took on board MacArthur, his acting Chief of Staff, Almond, the Commander of 10 Corps and the press. At least the confinement of all the chief reporters ensured security during the approach. The Group sailed on 13 September, an auspicious day for MacArthur, the 191st anniversary of Quebec.

On D-2, 13 September, a cruiser and destroyer squadron stood in to bombard Wolmi Do under cover of an air attack. It was considered vital to draw the enemy's fire so that naval and air bombardment might silence the defences for the assault crafts' run-in as it was appreciated that it was now too late for the North Koreans to reinforce the threatened area. The bulk of their Army, now increased to 13 divisions, was committed against the Pusan perimeter. It could not disengage and move any substantial force to oppose the Inchon landings in time in the face of American air power. The local North Korean sector commander's warning that a landing was imminent appears to have been disregarded by the high command. The following day the cruisers and destroyers bombarded Wolmi Do and Inchon again and stood out to sea before dark.

That night, 14/15 September, the same enterprising naval office, Lt Clark, went ashore again on Palmi Do to turn on the lighthouse to help the armada of assault shipping and bombardment groups negotiate Flying Fish Channel. The destroyer and cruiser squadrons opened up on Wolmi Do at 0545, followed by an air strike and a rocket ship bombardment. After forty-five minutes preparation the 3rd Battalion, 5 Marine RCT ran ashore on GREEN Beach to capture the island in an hour and a half. The tide receded and the Battalion remained isolated, but supported by the guns and aircraft of the Fleet, until late afternoon. Then at 1730 the remainder of 5 Marine RCT landed on RED Beach to the north of Wolmi Do and 1 Marine RCT ran ashore on BLUE Beach to the south. By midnight 5 Marine RCT had established itself on the vital high ground in Inchon city and 1 Marine RCT had secured the hill feature overlooking the road to Seoul. The landing had succeeded for the loss of just over 20 killed and 174 wounded. The intelligence estimate of the strength of the North Korean garrison had been correct.

On the 16th, the Marine Division pressed inland, 1 Marine RCT on the right directed straight for Seoul and 5 Marine RCT on the left towards Kimpo airport, while 1 ROK Marine Brigade came ashore to mop up Inchon behind them. A counter-attack with six tanks and 200 men was neatly ambushed by 5 Marine RCT on the following day and Kimpo was captured on the 18th. The airport could not be used fully for some days because insufficient thought had been given in the planning stage to the landing of vehicles, fuel and airfield equipment. It was also on the 18th that 7 Infantry Division started coming ashore. On the 20th 5 Marine RCT crossed the Han River to the west of Seoul and developed an attack on the capital from the north while 1 Marine RCT developed a second pincer movement from the south. The North Koreans reinforced their garrison to 20,000 and put up a desperate fight. 1 Marine Division's last RCT (the 7th) arrived on the 21st and an airborne regimental combat team was flown into Kimpo starting on the 24th. It was necessary to direct part of 7 Infantry Division from its right flank protection role to street fighting and it was not until 28 September that Seoul was finally cleared. Two days later Syngman Rhee's Government was restored to the capital.

Meanwhile Walker's 8th Army attacked on 16 September and broke out of the bridgehead four days later. On the 26th 1 Cavalry Division from the south linked up with 7 Infantry Division near Osan. The North Korean Army dissolved. The seizure of the only road to the north involved the loss of almost all its tanks, guns, vehicles and equipment. Many of its soldiers disappeared into the countryside with their small arms to act as guerrillas and became a nuisance which was difficult to eradicate. Only 25,000 escaped through the mountains to rally north of the 38th parallel. Some 20,000 casualties had been inflicted on the North Koreans and a further 135,000 were taken prisoner in contrast to 3,500 American casualties incurred in the Inchon landings and the capture of Seoul.

Although the operation was to be overshadowed by nearly three more dreary years of attrition it remains a dazzling success. In spite of speculation in the press the landings achieved surprise. By the time the naval bombardment and concentrated air strikes began at Inchon two days before the assault it was too late for the North Koreans to react. As in most surprises the self-delusion of the victim is an essential ingredient. Inchon was the one place where a decision could be gained but a landing there seemed so difficult that the North Koreans discounted the possibility. Until the last moment the dispersion of air attacks up and down the west coast and diversions helped to foster that illusion.

Bibliography

Heini, Robert Debs, *Victory at High Tide, The Inchon–Seoul Campaign*, Leo Cooper, 1972.

Langley, Michael, Inchon, *MacArthur's Last Triumph*, Batsford, 1979.

Long, Gavin, *MacArthur as Military Commande*r, Batsford, 1969.

Manchester, William, *American Caesar, Douglas MacArthur 1880–1964*, Little Brown, Boston, Mass, 1978.

Rees, David, *Korea, the Limited War*, Macmillan, 1964.

Ridgway, Matthew B, *The War in Korea*, Barrie and Rockliff, 1967.

APPENDIX 5 CONCENTRATION OF FORCE

THE BREAKOUT OF 1ST PANZER DIVISION KLIN-MOSCOW DECEMBER 1941

The Soviet counter-offensive started north of Moscow with a battle for the Klin bulge. This projecting arc of the front of 3rd Panzer Group was the most serious threat to Moscow. Indeed German troops had by 5 December 1941 reached the outer boundary of the city and could, just about, see the Kremlin. On the morning of 6 December the initial artillery bombardment north of Moscow by the Yakroma river began. Two Soviet armies had been assembled in this area with the purpose of driving directly westwards to cut the supply and communications life line for the German Third Panzer Group comprising some two Panzer Corps and units of an Army Group.

By 8 December, Soviet units had nearly achieved their task and had by-passed the small town of Klin from the north and were threatening the only route to safety at the small town of Nekrasino some 5km westwards. A large number of German combat units were still east of Klin and it became apparent that unless urgent action was taken they would be cut off. At this stage 1st Panzer Division (about 7,000 men)[1] was located at a point fifteen miles north of the Russian capital. It was immediately ordered back to Klin with the mission of keeping that town open for the withdrawal of other German armoured forces. Deep snow obstructed every movement, and the highway running through Klin was the only route over which the withdrawal of mechanised and motorised columns could be effected.

The Division reached Klin, after fighting the elements as well as the enemy, and succeeded in holding that important area against persistent Soviet attacks until the withdrawal of other German units through the town could be completed. The defence of the town of Klin proper, where thousands of wounded still remained awaiting evacuation, was in the hands of three ad-hoc: formations. Initially the town had been kept open for the withdrawing divisions by hurriedly organised emergency formations with sappers, road-building details, a few anti-tank and anti-aircraft sections, three self-propelled guns, Luftwaffe ground staff, workshop mechanics, and a few repaired tanks. During the next few days, however, every available man was roped in for active defence. Presently three mixed combat groups were fitted in along the north-eastern and north-western edges of the town. Klin by then was under Soviet artillery bombardment, and fires were burning everywhere. Five days later on 13 December, 3 Panzer Group, with Hitler's approval, ordered the abandonment of the positions east of Klin.

[1] Although established to have up to 15,000 men, casualties, hard fighting and lack of reinforcements had cut the numbers to about 9,000 men, about 60 tanks and about 30 guns. The number of vehicles then on the strength of the Division would be about half those of today's armoured brigade vehicle strength. By the end of the fighting around Klin, 1st Panzer division had about six available tanks and some 300 combat capable troops.

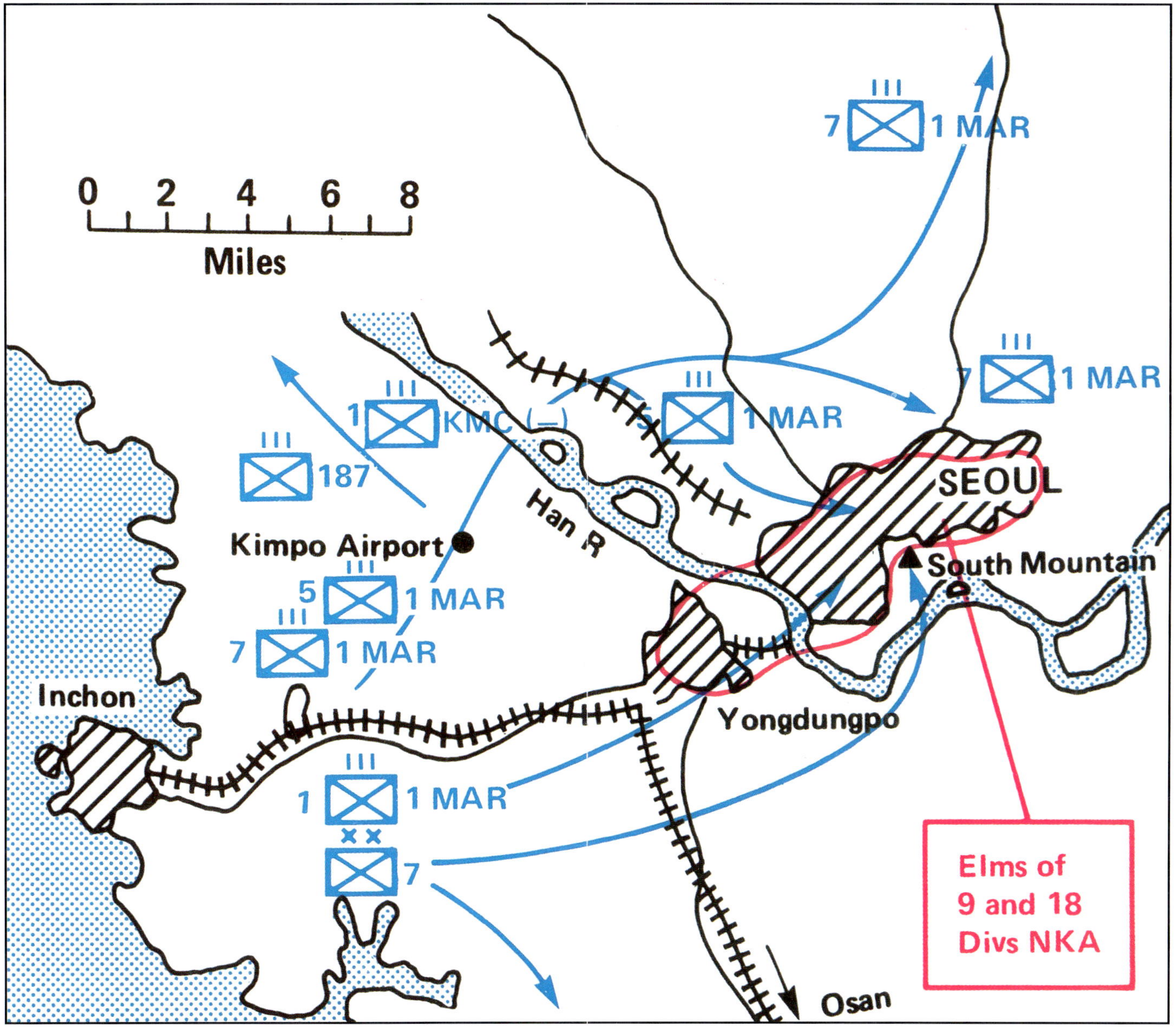

10 Corps Captures Seoul 20-27 September 1950

German troops in Klin. The last tramway stop from Moscow, December 1941.

Everything had to move back along a single road, the road through Klin. At that point, however, as the Division was ready to break contact and withdraw in the direction of Nekrasino, it found itself completely surrounded by strong enemy forces. The Division was ordered by 3 Panzer Group to abandon its vehicles if necessary, and to break through to Nekrasino where it would be able to link up with other German forces.

During these days of heavy fighting the road to Nekrasino had been cut by the enemy on several occasions. In these engagements other German units lost numerous vehicles and these wrecks had piled up all along the road leaving no more than a narrow lane between them.

Early on the morning of 13 December the Division discovered, by reconnaissance in force, that enemy resistance was weakest south-east of Klin, and that a breakout in this direction would be most likely to succeed. The terrain, however, was such that practically all vehicles would have to be left behind. There were from 800 to 1,000 wounded in Klin who could not be evacuated without transportation. Furthermore, despite considerable loss of equipment, the encircled force was still well provided with vehicles and not inclined to abandon them if that could possibly be avoided.

After short deliberation it was agreed that the Division, in order to retain its mobility, would have to break out along the road to Nekrasino, although it was now held by enemy forces in considerable strength. The main reason for this decision was the large number of casualties that had to be evacuated.

In preparing for the breakout, the Division made use of its experiences during a previous smaller encirclement at Kalinin. There, after executing a feint in a different direction which diverted some of the hostile forces, the Division had succeeded in making a surprise breakout, losing no equipment and suffering few casualties. The great flexibility of the artillery had been of decisive importance. By shifting their fire rapidly from one target to the other, all pieces were able to support the diversionary attack as well as the actual breakout. Equally important had been the commitment of all the tanks that survived the diversionary manoeuvre to the main effort.

After a careful survey of the situation around Klin, a similar plan was adopted. All available tanks, one company of armoured infantry and one rifle battalion were to conduct a diversionary break-through north of Klin, and then to proceed in a westerly direction towards the town of Goijadi. Turning sharply south after reaching Goljadi, these forces were to initiate an attack in the direction of the main road. The artillery was to remain in position around the railway station of Klin. The main breakout towards Nekrasino was to take place as soon as the Soviets reacted to the threat near Goljadi and began to divert their forces from the main road. The Germans calculated that the turning movement at Goljadi would force the enemy to shift his front towards the north in order to avoid envelopment from that direction. Initially, the entire German artillery and all available anti-aircraft weapons were to support the forces carrying out the feint.

While all remained quiet in the area designated for the main effort, the German units were assembled inside the encircled town. H Hour for the diversionary manoeuvre – actually an attack with limited objective – was set for dawn on 14 December. The time of the main break-through depended on the development of the situation.

The intended deception of the enemy was accomplished with success. A well-organised German task force fell upon the Soviet Forces at Goljadi and caught them by surprise. At the appearance of German tanks the Soviets immediately shifted their reserves to meet the diversionary attack which they assumed to be the main German breakout. The attacking German troops, incidentally, had not been informed that their effort at Goljadi was no more than a feint. It was felt that they would not fight with quite the same zeal if they knew that they were merely trying to deceive the enemy. Only the Division's artillery commander was entrusted with the full details of the plan, including the code word for shifting fire to his new targets on either side of the Klin – Nekrasino road. The German task force took Goljadi and pivoted south. As expected, the enemy began to pull out from the area of the main road and to move north across the railway line, determined to counter the threat of envelopment.

The withdrawal begins, 7 December 1941.

At about 1300 hrs a Soviet second lieutenant with a white flag appeared in front of a Captain Hingst, commanding a company along the south-eastern edge of the town as part of a combat group. The Soviet officer carried a letter signed 'Colonel Yulkhvin' and demanding the surrender of Klin. 'The position of the defenders is hopeless', the Soviet colonel wrote. It was the first Soviet invitation to surrender presented under a white flag on the Eastern Front. Captain Hingst treated the Russian very courteously and, having reported for instructions, sent him back at 1400 hrs with the answer that the colonel was mistaken as the situation was by no means hopeless for the defenders.

This was the appropriate time – about noon of the same day – to launch the main breakout along the road to Nekrasino. Upon a prearranged signal, the artillery and anti-aircraft weapons shifted their fire. Only one artillery battalion continued to fire on the old target so as to cover the withdrawal of the diversionary force

The withdrawal continues, 7-14 December 1941 (above and below).

from Goljadi. Simultaneously, on the road leading out of Klin towards the west, the main attack got under way. The Division's armoured infantry battalion drove the first gap into the lines of an enemy taken completely by surprise. Dismounted armoured infantry and motorcycle troops followed and widened the penetration. Some of the tanks initially engaged in the diversionary manoeuvre had made their way back to Klin and were now committed on both sides of the road. Under their protection, the wounded on trucks and sleds and accompanied by armoured personnel carriers were moved out of the town.

By now the artillery was covering the flanks of the main break-through column. In the eastern part of the town combat engineers held off the enemy while the evacuation took its course. With the rate of progress determined by the movement of numerous vehicles, and by the need for the gradual withdrawal of the artillery north and south of the road, the entire force fought its way through to Nekrasino, where it linked up with other German units during the evening of 14 December.

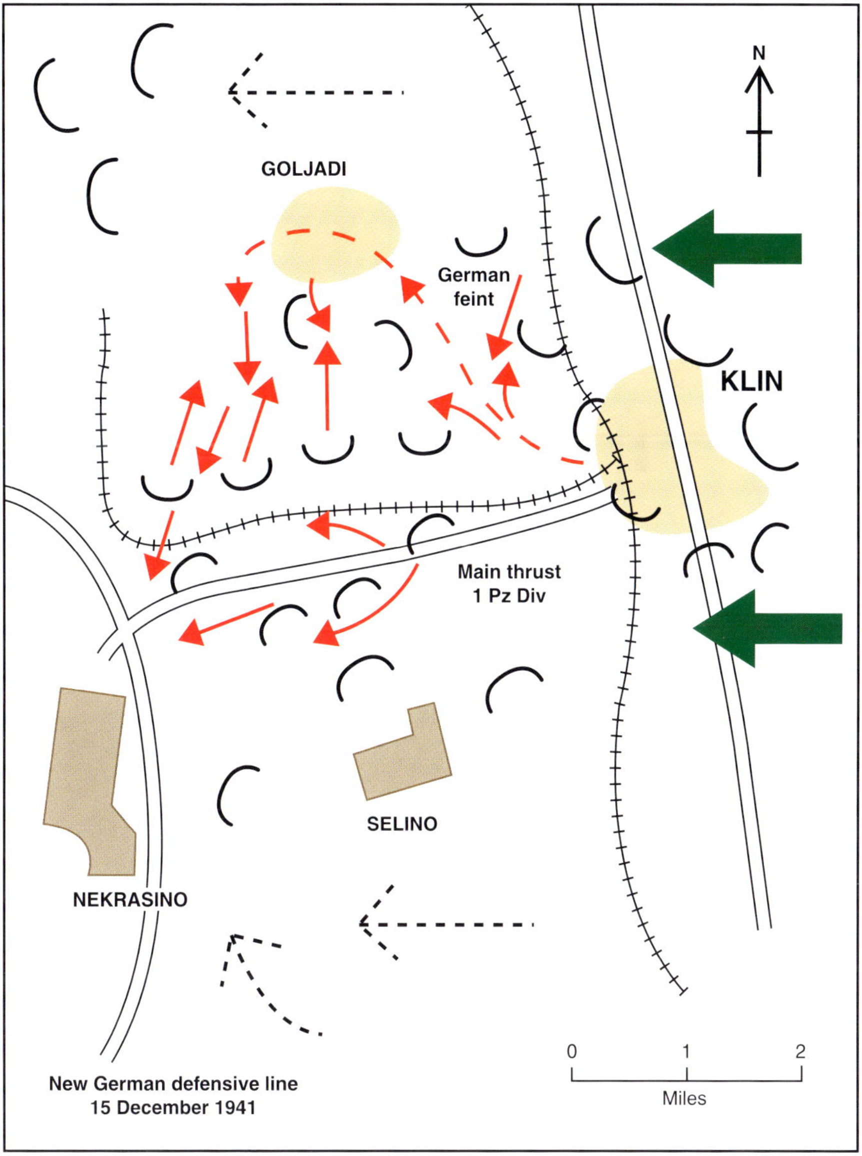

The Encirclement and Breakout at Klin 14-15 December 1941

The withdrawal ends, 15 December 1941.

Undoubtedly the Division owed much of its success to the employment of its combat elements, but it was primarily the maintenance of strict traffic control that permitted the evacuation of an unusually large number of vehicles and this determined the outcome of the entire operation. All vehicles that broke down were immediately pushed off the road to keep the column moving without interruption. A large number of officers and non commissioned officers with minor combat injuries had been added to the military police to assist in the strict enforcement of traffic discipline. The Division's staff, at first located at the western edge of Klin and later with the main body of the Division, directed the initial break-through and the subsequent movements of individual elements with the use of radio and messengers, but without telephone communications.

Substantially intact, although much reduced in fighting strength, the Division broke out from Klin, taking along its casualties and nearly all of its equipment. Twenty- four hours later, on a different sector of the front, it was again in action against the enemy. The breakout demonstates the principle of concentration of force, even in the most perverse of battle conditions.

Bibliography

Carell, Paul, *Barbarossa,* Harrap, 1970.
Stoves, R, *History of the 1st Panzer Division*, Verlag.

APPENDIX 6

ECONOMY OF EFFORT
VON MANSTEIN'S COUNTERSTROKES FEBRUARY – MARCH 1943

The Russian Winter Offensive

The Stavka took advantage of the exhaustion and overstretch of the Axis armies between the Arctic Circle and the Caucasus in the autumn of 1942 to plan a massive counter-offensive for the winter. After the loss of so many guns in the first eighteen months of the war it was necessary to concentrate the remaining artillery against each sector in turn. To make the most of the frozen ground the attacks were to start in the south with the encirclement of Paulus' 6 Army at Stalingrad and continue northwards as far as Leningrad.

Operations began on 19 November 1942 to surround Stalingrad. These were ultimately successful, despite a relief attempt in mid December, and resulted in the surrender of von Paulus' 6 Army in early February 1943. In the meanwhile during these three months, attacks had developed all along the German front lines and a large wedge had been driven between Army Group B (von Weichs) on the upper Don river and Army Group A (von Kleist).

In the early days of 1943 von Manstein's first task was to stabilise a line and to hold the bridges at Rostov to keep the communication and logistic supply for 1st Panzer Army open until this formation could move to the Donets River area.

The Battles to Hold Rostov

2 Guards Army started probing the gap south of the Don in early January. A small force crossed the lower Don to threaten von Manstein's Headquarters at Novocherkassk on the 7th and was only beaten off by a scratch force using tanks hurriedly repaired in workshops. However, a more immediate threat was posed by Russian crossings of the Don at Potemkinskaya and Tsymlyanskaya which forced the Germans to abandon the Chir and fall back on the Kagalink river by the 8th. Holding the river with reduced forces the Corps Commander (Hollidt) swung two panzer divisions in turn against an attempt to break through frontally by 5 Shock Army (South Front) and a Russian tank concentration threatening his northern flank on the Bystraya. For the moment, Hollidt, and the Fretter-Pico Group to his left, were secure and von Manstein seized the opportunity to bring Hollidt behind the Donets unmolested and to move his Army Group Headquarters to Taganrog. South of the Don a serious threat developed as 2 Guards Army crossed the Sal and Manych rivers to seize Rostov airfield. While 4 Panzer Army, reinforced by a panzer division from Army Group A, held the Manych river in the Spornii – Proletarskaya area and counter-attacked the Russians from the south, Hollidt left only infantry to hold the Donets bend against renewed attacks by 5 Shock Army and counter-attacked southwards

across the frozen Don on the 25th with two panzer divisions to catch 2 Guards Army in flank. The Russians withdrew and the German communications through Rostov were saved. The policy of economising in effort on a less vital sector to concentrate a force large enough to obtain a decision where it mattered had paid off once again.

Two days later, Headquarters 1 Panzer Army was withdrawn from Army Group A and switched to the Donets on von Manstein's west flank, ready to receive its divisions, together with some of 4 Panzer Army's, as they were released from south of the Don. On the 29th von Manstein moved his Headquarters to Stalino as the point of main effort switched from the Don to the Donets.

Planning for the Counterstrokes

From the end of January, von Manstein had been advising Zeitzier, Chief of Staff, OKH, that to comply with Hitler's wish to retain the whole of the Donbas area would tie up all the formations of his Army Group, a most uneconomical use of resources. In particular, 4 Panzer Army would have to be committed to the defence of the Donets-Don salient. It was necessary to withdraw from the east end of the salient to the Mius in order to shorten the line to free a sizeable armoured force for use as a mobile reserve. Without this, von Manstein explained, the Russians would be able to break through the defensive crust to pin Army Group Don against the Sea of Azov and cut off Army Group A. With the Russians threatening Kharkov and the likelihood that Rokossovski's troops, now freed from Stalingrad, would appear within the next two or three weeks, von Manstein predicted a thrust to the Dnieper bend to cut the railways supplying the two Army Groups. Hitler had wished to commit the SS Panzer Corps piecemeal as it arrived in Army Group B's area in a series of counter-attacks across the Donets due east of Kharkov. Von Manstein wanted the counter-attack delayed until all three divisions were concentrated and directed south-east on the west bank of the river to trap the Russians who had already crossed and who would continue to expand the bridgeheads in the next fortnight. He also called for the concentration of 7 Anti Aircraft Division, dispersed throughout the communication zone, to protect the road and rail crossings of the Dnieper at Dnepropetrovsk, and for the preparation of an airlift in case the crossings were lost. He suggested to the OKH that reinforcements might be provided by transferring the combat arms of three divisions from the Kuban bridgehead and marrying them up-with the now idle logistic units of Paulus' 6 Army which had escaped encirclement. These proposals, and a threat to resign, led to a conference with the Fuhrer in East Prussia on 6 February.

Hitler, always averse to giving up ground, wanted to retain the Donbas coking coal for German industry and deny it to the Russians. He expressed concern for the effect of any further withdrawals on neutral Turkey. He argued that an enemy forced to fight bitterly for every inch of ground would be seriously weakened. As the Russians had been attacking for two and a half months their losses and supply problems would no longer enable them to launch ambitious

Erich von Manstein, CinC Army Group South.

outflanking operations. There was a germ of truth in the latter argument. Von Manstein's counterstroke succeeded largely because the Russians were short of fuel and reduced in strength. Living from day to day with little appreciation of an army group commander's need to think three weeks or more ahead, Hitler refused to accept von Manstein's forecast of what might happen. Troops released by shortening the front, Hitler argued, would merely release Russian forces. Von Manstein explained the advantage accruing to the side which made the first move in gaining the initiative. Interior lines would help. A relatively small force used quickly would gain a victory. At last, Hitler agreed to withdraw to the Mius and the basis for von Manstein's counterstroke was laid. 4 Panzer Army's move to the west was confirmed but its deployment on 1 Panzer Army's left would take a further two weeks.

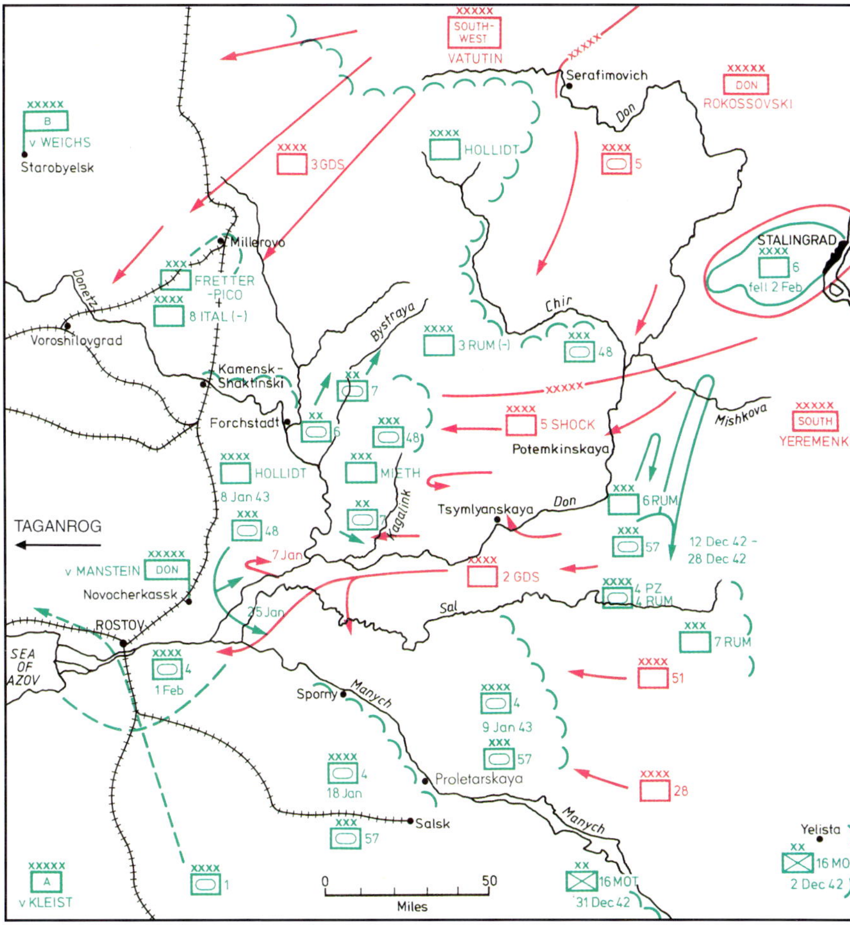

The Don and the Donetz: Stabilising the Front 12 Dec 1942 – 2 Feb 1943

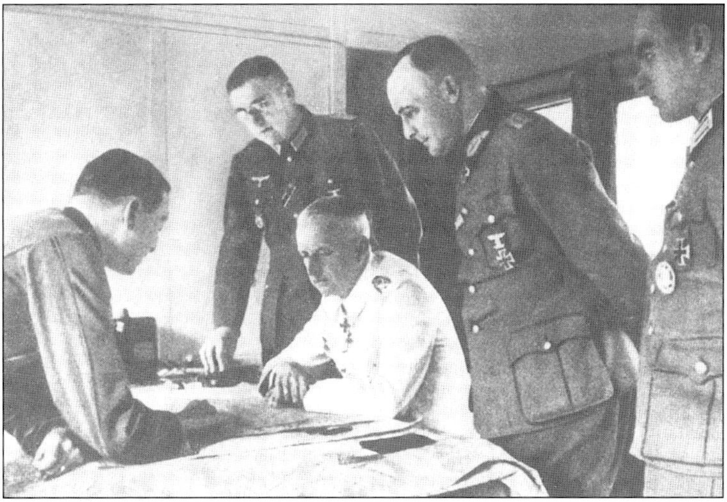

The CinC with his staff in his command train.

The next day the Russians reached the south bank of the Don at Rostov and Hollidt prepared to withdraw to the Mius. The following day, 8 February, 3 Guards Army broke out of the Voroshilovgrad bridgehead and its leading cavalry corps reached Debaltsevo, where it was stopped, surrounded and eventually forced to surrender. In Army Group B's sector to the north Das Reich, the first division of SS Panzer Corps to arrive at Kharkov, launched the counter-attack Hitler had demanded. The operation failed and the Division retired behind the Donets. Golikov's Voronezh Front pushed the assembling SS Panzer Corps back into Kharkov and took Belgorod and Kursk to the north. To hold the Kharkov area Army Group B had only the remnants of 2 German Army to oppose the Russian thrust through Kursk to Rylsk and Army Detachment Lanz, consisting of Hausser's incomplete SS Panzer Corps and Rauss' 11 Corps of two infantry divisions. Hitler ordered the SS Panzer Corps to defend Kharkov to the last man but, when the city was almost surrounded on the 15th, Hausser took the decision to break out. In doing so he saved the mobile forces which were to provide an essential part of von Manstein's later counterstroke but Lanz, a mountaineer, was replaced by Kempf, a tank specialist. That same day Army Detachment Kempf was transferred to Army Group Don. Von Manstein's order of battle for the counterstroke was now complete but, with the demise of Army Group B on 12 February, his front had been extended north to Belgorod. There were two further changes; Army Group Don was renamed Army Group South and von Manstein moved his Headquarters to Zaporozhe, the better to control operations where the crisis was developing on the Donets between Kharkov and Slavyansk.

Hitler had left the decision to fall back to the Mius so late that 1 Panzer Army's left faced encirclement by Popov's Group and 1 Guards Army, while 6 (Russian) Army raced for the Dnieper bridges at Dnepropetrovsk and Zaporozhe. It was feared that a further threat might develop from Golikov's 3 Tank Army from Kharkov south-westwards across the Dnieper at Kremenchug to Kherson on the Black Sea.

General Hausser, SS Panzer Corps.

By 17 February the spearhead of Popov's Armoured Group, four tank corps, two armoured brigades and three infantry divisions, all much reduced in strength and running out of fuel, reached Grishino and Krasnoarmeyskoye, where it was stopped by Heinrici's 40 Panzer Corps. In a successful action SS Viking Panzer Grenadier Division held the spearhead while 333 Infantry Division, supported by 3 Panzer Corps, held the right shoulder of the penetration at Slavyansk. Simultaneously 7 and 11 Panzer Divisions launched a counterstroke at the flanks of the moving columns between Grishino and Slavyansk. These moves cut off the spearhead and halted the Soviet thrust. To the west there was nothing to stop the advance of 6 Army (two tank corps, with perhaps 150 tanks left, two rifle corps and a cavalry corps from Izium) down the railway towards the Dnieper bridges. By the 17th one spearhead had reached Pavlograd and another, a little to the east, was within 60 miles of Zaporozhe. Army Detachment Kempf was

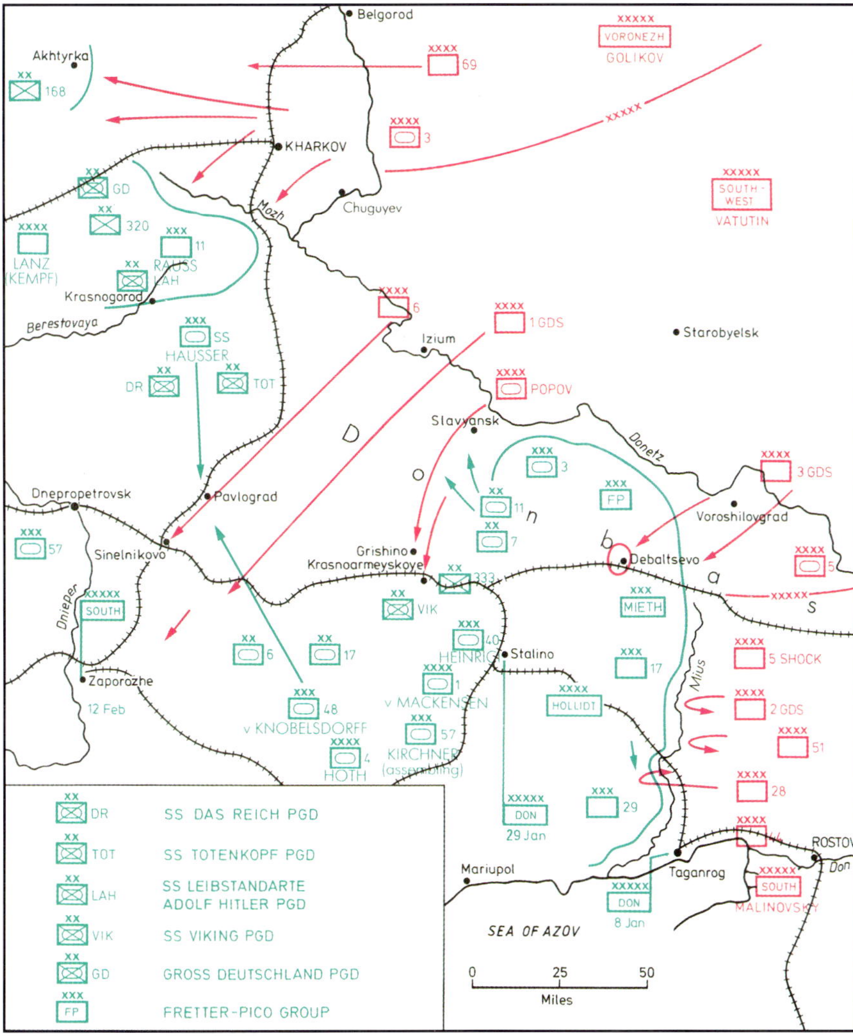

Vatutin's Offensive across the Donetz and Von Manstein's First Counterstroke

The SS Panzer Corps on the outskirts of Kharkov.

Soviet artillery moving into position.

rallying on the Mozh river south-west of Kharkov, threatened by 3 Guards Army and by an outflanking move westwards to Akhtyrka. To the east, Hollidt was holding the Mius. 4 Panzer Army would be concentrated between Stalino and Zaporozhe by the 19th.

Final Preparations

This was the situation when Hitler arrived at von Manstein's Headquarters on the 17th. The Army Group Commander explained his plan for the counterstroke. SS Panzer Corps was to concentrate at Krasnograd and strike south-eastwards with two Panzer grenadier divisions (SS Totenkopf and SS Das Reich) to meet Hoth's 4 Panzer Army striking north-westwards at Pavlograd. Hoth was to co-ordinate the attacks of both formations. Army Detachment Kempf, with Rauss' 11 Corps, reinforced by SS Leibstandarte Adolf Hitler and Gross Deutschland Panzer Grenadier Division, would hold the left shoulder. 57 Panzer Corps was still assembling in the Dnieper bend but would provide a reserve and be available for the next phase, the advance on Kharkov. 1 Panzer Army would deal with Popov and hold the Donets to the point where Fretter-Pico's Group provided the hinge between 1 Panzer and Hollidt on the Mius. Hollidt was to be stripped of his panzer and motorised troops to strengthen the decisive blow. The greatest economies of effort were to be enforced on the flanks to effect the maximum concentration of force in the centre. Massive air support was to be provided by von Richthofen's Luftflotte 4.

Hitler wanted to recapture Kharkov first but von Manstein pressed his case for destroying the spearheads of the Russian breakthrough and dealing with the city afterwards. As 4 Panzer Army's concentration would not be complete for another two days and seeing that Hitler was obstinate, von Manstein could afford to defer the decision. On the 18th the remnants of an Italian division abandoned Pavlograd to the advancing 6 Army. Totenkopf Division was stuck in the mud on its way to join the SS Panzer Corps. The impossibility of an immediate attack on Kharkov and the need to deal with 6 Army persuaded Hitler to accept von Manstein's plan. Von Manstein broached the question of a large scale offensive further north after the thaw to enable Army Group South to maintain its salient on the Donets but Hitler would not discuss operations so far ahead. However, he did agree to abandon his project for another offensive from the Kuban bridgehead into the Caucasus and to reinforce von Manstein from Army Group A.

On the 19th 6 Army took the vital rail junction at Sinelnikovo, only 40 miles from Zaporozhe. Fortunately for the Germans, a local initiative restored the situation. 15 Infantry Division was arriving at Dnepropetrovsk after a nine day rail journey from La Rochelle on the Atlantic coast. Two trains, each carrying a battalion, were sent on at midnight to capture the junction by coup de main. Hitler departed from Zaporozhe before other Russian spearheads could menace the airfield, leaving von Manstein free to issue the final orders for the counterstroke. On 20 February, Malinovsky's South Front pierced Hollidt's line on the Mius in three places but the defenders managed to halt two of the thrusts and cut off the assault troops of the third by the following day. Von Manstein's risk had been nicely calculated.

On the Russian side there was some confusion. The dangers of being caught scattered and running out of fuel had alarmed Popov sufficiently to ask for permission to withdraw. At Front and Stavka levels air reconnaissance reports of the westward concentration of 4 Panzer Army were interpreted as preparations for a withdrawal behind the Dnieper. The breakout of the SS Panzer Corps from Kharkov was interpreted as confirmation of Hitler's concession of defeat. Vatutin's reply to Popov was, 'No. Attack the enemy. The enemy is retreating. He must not escape across the Dnieper.' As late as the 23rd, the fourth day of the German counterstroke, when Vatutin was trying to impress Stavka with the reality of the situation. Stalin replied sharply. 'Get that left wing of yours moving!'

The Counterstroke to the Donets

The counterstroke opened on 19 February with Hausser's attack from the Krasnograd area with his two Panzer Grenadier divisions abreast, SS Totenkopf on the left, SS Das Reich on the right, supported by the concentrated might of Luftflotte 4. The following morning von Knobelsdorff's 48 Panzer Corps of 4 Panzer Army advanced northwards from its concentration area two divisions abreast, 6 Panzer on the left with 17 Panzer on the right. Von Manstein's 'armoured shears' cut through Kharitonov's overextended 6 Army to meet at Pavlograd on the 23rd. On Hoth's right Heinrici's 40 Panzer Corps of 1 Panzer Army joined in to defeat Popov's Group at Krasnoarmeyskoye on the same day and to drive the remnants over the Donets between Slavyansk and Izium by the evening of the 28th. On the Mius, Hollidt beat off Malinovsky's infantry attacks floundering through the mud of the thaw.

By 2 March, 6 Army, Popov's Armoured Group and 1 Guards Army had lost a tank corps and three rifle divisions. Their remaining formations had been badly mauled and the Germans claimed 615 tanks, 354 guns and 69 anti-aircraft guns destroyed or captured, plus 23,000 Soviet dead and 9,000 prisoners.

The Counterstroke around Kharkov

Having beaten Vatutin, von Manstein set about Golikov's Voronezh Front. The approaching thaw made an encircling movement to the east of the Donets to trap Golikov's troops beyond the river impracticable. The melting ice would have made pontoon bridging impossible, isolating the panzer spearheads.

A direct attack on Kharkov would have required large forces, wasted much time and cost heavy casualties, altogether a most uneconomic use of effort. Von Manstein's orders, issued on 28 February, two days before the closure of the Donets battle, called for the SS Panzer Corps at Pavlograd to wheel left, almost through 180 degrees, and advance northwards alongside 4 Panzer Army. Hausser's SS Panzer Corps was to move to the west of Kharkov. 48 Panzer Corps, with 57 Panzer Corps now coming into action on its right, would move to the east of the city.

Seeing the threat to his flank, Golikov moved two tank corps and three rifle divisions from 3 Tank Army south to the Krasnograd area to oppose it. The group was sandwiched between SS Leibstandarte Division, holding the south-eastern face of Kempf's left flank protection group and Hausser's advancing SS Panzer grenadiers. Wheeling in his two divisions and well supported from the air, Hausser closed the trap on 5 March. The fighting between the elite troops of Hitler and Stalin was fierce and a Russian corps commander was killed within a hundred yards of Hausser's command post. The Russians lost 12,000 killed, 61 tanks and 225 guns.

The weather changed suddenly and, in the mud of the thaw, a Soviet rifle division held up 48 Panzer Corps for five days on the Mozh river 25 miles south of Kharkov. With nothing left to oppose them, Hausser's three SS Panzer Grenadier divisions advanced west and north of Kharkov to encircle the city and reach the Donets at Chuguyev by 15 March. Exploiting what appeared to be a chance to seize the city by *coup de main* the SS Panzer Grenadiers became heavily involved in street fighting. Resistance was crushed by the 15th although the garrison could have been left to starve. Meanwhile, Army Detachment Kempf advanced northwards up the Donets to capture Belgorod on the 18th. Golikov pulled the remnants of 3 Tank Army, and 69 Army to its north, back across the Donets and called for reinforcements to patch up his front.

A Lost Opportunity and Lessons

There remained the possibility of a further advance to Kursk to pinch out the huge Russian salient in conjunction with a drive by von Kluge's Army Group Centre from the north. But von Kluge insisted that his troops were too exhausted and von Manstein's pleas were in vain. The chance of inflicting a further major defeat on the disorganised Soviet forces was missed and when the offensive was finally launched in July, the Soviet Defences were too strong. The German defeat at Kursk, the largest tank battle of the war, became the turning point of the war on the Eastern Front.

Von Manstein's withdrawal from the Chir to the Mius and the leap-frogging of 1 and 4 Panzer Armies from south of the Don to the Donets was a masterly operation. At each stage he held the line with as few troops as possible to provide local reserves. To concentrate sufficient forces to mount the Donets and Kharkov counterstrokes he denuded his eastern flank of its mobile divisions. Hollidt was left with just sufficient troops to defeat all attempts to cross the Mius. The early thaw was exploited to economise in troops on the less important sector. As an example of economy of effort to achieve a decisive concentration von Manstein's winter campaign is a classic.

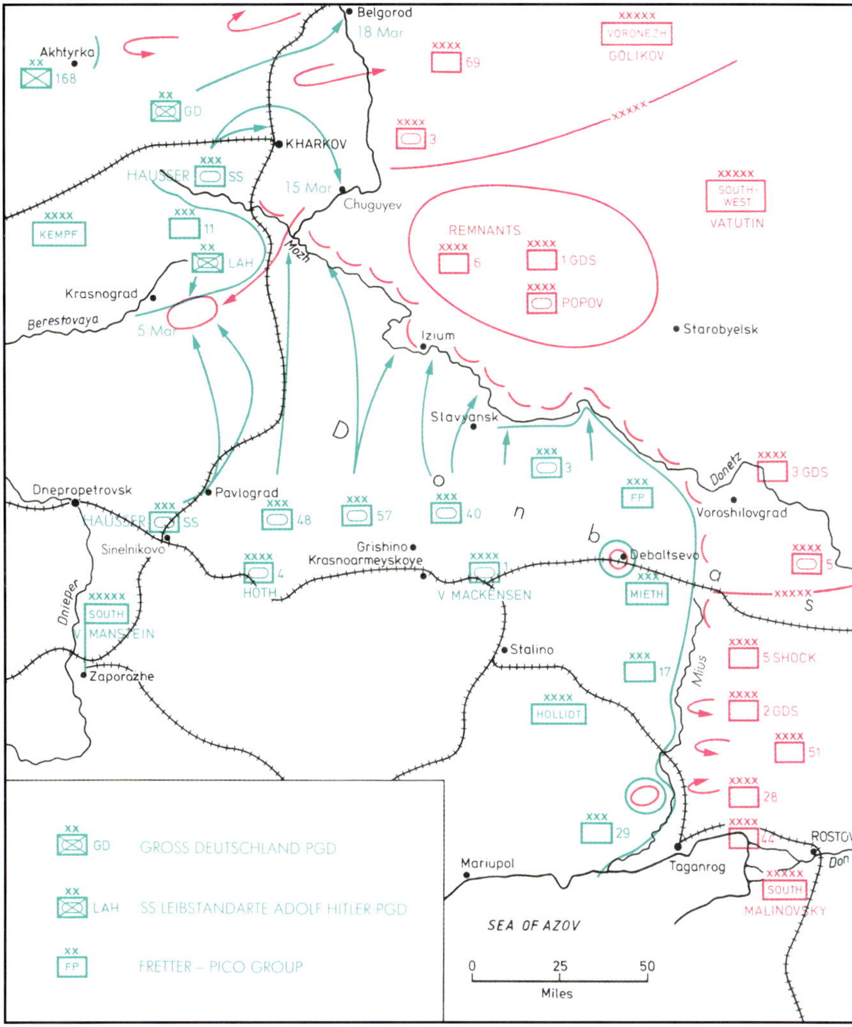

Von Manstein's Second Couterstroke around Karkov and to the Donetz

Bibliography

Brett-Smith, Richard, *Hitler's Generals*, Osprey, 1976.
Carell, Paul, *Scorched Earth*, Harrap, 1970.
Erickson, John, *The Road to Berlin*, Weidenfeld and Nicolson, 1983.
Keitel, Field Marshal, *The Memoirs of William Kimber*, 1965.
Manstein, Erich von, *Lost Victories*, Methuen, 1955.
Mellenthin, Major General F W von, *Panzer Battles 1939–1945*, Cassell, 1956.
Perrett, Bryan, *A History of Blitzkrieg*, Hale, 1983.
Seaton, Albert, *The Russo-German War 1941–1945*, Arthur Barker, 1971.
Seaton, Albert, *Stalin as Warlord*, Batsford, 1976.
Warlimont, Walter, *Inside Hitter's Headquarters, 1939–45*, Weidenfeld and Nicolson, 1964.

APPENDIX 7 **SECURITY**
THE SUEZ CANAL, OCTOBER 1973

Political Background

After victories in the June War of 1967 Israel was determined to retain her gains in Sinai, the Gaza Strip, the West Bank, Jerusalem and the Golan until a settlement could be negotiated with her Arab neighbours to protect vulnerable frontiers and obtain recognition. Holding on to the 1967 territorial gains afforded a tangible measure of security but at the price of peace. Withdrawal would have been popular internationally but unacceptable internally.

President Nasser, of Egypt, also had a problem. As the main defender of Arab dignity, he was pushed by public opinion and his Arab paymasters into demanding Israeli withdrawal from Arab territory, 'legal rights' for the Palestinian refugees and 'no surrender'. In no position to fight after the 1967 defeat he opted for a long-term strategy, but not too long, or he would be unable to control his people. He was obliged to stay on the defensive while he re-equipped and retrained his forces before turning to a more aggressive strategy. The Russians readily agreed to provide the equipment, including SAM systems, to protect Egyptian Air Force bases and to prevent a repetition of the 1967 debacle. Their price was Soviet naval facilities in Egypt and Syria. Nasser and Assad agreed because they hoped that the presence of the Russian 5th Fleet would reduce the influence of the American 6th Fleet.

When Nasser died in November 1970 there was a period of uncertainty before Sadat defeated the extreme pro-Soviet faction under Ali Sabri to emerge as undisputed leader the following Spring. Sadat was careful to warn the Russians in advance that the removal of their chief supporter would not involve a reversal of alliances. The collateral was a 15 year Treaty of Friendship and Co-operation.

Egyptian War Aims

To fight a successful war Sadat needed allies, attainable war aims and arms. He appreciated that Jordan lacked an adequate air defence system and that King Hussein could not afford to risk his throne by intervening directly. However, he hoped to secure the King's goodwill, without letting him into the secret war planning, and to rally Syria to Egypt's side for an attack on their common enemy. Egypt and Syria had both lost territory in 1967 but their aims were different. Egypt had accepted Resolution 242, and was prepared to recognise Israel; Syria was not. Egypt was ready to settle for the return of Arab territory lost in 1967; Syria, like the PLO whom she harboured, aimed unrealistically at Israel's destruction.

Sadat persuaded Assad to agree to more limited objectives: the evacuation of Arab territory occupied in 1967, a 'just settlement' of the refugee problem and the recognition of a Palestinian entity. The means were to be the seizure of the Golan Heights and the east bank of the Suez Canal as a demonstration of determination to enlist world sympathy and to precipitate an oil embargo sufficiently damaging to European nations to compel these governments to persuade America to force Israel to a settlement. Such limited aims, offering no menace to Israel's vital interests, were considered unlikely to provoke retaliation with the nuclear weapons which the Arab leaders feared the Israelis might possess.

Additional arms were obtained in exchange for an extension of the Soviet Egyptian Naval Agreement. Meanwhile, to provide security the two countries built up the densest system of SAM 2, 3 and 6 missiles in the world to protect their capitals and major cities, to cover the Golan Heights and both banks of the Suez Canal. A combination of the SAM 7 and the ZSU 23-4 anti-aircraft gun gave their ground forces a considerable measure of protection in the forward combat zone. Both air forces hardened their airfields to prevent a repetition of the 1967 disaster and special attention was paid to all-arms training.

On 24 October, 1972 Sadat explained his aim of securing a lodgement on the Sinai bank of the Canal as a bargaining counter available to the Egyptian Supreme War Council of the Armed Forces. When General Sadiq, the Minister for War, complained that he had insufficient equipment he was replaced by General Ismail. General Shazli became Chief of Staff and General Gamasi Director of Operations.

Ismail was a cautious and stolid infantryman. Though not clever and rather narrow minded he was conscientious, determined and strictly non-political. He was just the man for a limited, set-piece enterprise. Shazli was a paratrooper who had a reputation for panache. He had managed to escape from Sinai with some of his brigade in the 1967 debacle; sophisticated and urbane he had been a military attaché in London and at the United Nations. In 1960 he had commanded the Egyptian contingent with the United Nations force in the Congo. There he had been inspected by General Ismail; he resented it and the two fell out. Gamasi was able, quiet, intellectual and rather prim. He provided the brains of the high command.

Egyptian War Plans

By taking the initiative Ismail counted on achieving a sufficient degree of surprise to gain and consolidate their limited objectives before the Israelis could react. A simultaneous attack on two fronts would prevent the Israelis from concentrating first on one ally and then on the other as they did in 1967.

Timing was all important. The most difficult task faced the Egyptians on the Suez Canal. A steady current flows through the Canal from south to north to replace water lost in the Mediterranean by evaporation. The current is especially strong during spring tides. A period of slack current during the neap tides was desirable for the assault crossing and the assembly of the Russian PMP and pontoon bridging. Sufficient daylight was required to move the assault echelons across the Canal quickly against relatively light opposition. Moonlight was needed to assist the bridge building in the first half of the night and darkness to hide the subsequent crossing of the assault divisions' vehicles and armour. A convenient gap in the American satellite coverage and a good deception plan were necessary to maintain secrecy and obtain surprise. Such was the basis of Operation 'Badr'.[1]

The only suitable dates were in May, September and early October. As neither Egypt nor Syria could absorb their new weapons in time for a May attack, the two remaining periods were considered at the last major co-ordinating conference on 22 August.

The staffs needed a minimum of 15 days' notice to complete their deployment. This ruled out September. The Syrians needed five days' warning to pump out the Homs refinery. The Egyptians chose Saturday, 6 October as Y-Day[2] on 21 September and told the Syrians the following day, but for some undisclosed reason the Syrians failed to empty the Homs refinery. The Egyptians selected 1800 for H hour so that they could cross the Canal with the sun behind them. When the Syrians objected, because they would be attacking into the sun on the Golan, the Allies compromised on 1400.

Israeli War Aims

In the event of war the Israelis aimed to inflict a defeat on the Arabs severe enough to deter further attacks, to maintain their 1967 security borders and to achieve recognition of the Israeli state. It would be necessary to achieve a decision before the superpowers imposed a cease-fire, occupying additional territory if possible as a bargaining counter.

The Defence of the Suez Canal – A Security Dilemma

From the military point of view it would have suited the Israelis to have used a mobile screen to watch the Canal and to have held their armour well back in reserve ready to counter-attack once the Egyptians were committed across the obstacle. However, the political need to prevent the Egyptians from staking out a presence in Sinai, however shallow, demanded a forward defence on the water line. This was to carry severe military penalties.

A former Israeli Chief of Staff, Barlev, gave his name to the defensive system. However, it was not just a linear defence. A line of fortified posts along the east bank gave observation along the water obstacle and beyond, until the Egyptians built a ramp on their side. Each post had a garrison of half a platoon in quiet

[1] Named in honour of Mohammed's victory over the Qura ish in AD 624.
[2] Y = Yom = Day.

General Shazli, President Sadat and General Ismail, at the Underground Command Centre.

periods, to be doubled in an emergency. A troop of three tanks was available to support each post from firing ramps which gave an enfiladed shoot along the waterway. Along the first ridge of sand dunes, some 5 to 8 kilometres behind the Canal, large strong points were constructed to take an infantry company apiece on mobilisation. Small reserves of tanks were held behind the ridge ready to move forward to firing positions about 500 to 1,000 metres behind the Canal to support the bank posts and cover the gaps between them. Just behind the ridge the Artillery Road was built so that guns and local reserves could be switched across the front. A further 10 to 15 miles back the Lateral Road was constructed as part of a communications network to move major reserve forces and supplies across the soft sand. Further back still, positions had been selected to guard the passes through the Western Hills, the Khatmia, the Giddi, the Mitla and the Sudr, which could be occupied by reserve infantry brigades on mobilisation. The main command and administrative centre for the Sinai Division was based at Refidim (Bir Gifgafa) in the centre of the peninsula and shielded by the Western Hills.

So, while the system as a whole provided for a mobile, elastic defence, political considerations concerned with the security of a disputed border made for a rigidity which the Egyptians would exploit.

A Matter of Intelligence

The strategic surprise achieved by the initial Egyptian and Syrian attacks was perhaps the most outstanding feature of the war. It was the fruit of an elaborate deception plan and good security on the part of the Arabs and the consequence of becoming the victim of preconceived ideas on the part of the Israelis.

The Israeli Military Intelligence Branch had an enviable reputation and under a strong Director of Intelligence, Major General Yariv, it spread its interests into the fields of political and economic intelligence, properly the field of Mossad. The latter organisation gradually lost influence to the Military Intelligence Branch which openly boasted of its ability to read the Arab mind. Six months before the Yom Kippur War, Yariv was replaced by his deputy, Major General Zeira, an inflexible man unwilling to change his views once his mind was made up.

Israeli military intelligence developed a theory that Syria would not move without Egypt and Egypt would not be in a position to attack until her Air Force had developed an effective medium range capability. It was estimated that such a force could not be built up and trained before 1975 and it was assumed that there would be no war before then. For political reasons Sadat could not afford to wait so long, hence the Egyptian and Syrian investment in SCUD and FROG missiles. Israeli intelligence failed to perceive the significance of these weapon deliveries in April and July 1973. The Israelis placed much faith in the 'deterrent borders' which they had won in 1967. They assumed that the Arabs would appreciate that they would prove too costly to assault although the Egyptians and Syrians had already manned their sectors in strength thus making it easier to build up a concentration for an offensive undetected.

There were numerous minor alarms and three major scares between December 1971 and May 1973. In each of the major scares the Egyptians mobilised sections of their reserves, moved bridging material to the Canal, prepared crossing places and concentrated tanks, artillery and troops. Israeli intelligence became accustomed to the pattern of concentration and dispersal. Trusting to their reputation for obtaining early warning, their assumption that their Air Force and small Active Army could hold the frontiers while they mobilised, and their belief in 'the concept', the intelligence staff grew increasingly dismissive of each scare. Nevertheless, the Chief of the General Staff, Lieutenant General Elazar, took the May scare sufficiently seriously to persuade the Israeli Cabinet to order a partial mobilisation. But mobilisation is expensive, disrupts the economy and is politically provocative. When nothing happened the CGS was discredited in the eyes of the Cabinet and in particular with Moshe Dayan, the Minister of Defence, the man who had appointed Zeira as Director of Intelligence.

In mid-1973 the Americans became aware of Operation 'Badr' but they appear not to have taken it seriously. Apart from this lapse Arab security was good; so was their deception plan. Doubts were spread about the efficacy of the SAM missile force. Rumours of Arab disunity and friction with the Russians were not discouraged. Although Sadat did not believe that the 'oil weapon' would prove effective until Arab blood was shed, the Arabs threatened its use throughout the summer until Western governments and oil companies became seriously worried. It appeared that the Arabs were concentrating on political and economic pressure. Diplomatic statements in the United Nations and elsewhere lent credence to the idea.

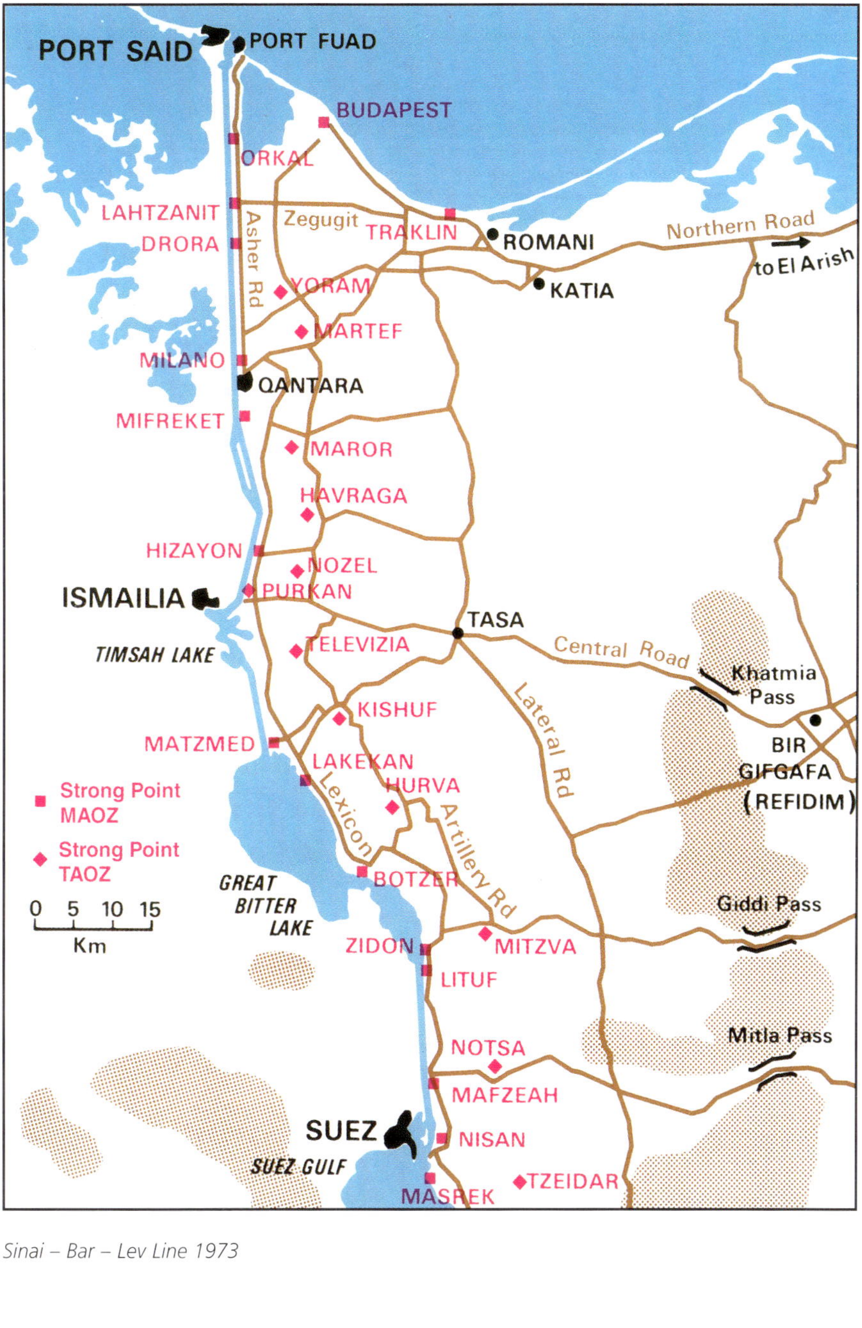

Sinai – Bar – Lev Line 1973

President Sadat and General Ismail inspecting a SAM 3 missile site.

The Egyptians were able to turn their contacts with America to good account. They had commissioned an American team to advise on the feasibility of an opposed Canal crossing. When the team reported unfavourably the Egyptians leaked the report to Israeli intelligence. They gave wide publicity to an American contract to build an oil pipeline from the Gulf of Suez to the Mediterranean, close to the intended war zone.

Countdown to War

On 13 September Syrian fighters were scrambled to intercept an Israeli reconnaissance aircraft photographing Russian shipping approaching Latakia in Syria. In the battle with the Israeli top cover, 13 Syrian aircraft were shot down for the loss of one Israeli. The Syrians' well advertised preparations to meet further alleged aggression provided a fortuitous cover plan for their concentration on the Golan. Nevertheless, the concentration was sufficiently large for Moshe Dayan to order 7 Romani Armoured Brigade to the Golan at the end of the month.

The Egyptians concentrated under cover of Exercise 'Tahrir 73' ('Liberation 73), the annual autumn manoeuvre. All classes of reservists were called up towards the end of September with the promise of release by 8 October. Activity along the Canal was kept as normal as possible. Mines were lifted and routes opened in some places and routes closed elsewhere in a seemingly random pattern. Units were brought up behind the Canal at night and their transport sent back the next day. The bridging was not brought up until the night before the attack. The troops were only briefed the next morning. An exercise during Ramadan, when Muslims avoid strenuous activity during the day, was unusual but unremarked by Israeli intelligence. However, as a routine precaution during the autumn exercises an Israeli division in the South went on to the first stage of alert on 1 October. On the same day a subaltern on the Southern Command Intelligence Staff at Beersheba, who had made a careful analysis of Egyptian activity, informed his branch chief that an attack was imminent. Because his conclusions did not fit the overall concept they were rejected.

On 2 October Major General Gonen, GOC Southern Command, toured the Bar-Lev Line. He ordered a higher state of alert and a review of Operation 'Shovach Yonim', the contingency plan to meet an attack in Sinai with the forces in place. News of Gonen's visit reached Egyptian GHQ that evening, causing some concern.

The next day, 3 October, *El Ahram*, Egypt's leading newspaper, mentioned that the CinC was opening a list for officers who wished to go on the short pilgrimage to Mecca. It announced a meeting between General Ismail and the Rumanian Minister of Defence scheduled for 8 October. Finally, it referred to the move of the Israeli 7 Romani Armoured Brigade to the Golan, accusing them of provocative action. At HQ Southern Command a further report by the persistent intelligence subaltern was ignored. The Russians launched the first of a series of surveillance satellites to watch the Middle East. That same day Mrs Golda Meir returned from a visit to Europe which had been extended by an incident in Austria. There, on 29 September, Saiqa, a terrorist organisation discreetly handled by Syrian military intelligence[3] had held up a Jewish refugee train at the border and demanded the closure of the Jewish emigrant route from Russia through Austria. Chancellor Kireisky capitulated. Israeli public opinion was inflamed and Mrs Golda Meir left the Council of Europe at Strasburg for Vienna in an unsuccessful attempt to change the Chancellor's mind. Whether a coincidence or good timing the Saiqa raid diverted Israeli attention from the military build-up on her borders. There were other distractions. The Israelis were preparing for elections and the Americans were immersed in Watergate.

On 4 October Sadat informed the Russian Ambassador. This was a calculated risk. Unless the Russians were told in advance they might be offended and act unpredictably, even informing the Americans in the interests of detente. Moscow gave the Arabs tacit support but insisted on sailing its shipping from Egyptian and Syrian harbours and withdrawing its civilian advisers and their families. The arrival and departure of half a dozen Tupolevs at Cairo and Damascus during the night and the sudden departure of Soviet vessels was noted by Israeli Naval Intelligence, who warned the CGS that war was imminent. Mossad came to the same conclusion but Military Intelligence banked on detente. If the Arabs were bent on war they reasoned that the Russians would have warned the Americans, who would have told the Israelis.

On 5 October Major General Magen arrived in Sinai to take over the Armoured Division from Major General Mandler on routine relief but, because air reconnaissance reported the arrival of 56 batteries opposite the Canal, amongst other warlike preparations, the two generals decided to postpone the handover.

[3] Saiqa (Thunderbolt), the military arm of the Vanguards of the Popular Liberation War, a fedayeen organisation formed by the Syrian Ba'th regime in 1968 to promote a Palestinian state as part of a united Arab entity under Syrian leadership.

General Ismail crossing the Suez Canal on a pontoon bridge.

Requests for reinforcements and permission to implement Operation 'Shovach Yonim' were refused because they might be construed as provocative. The Syrians also moved their guns forward in the night but military intelligence missed the significance of this. Major General Zeira's estimate of the threat was 'the lowest of the low'. Nevertheless, the CGS put the Active Army on the highest state of alert.

The Egyptians Attack

Early on the morning of 6 October Israeli Military Intelligence got hold of the 'Badr' plan but with the original H hour of 1800. At 0430 the General Staff met. Preliminary arrangements were made to prepare for mobilisation, alert the Civil Defence and evacuate the exposed settlements on the Golan. Preparations were also made to launch a pre-emptive air strike against the Syrian airfields and SAM sites.

By 0715 the GOCs of Northern and Southern Commands had been called in to GHQ at Tel Aviv. General Elazar, the CGS, told them to be ready for war at sunset and to be prepared to launch a major counter-attack in two days' time.

The Inner Cabinet met at 0800. The CGS proposed full mobilisation. Moshe Dayan opposed it, suggesting only two divisions. The Cabinet compromised on 100,000 men and at 1000 the CGS, on his own initiative, sent out orders to mobilise many more. As there would be no time to complete the mobilisation and assembly of brigades and divisions Tal, the Deputy CGS, ordered that companies should be despatched to the front as soon as they were ready. Mrs Golda Meir vetoed the proposed pre-emptive strike against Syria. She had been warned through the American Ambassador that United States diplomatic and material support were contingent on Israel being unequivocally the victim of aggression.

Egyptian troops in a captured OP of the Bar-Lev Line.

At 1330, half an hour before the crossing, Cairo Radio interrupted its programme with a false news flash about an Israeli raid on Zafarani on the Red Sea coast. A complaint was lodged with the Security Council at H Hour and half an hour later Radio Cairo released another news flash announcing that Egyptian troops were crossing the Canal as a reprisal. Israel had been surprised.

The Egyptians Secure the Crossing

The assault elements of five Egyptian infantry divisions faced a depleted Israeli reserve infantry brigade garrisoning the bank posts on the Canal backed by only one armoured brigade. The other two armoured brigades of the Sinai Division were well to the east, hours from the battle. The Egyptian assault waves started crossing the Canal soon after 1400, indirectly supported by numerous helicopter borne commando raids on choke points and radar sites. By last light, 1930, the Egyptians had 80,000 men on the east bank for the loss of 208 killed.

Although the other two Israeli armoured brigades arrived late that afternoon and evening they were unable to do more than delay the Egyptian build-up. All Israeli attempts to drive in the Egyptian bridgeheads with local counter-attacks failed against the Egyptian tanks and anti-tank missiles ranged on the Canal ramps and the hand-held anti-tank weapons of their infantry. The SAM system protected the bridgeheads from air attack to provide the assault forces with maximum security. That night the Egyptians bridged the Canal in numerous places so that they could move the follow-up echelons of their assault divisions across to the east bank. Most of the bank posts were evacuated in the course

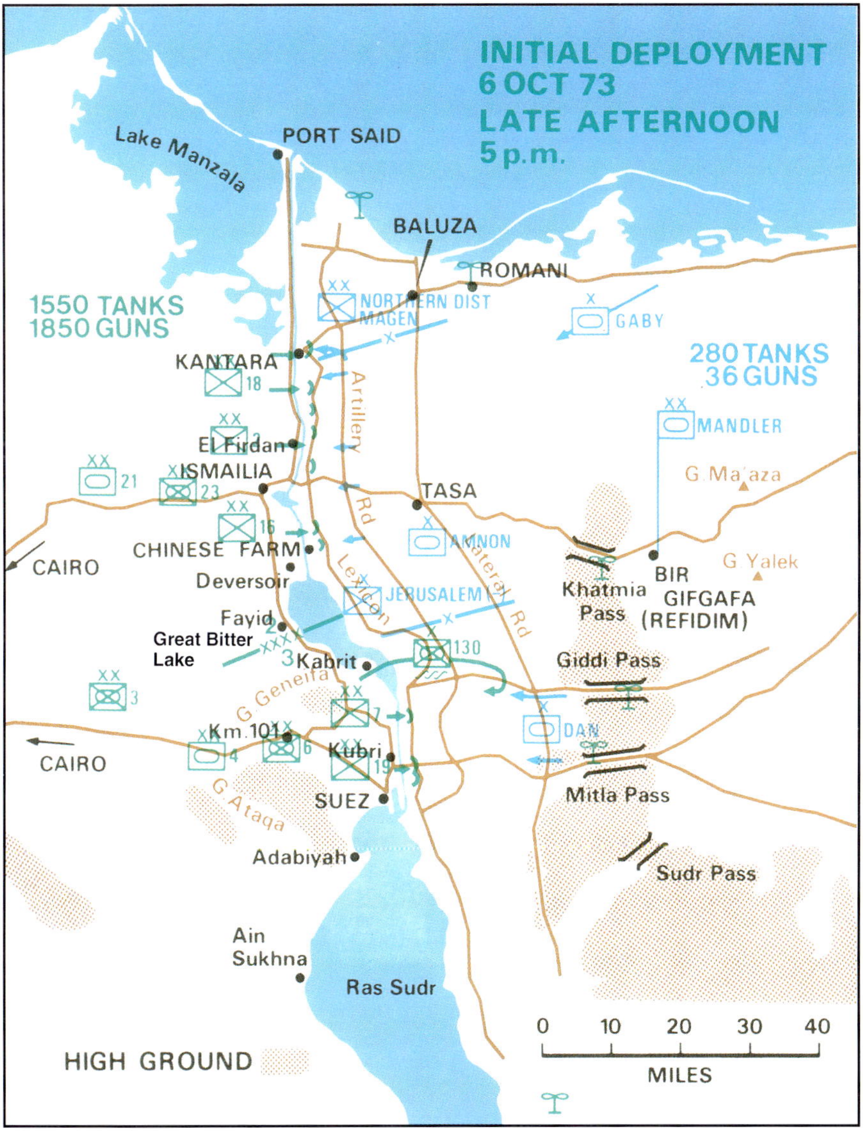

Suez Canal Front 6 October 1973

of the next 24 hours. The information reaching HQ Southern Command was one of crossings and pressure everywhere with no indication of any main thrust lines. The Sinai Armoured Division was hard pressed and had sustained heavy casualties.

The only sizeable losses suffered by the Egyptians were the consequences of operating outside the security of their anti-tank missile and SAM umbrella. Many of the helicopters carrying commandos to block the Khatmia, Giddi and Mitia Passes through the Western Hills were shot down by the IAF. Nevertheless, enough arrived to cause the Israelis a considerable amount of trouble before sufficient infantry could be mobilised and sent up to deal with them. 130 Marine Amphibious Brigade swam across the Great Bitter Lake in an effort to link up with the commandos and cause a diversion. The Brigade's PT 76 tanks and amphibians ran into one of the Sinai Division's armoured brigades on its way up to take over the southern sector, and were destroyed. In the evening the third Israeli brigade arrived to take over the northern sector, allowing the original brigade to concentrate in the centre.

On the morning of Sunday, 7 October the Egyptians started to pass the armoured brigades attached to their infantry divisions across the Canal. The Israeli Air Force did its utmost to interfere with the crossing but the Egyptians either repaired the pontoon bridges or moved them elsewhere. By first light the Israeli Sinai Division had been reduced from 280 tanks to 90 runners and losses continued to mount during the day. However, the sacrifice had not been entirely in vain. By evening the Egyptians had only 450 of the planned 1,100 tanks across the Canal and they had failed to secure the ridge protecting the Artillery Road.

Summary

With a realistic appreciation of their inability to conduct mobile operations outside their SAM umbrella the Egyptians had opted to seize a limited bridgehead which they could hold against any anticipated counter-attack. A combination of tanks and Saggers firing from the Canal ramps could protect an infantry force along the east bank supported by short range anti-tank weapons, tanks and artillery. The two armoured divisions on the west bank would be able to counter-attack any crossing without serious interference from the Israeli Air Force. The Egyptian plan and dispositions provided a very high degree of balance and security. The Egyptian defence succeeded in beating off a major counter-attack on 8 October and minor ones the day before and the day after. Only when the Egyptians left the security of their SAM and Sagger defences on the 14th did they give the Israelis the opportunity to inflict a crushing defeat and open the way for a major counter-attack across the Canal.

From the point of view of security of information and deception the Egyptians had pulled off a classic of surprise which will rank with the two German attacks through the Ardennes in 1940 and 1944. Seldom has the secret of an operation been so well kept and a defender so completely hoaxed.

Bibliography

Adan, Avraham (Bren), *On The Banks of the Suez*, Arms and Armour Press, 1980.

Carver, Field Marshal Lord, *The Apostles of Mobility*, Weidenfeld and Nicolson, 1979.

Creveld, Martin van, *Command in War*, Harvard University Press, Cambridge, Mass, 1985.

Dan, Uri, *Sharon's Bridgehead*, Special Edition, Tel Aviv, 1975.

Dayan, Moshe, *The Story of My Life*, Weidenfeld and Nicolson, 1976.

Heikal, Mohamed, *The Road to Ramadan*, Coffins, 1975.

Heikal, Mohamed, *Sphinx and Commissar*, Coffins, 1978.

Herzog, Major General Chaim, *The Arab-Israeli Wars*, Arms and Armour Press, 1982.

Hogg, Ian V, *Israeli War Machine*, Hamlyn, 1983.

Insight Team, Sunday Times, *The Yom Kippur War*, André Deutsch, 1975.

Luttwak, Edward and Dan Horowitz, *The Israeli Army*, Harper and Row, New York, 1975.

Messenger, Charles, *The Art of Blitzkrieg*, Ian Allan, 1976.

Osman, Hassan and Major General Hassan al Badry, *October War*, GEBO, Cairo, 1977.

Pimlott, John, editor, *The Middle East Conflicts from 1945 to the Present*, Orbis, 1983.

Pry, Peter, *Israel's Nuclear Arsenal*, Croom Helm, 1984.

Rafael, Gideon, *Destination Peace. Three Decades of Israeli Foreign Policy*, Weidenfeld and Nicolson, 1981.

Sadat, Anwar el, *In Search of Identity, An Autobiography*, Harper and Row, New York, 1977.

Sellers, Colonel J A, *The War of Yom Kippur*, RN Staff College, Greenwick (Principles of War Series), 1983.

Shazli, General Saadal, *The Crossing of the Suez, The October War (1973)*, Third World Centre for Research and Publishing, 1980.

APPENDIX 8 FLEXIBILITY

CROSSING THE MEGHNA, 1971

The crossing of the River Meghna by 57 Mountain Division of the Indian Army during the campaign to liberate East Pakistan in 1971 provides an excellent example of flexibility in furtherance of the aim.

The complex of waterways forming the Ganges delta dominated operations. Dacca, the capital, lies in the middle protected on three sides by major rivers several miles broad, the Ganges to the south, the Jamuna to the west and the Meghna to the east. The easiest approach is from the north where the only major obstacle is the smaller Old Brahmaputra which completes the circle of water around the capital. Although there were fewer water obstacles in the north the lack of communications through the Shillong Hills on the Indian side of the border made a major effort from that direction difficult. The approaches from the west on either side of the Ganges were blocked by numerous waterways apart from the main rivers. The Calcutta approach was considered to be the most obvious. Only two railway bridges crossed the major rivers, the Hardinge Bridge over the Ganges in the west and the former King George V Bridge over the Meghna at Bhairab Bazar in the east. Only the latter could be used for an advance on Dacca and, even if captured intact, it would have to be decked for motor vehicles.

The Pakistani forces in the east consisted of five understrength infantry divisions organised primarily for counter insurgency against the Bengali Mukti Bahini resistance movement. Nevertheless, their defensive potential in such difficult country was considerable. However, the Pakistani Government's insistence on holding forward on the frontier with India in an attempt to prevent the Mukti Bahini from forming lodgements, which could be exploited politically as Bengali liberated areas, led to a lack of flexibility in the defence of the Province. Insufficient troops were available to garrison the towns, which had been designated as fortresses, let alone to provide a mobile reserve for counter-attack or to secure the area round Dacca behind the main rivers as a central keep. Further inflexibility was built into the Pakistani repair and replacement organisation by the diversity of equipment. The resident formation, 36 Pakistan Infantry Division, had British equipment whereas the reinforcing divisions had Chinese.

The five Pakistani divisions were deployed one to each sector in the south-west, north-west and centre and two in the east. In the east, 14 Pakistan Infantry Division held the northern half of the sector between Sylhet and Akhaura while to the south, 39 Pakistan Infantry Division held the river ports of Daudkandi and Chandpur, and East Pakistan's main seaport of Chittagong.

The Indians deployed the equivalent of seven divisions organised in three corps and a communication zone around the borders of East Pakistan. While 2 and 33 Corps were to overrun the two western sectors and close up to the Jamuna and the Ganges, the main effort was to be made by the three divisions of 4 Corps in the east. This was the direction from which the Pakistanis would least expect it because of its remoteness from the main base at Calcutta and the subsidiary bases along the Brahmaputra in Assam facing the Chinese in the Himalayas. It took four months to build up sufficient stocks. In the north, 101 Communication Zone, designed to support the Himalayan front, was given two brigades for an advance between the Jamuna and the Meghna.

The campaign against East Pakistan was commanded by Lieutenant General Jagjit Singh Aurora from HQ Eastern Command in Calcutta. He aimed to destroy the coherence of the Pakistani defence. His plan called for a simultaneous advance in all sectors to pin down all the Pakistani divisions, including any local reserves, break through their crust defence on selected narrow frontages, and disrupt their communications and control organisation. It called for flexible infiltration tactics to bypass the main centres of resistance, particularly the fortress towns, and the use of local resources to supplement the engineers' limited bridging to cross the rivers. The Mukti Bahini could be relied on to provide boats, porters, guides and intelligence. The aim was to close up to the main rivers, the Ganges, the Jamuna and the Meghna, and to exploit any opportunities for using the ferry sites to cross into the central Dacca sector. Because there were fewer water obstacles north of Dacca it was expected that the relatively weak force under 101 Communication Zone would occupy the capital if the other corps succeeded in tying down the bulk of the Pakistani forces. Should the northern thrust be held up it was considered that 4 Corps would have the best chance of crossing the Meghna into the Dacca sector using the bridge at Bhairab Bazar or the ferry sites at Daudkandi and Chandpur.

In 4 Corps' sector each of its three divisions was to hold the Pakistanis to their immediate front and attack south-westwards to get behind their opponents. The aim was to cut their escape routes to Dacca and capture the main river ports and the seaport of Chittagong. In the north 8 Indian Mountain Division was to capture Sylhet and then release a brigade to reinforce 57 Indian Mountain Division in the centre, which was to make the main effort. 57 Mountain Division was to seize the road and rail bridges over the Titas near Akhaura, contain 27 Pakistan Infantry Brigade in the Brahmanbaria area and move south-west to capture the ferry port at Daudkandi with a view to crossing the Meghna and threatening Dacca. One of its brigades (61 Mountain Brigade) was despatched to the south to protect the Division's left flank and to help its neighbour, 23 Indian Mountain Division, capture Maynamati and guard its flank as it advanced on Chandpur.

The commander of 57 Division, Major General Gonsalves, was an exceptional man. An ex-air OP pilot and parachutist, he had recently conducted a successful counter insurgency operation on the North-East Frontier. After the detachment of the brigade on flank protection he was left with two mountain brigades and

Lieutenant General Aurora, Eastern Command.

S Force, a Mukti Bahini brigade. While S Force threatened Akhaura from the north his other two brigades (73 and 311 Mountain Brigades) approached from the south, avoiding the obvious route up the main road from Agartala, crossed the Titas behind the Pakistanis and entered Akhaura on 5 December. The final attack was postponed three times owing to the difficulty of arranging air support because HQ Eastern Command and HQ Eastern Air Force[1] were not

[1] While HQ Eastern Command controlled ground operations from its peacetime location at Calcutta, HQ Eastern Air Force remained at Shillong, convenient for the counter-insurgency campaigns on the north-east border and for defending the frontier with China. The time, effort and expense involved in re-siting the line and radio communications was not considered worthwhile for a short campaign in which the air threat was minimal. Although the Indian Air Force established an air commodore with a small staff at HQ Eastern Command, misunderstandings arose because Air HQ at New Delhi allocated much of the air effort without consulting Calcutta and Shillong. The two Services took the lesson to heart after the war.

Lieutenant General Singh, 4 Corps.

collocated. With commendable flexibility Gonsalves changed his plans and took the town in a night attack. The road bridge had been blown and the rail bridge was not decked for wheeled traffic. Vehicles were ferried across the river and the railway on the far side was used as a road after one of the tracks had been removed.

The Pakistanis abandoned Brahmanbaria in order to make sure of reaching Ashuganj on the eastern side of the Bhairab Bazar bridge over the Meghna before the Indians. With the collapse of the Pakistani position in the Titas bend and with operations further to the south going well, Gonsalves obtained Commander 4 Corps' agreement to abandon the advance on Daudkandi in favour of bouncing a crossing of the Meghna at Ashuganj. However, Pakistani demolitions prevented the Indians from bringing up their artillery and an

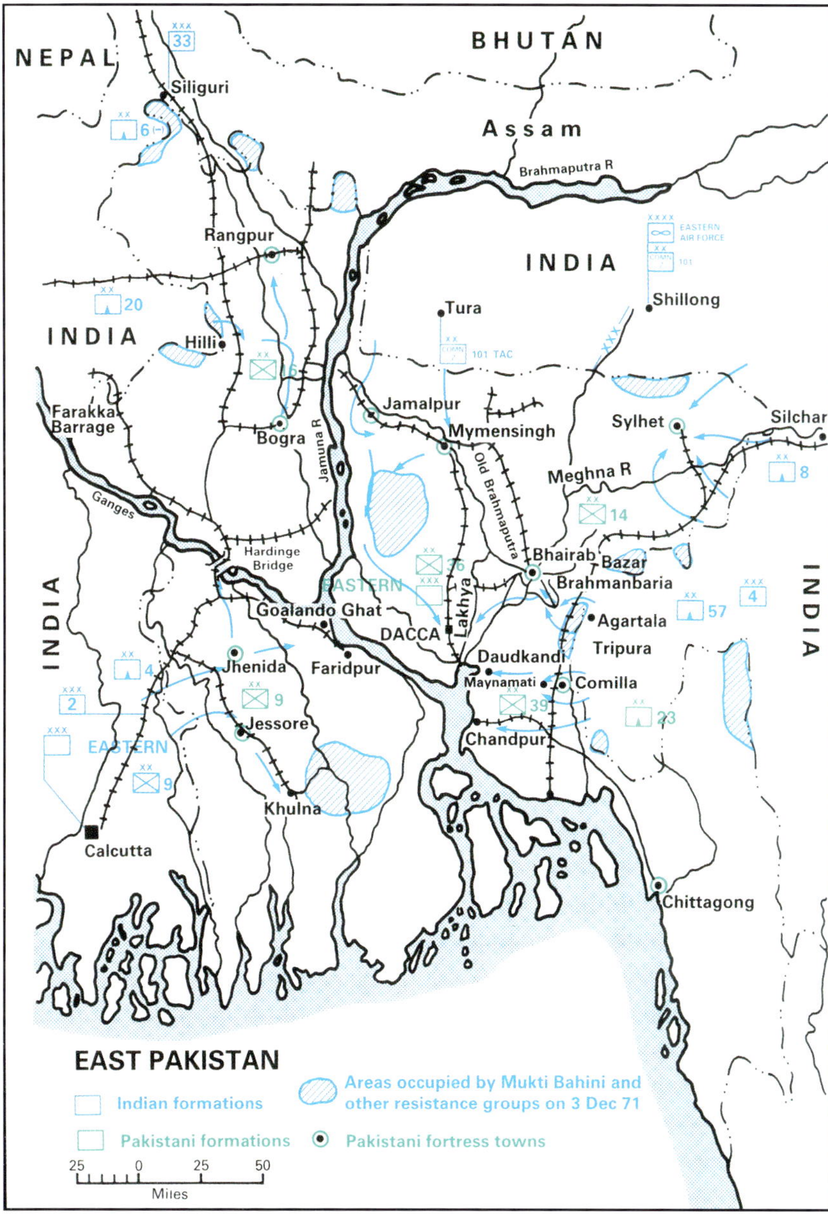

Deployment on 3 December 1971

Major General Gonsalves, 57 Mountain Division.

unsupported attack on Ashuganj on 9 December failed. 27 Pakistan Infantry Brigade fell back behind the Meghna that night, blowing the Bhairab Bazar bridge behind it.

Thwarted at Bhairab Bazar the Corps Commander, Lieutenant General Sagat Singh, decided to improvise a crossing of the Meghna at a point where there was no opposition. Reconnoitring the far bank from the air, he decided to land a force by helicopter at Raipura, 9 miles downstream, with the object of seizing the minor river port of Narsingdi a further 12 miles to the south-west. The proposed landing zone was unoccupied, out of range of Pakistani artillery in the Bhairab Bazar area and secure because there was no road along the west bank of the Meghna down which the Pakistanis could launch a counter-attack. Sagat Singh gave out his orders at noon. To provide the lift all the 14 Mi 4 Hound

Indian Engineers improvised crossings over water obstacles with local boats and bridging material.

helicopters still available to 4 Corps were allotted to 57 Division. By 1530 hours the first wave of helicopters was taking off from Brahmanbaria sports stadium under the direction of the Corps Air Liaison Officer.

Gonsalves' plan was to use 311 Mountain Brigade, reinforced by S Force, to seize the airhead at Raipura and 73 Mountain Brigade to seal off 27 Pakistan Infantry Brigade at Bhairab Bazar. One of 73 Brigade's battalions was transferred to 311 Brigade to strengthen the bridgehead. The first battalion to be airlanded secured the landing zone before sunset and the airlift went on till moonset. Next morning the leading battalion of 311 Brigade advanced down the railway to seize the jetty at Narsingdi against light opposition. A new landing zone was established at the river port and the next battalion to arrive seized the road and rail bridges over the Old Brahmaputra west of the town. The build-up was pressed with the utmost energy by helicopter and country boat, using the small river ports, Charlalpur and Gokarna on the Meghna and Titas. The headquarters of a heavy mortar regiment was used to organize the water movement. Engineers freed motor launches trapped by a broken bridge in a stretch of the Titas to tow rafts carrying heavy equipment.

The river voyage was 30 miles to Narsingdi. The first infantry battalion to go by water did not arrive until late in the evening of the 10th and the heavy equipment not until the 13th. Meanwhile, the first mountain artillery regiment was flown in by helicopter on the 12th. The Mukti Bahini pressed every form of transport into service to help the Indians and provided thousands of porters. The Divisional Commander's rover was a motorised rickshaw and the Divisional Fire Direction Centre was mounted on a trailer pulled by a tractor. Buses, lorries, cars and trishaws were commandeered to move troops, stores and radios. A squadron of amphibious PT 76 tanks arrived on the 14th after an eleven hour swim.

The previous day the leading troops of the Division reached the Lakhya, the last water obstacle in front of Dacca. The speed with which the Division crossed the Meghna posed a serious problem for the Pakistani Eastern Command. To block the Lakhya crossings the last reserves of 36 Pakistan Infantry Division, mostly logistic troops, were committed. This eased the pressure facing Major General Nagra's scratch division advancing from 101 Communication Zone in the north and allowed his troops to enter Dacca on the 16th.

Flexibility was a major factor in the Indian success. The defeat of 27 Pakistan Infantry Brigade at Akhaura offered a fleeting opportunity to capture the Bhairab Bazar bridge intact. When this failed the Corps Commander's decision to cross the river away from enemy interference at Raipura demonstrated flexibility of mind and enterprise. All the remaining helicopters in the Corps area were concentrated for the purpose and special arrangements were made to co-ordinate the river crossing. Ingenuity and improvisation were employed in collecting and organising river and road transport. 57 Mountain Division's original mission had been to capture the river port of Daudkandi with the aim of menacing Dacca. When a better solution offered the method was changed but without altering the main aim.

Bibliography

Aurora, Lieutenant General Jagjit Singh, *The Fall of Dacca*, Illustrated Weekly of India, New Delhi, 1973.

Bacon, Wing Commander G McA and Lieutenant Colonel J A Sellers, *Notes on the Indo-Pakistan War, 1971*, NDC, 1973 (Confidential).

Jackson, Robert, *South Asian Crisis, India-Pakistan-Bangladesh*, Chatto and Windus, 1975.

Lachman Singh, Major General, *Victory in Bangladesh,* Natraj, Dehra Dun, 1981.

Mankekar, D R, *Pakistan Cut to Size*, Indian Book Company, New Delhi, 1972.

Muqeern Khan, Fazal, *Pakistan's Crisis in Leadership*, National Book Foundation, Islamabad, 1973.

Palit, Major General D K, *The Lightning Campaign*, Compton Press, Faridabad and Salisbury, 1972.

APPENDIX 9

CO-OPERATION
THE RELIEF OF MALTA, AUGUST 1942

The Influence of Logistics

The strategic location of Malta in the Mediterranean provides a useful illustration of the principle of co-operation both at tactical and operational levels within the Army and at the strategic level between the three Services.

A major factor in the North African campaign was the influence of logistics. When Italy entered the war in June 1940 the direct route to Egypt through the Mediterranean was at first severely restricted by the Italian Air Force and Navy and then virtually closed with the arrival of the Luftwaffe in Sicily and southern Italy in January 1941. The capture of Crete by an airborne invasion in May gave the Luftwaffe a base from which to control much of the eastern Mediterranean, attack the British base in Egypt, mine the Suez Canal and attack shipping in the Red Sea. Although occasional convoys could be fought through the Mediterranean with heavy naval escorts the British supply route to the Middle East was lengthened from 4,000 to 14,000 miles or, in sailing time, from two or three weeks to two or three months as convoys were obliged to use the Cape route. In contrast, Axis shipping could use the short routes across the Mediterranean from the southern Italian ports to Tripoli, a mere 500 miles. When Axis forces controlled Cyrenaica merchant ships could dock at Benghazi and destroyers run urgent supplies through to Tobruk. Consequently, the Axis were able to reinforce and supply their forces in North Africa more quickly than the British.

The Importance of Malta and Tri-Service Co-operation

The fortunes of the campaign in the Western Desert largely turned on our ability to sustain Malta as an offensive base athwart the Axis communications in the teeth of Axis air and sea power. The controlling factor was air power. With the limited range of contemporary fighters it was only possible to provide air cover for westbound convoys from Egypt to Malta in the central Mediterranean from Cyrenaica. The seizure of the Cyrenaican airfields by 8th Army was of cardinal importance.

The situation in November 1941 was favourable. Following the victory at Sidi Rezegh, Cyrenaica had been reoccupied, Malta was resupplied and could be used once more as a base for aircraft, submarines and Force K, a cruiser and destroyer squadron, to attack Axis shipping. In that month 62% of Axis traffic to North Africa was sunk. In the eastern Mediterranean, half a dozen reconnaissance and long-range fighter squadrons were formed into a specialist 201 Group, RAF, to co-operate with the Navy.

Rear Admiral Vian (left).

The Eclipse of Malta

Unfortunately, a series of events rapidly changed the situation for the worse at the turn of the year. Giving priority to the Mediterranean, Hitler ordered nine U-boats to the theatre. The first victims were *Ark Royal* in the western basin and *Barham* off Sollum. *Queen Elizabeth* and *Valiant* were severely damaged by Italian human torpedoes in Alexandria harbour. With the Japanese entry into the war and the sinking of *Prince of Wales* and *Repulse* off Malaya no naval reinforcements could be spared for the theatre, and for the first time in the war there was no carrier with the Mediterranean Fleet based on Alexandria.

The unexpected success of Rommel's spoiling attack at El Agheila on 21 January encouraged him to exploit eastwards into Cyrenaica, reaching Gazala at the end of the first week of February. The Axis regained Benghazi as a forward supply port and the British lost the western group of airfields in Cyrenaica. Lastly, in Directive 38, issued on 2 December 1941, Hitler ordered Fliegerkorps 11 with its 335 aircraft from Russia to the Mediterranean to join Fliegerkorps X under Luftflotte 2, the latter commanded by Field Marshal Kesselring. Fliegerkorps 11 took over Sicily and North Africa to operate in the central basin allowing Fliegerkorps X to concentrate in Greece, Crete and the Dodecanese for operations in the eastern basin. The Directive appointed Kesselring Commander-in-Chief South and gave him the following tasks:

> To secure mastery of the air and sea in the area between Southern Italy and North Africa in order to secure communications with Libya and Cyrenaica and, in particular, to keep Malta in subjection.
>
> To co-operate with German and allied forces engaged in North Africa.
>
> To paralyse enemy traffic through the Mediterranean and British supplies to Tobruk and Malta.

Discussing Operation 'HERCULES' at Berchtesgaden. From left to right: Kesselring, Hitler, Mussolini and Keitel.

So began Malta's ten month ordeal to which she nearly succumbed. Had the Directive been carried through with single-minded vigour to its logical conclusion the victory at El Alamein might not have been possible.

In mid-January 1942 a convoy of five ships out of six reached Malta from Alexandria, supported by Admiral Vian's light cruisers[1] and fighters based in Cyrenaica. But the suppression of Malta by Fliegerkorps 11 and the neutralisation of the Mediterranean Fleet allowed the Italian Navy to escort two large convoys to Libya with 66,000 tons of supplies, including 54 tanks. 201 Group, using Cyrenaica just before the withdrawal, only managed to torpedo one ship.

In January, 669 tons of bombs fell on Malta, damaging all three airfields, reducing the fighter defence to 28 serviceable Hurricanes and sinking a destroyer in harbour. In February the bomb tonnage increased to 1,020, a convoy from Alexandria was turned back after two thirds of its merchantmen had been sunk and the fighter force was reduced to 11 aircraft.

Changes in Axis Strategy

The Commando Supremo in Rome, backed by Kesselring and Grand Admiral Raeder, proposed operation HERCULES, the capture of Malta by a combined air and seaborne assault. Hitler and OKW were of the opinion that the air and land

[1] 15th Cruiser Squadron.

Admiral Harwood, CinC Mediterranean Fleet, from April 1942.

forces required were better employed in Russia or in North Africa. They also remembered the cost of the capture of Crete, 6,000 casualties and 360 aircraft lost or damaged. Temporarily, Operation HERCULES was shelved. In the meanwhile, an all-out assault on the island by the Luftwaffe was planned for 20 March. Three weeks' bombardment were considered sufficient to reduce the island's offensive capacity after which a lower scale of effort would keep it neutralised. 2,000 tons of bombs fell on Malta in March and all the merchantmen of a convoy from Alexandria were sunk by air attack. Axis convoys reached Libya with regularity, only 21 ships being lost to air and submarine attack in the first three months of 1942. Malta had been neutralised.

Air Marshal Tedder, AOCinC Middle East Air Forces, 1942.

In April the bomb tonnage rose to 6,700, the dockyard was wrecked and the surviving submarines were withdrawn after four had been sunk in harbour. The fighter strength was reduced to six and only one Italian ship was sunk by one of the four remaining torpedo-bombers. On 20 April the US carrier *Wasp* flew in 47 fighters from the west but within three days the serviceable strength had been reduced again to six.

The reduction of Fliegerkorps 11 activity from the end of the month eased the situation. A further 81 fighters flown in from aircraft carriers enabled Malta's air defences to regain a measure of local air superiority.

The bomb tonnage dropped in May fell to 520. Even so, the Luftwaffe still controlled the air over the central and much of the eastern basins and an attempt to intercept an Italian convoy bound for Benghazi on the 11th was defeated with the loss of three British destroyers to dive bombers.

The subsequent withdrawal of Fliegerkorps 11 was the consequence of a reappraisal of Axis strategy. The subjugation of Malta had become of less immediate concern than the Russian and North African theatres. On the one hand it was necessary to nominate squadrons for a possible reinforcement of the Eastern Front. On the other was the need to beat 8th Army in Cyrenaica before it became too strong, in order to open the port of Tobruk and shorten the land section of the supply route. At a meeting between Hitler and Mussolini at the end of April the dictators agreed that Rommel's offensive, due to start on 26 May, should have priority and that Operation HERCULES should be put off until 10 July. As a guard against Rommel's tendency to short-sighted optimism his offensive was to stop at the Egyptian frontier and was to be concluded by 20 June.

Thereafter, preparations for HERCULES were to take priority. Three Italian parachute battalions and a German parachute division were earmarked for the initial assault. They were to be followed by some German armour and Italian infantry in German landing craft. In all, 35,000 men were to be involved. Once the Libyan supply line was secured Rommel would be authorised to advance on the Nile Delta.

Strategic Complications

On the British side Churchill was pressing Auchinleck to anticipate Rommel's offensive and reoccupy western Cyrenaica to make use of its airfields. Sir Stafford Cripps and the VCIGS, who flew out to Egypt to bring pressure to bear on Auchinleck, reluctantly agreed that mid May was the earliest date.

A month before, Admiral Nagurno's incursion into the Indian Ocean threatened not only the British position in the Far East but the Cape route to Egypt. RAF reinforcements were hurriedly despatched from the Middle East, forcing the postponement of Auchinleck's offensive until mid-June when it would coincide with an attempt to fight a convoy through to Malta.

Operational Opportunities and Logistic Constraints

Although the Axis sea communications to Libya were now virtually unmolested Rommel still faced serious logistic problems. Axis shipping losses before Malta was suppressed had left a shortage of vessels suitable for transporting tanks, vehicles and fuel. Because the capacity of Benghazi was restricted by damage and bad port organisation, Tripoli was still the major sea terminal. Rommel had to rely on the coastal road but there was a chronic shortage of trucks for the 940 mile haul. In May the Germans reorganised Benghazi and took over Derna, only 70 miles behind the front, quadrupling the latter's capacity to 11,000 tons

Enemy Attack on HMS Illustrious in Grand Harbour, Valetta.

The tanker Ohio, *escorted into Grand Harbour, Valetta.*

a month in June. By the end of May sufficient fuel, ammunition and rations had been accumulated for a limited offensive to capture Tobruk. On the 26th Rommel attacked at Gazala. After a three week battle Ritchie's 8th Army withdrew and Tobruk fell on 21 June, yielding some fuel ., large quantities of British and German ammunition, 5,000 tons of rations and 2,000 serviceable trucks, the latter a valuable windfall.

Seizing the fleeting opportunity, Rommel bypassed the Commando Supremo in Rome, appealing direct to OKW to prevail upon the Italians to authorise an advance to the Delta. Hitler persuaded Mussolini against his better judgement and Operation HERCULES was put off again until September. So Rommel's success and Ritchie's failures at Gazala and Tobruk saved Malta from an assault it was no longer in a position to resist, with immeasurable benefits to the Allies.

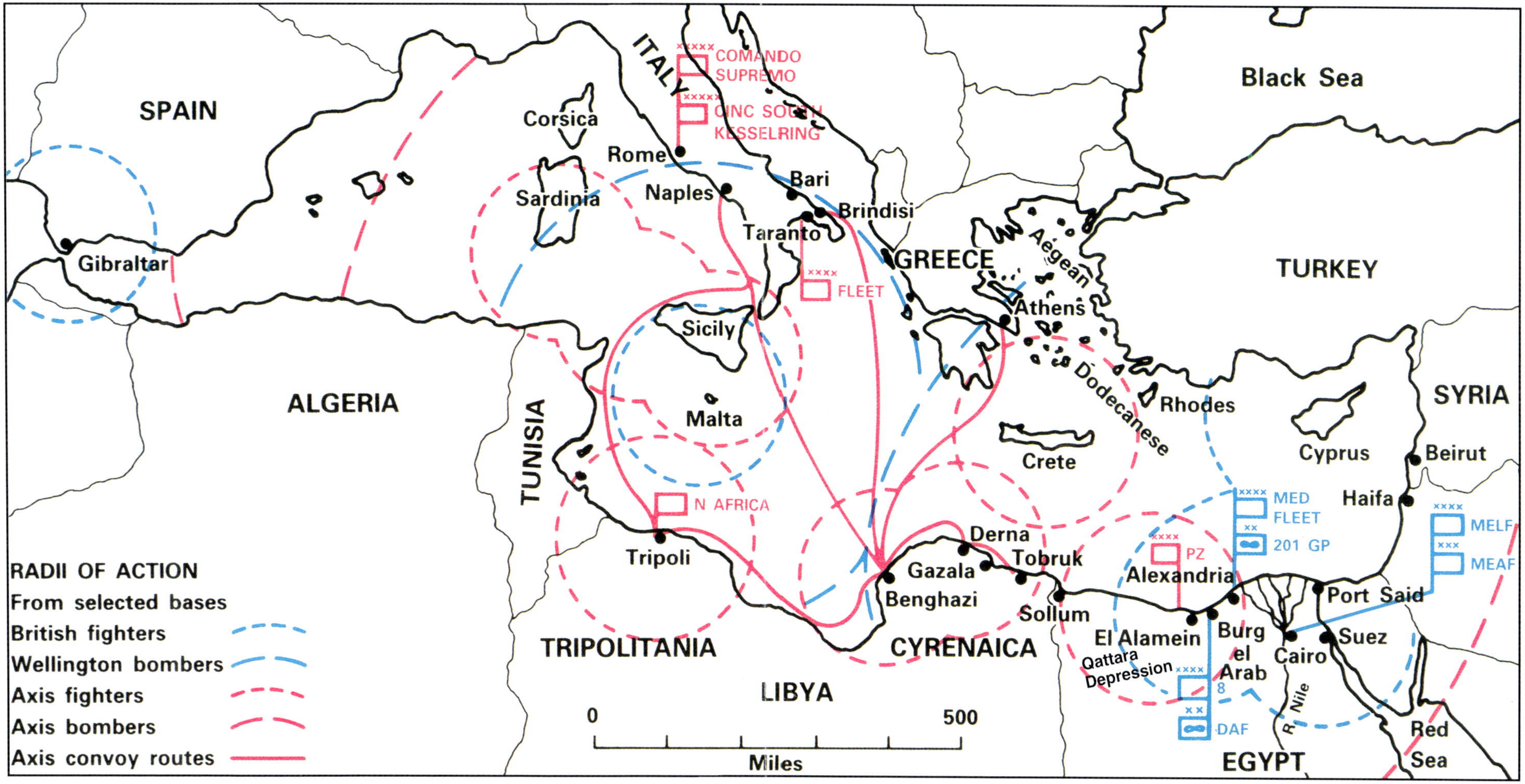

The Mediterranean July – October 1942

On 23 June Rommel advanced across the frontier into Egypt. The Mediterranean Fleet was dispersed from Alexandria to Port Said, Haifa, Beirut and Suez, the RAF was forced back on to the Canal Zone air bases and Malta was further isolated. Auchinleck took over the command of 8th Army and in a series of skilful mobile operations fought Rommel to a standstill at El Alamein in the first three weeks of July. Meanwhile, an attempt to fight two convoys through to Malta from Gibraltar and Alexandria in the teeth of the Luftwaffe based in Cyrenaica and Crete, and the Italian surface fleet, was unsuccessful. Only two of the 17 merchant ships arrived. Malta had only enough fuel for its fighter aircraft and the torpedo-bombers had to be grounded.

Malta Recovers

Nevertheless, the strengthening of the Malta fighter defences caused the recall of part of Fliegerkorps 11 from North Africa to Sicily to renew the air offensive on the island. This time the defending Spitfires broke the attack and the only direct consequence of the withdrawal of the German aircraft was the surrender of Axis airpower over Egypt to the RAF. In future, Rommel would lack effective air support and his Panzerarmée would be subjected to constant air strikes. Although the 26,000 tons of supplies, including 12,000 tons of fuel and 1,370 vehicles, which reached Rommel in July were a record they only met his immediate needs. The price was seven merchant ships sunk as the air situation allowed our submarines to return to Malta and fuel could be spared for attacks on shipping. With the problem of supplying Rommel 1,420 miles east of Tripoli, Operation HERCULES was finally abandoned on 21 July. Some of the parachute troops allocated to HERCULES were sent as reinforcements to Rommel to help him hold the 40 mile line between the sea and the Qattara Depression; they also added to his supply difficulties.

By August Malta's supply position was once again critical. The PEDESTAL convoy was fought through from Gibraltar, opposed by 600 aircraft, 21 U-boats, 23 MTBs, six cruisers and 11 destroyers. Fortunately, the Italian battleships were immobilised for lack of fuel. Although only five of the fourteen merchant ships arrived, the island was stocked until December, but that proved sufficient. Naval and air forces based on Malta began to exact an increasing toll of Axis shipping.

The Strategic Pay-Off

The changes in Malta's fortunes had immediate impact on the operations in the Western Desert. Rommel's supply situation became more serious and well known to our own higher command through the ULTRA intercepts of the German strategic radio network. The first battles of El Alamein in July and Alam Halfa in August had run down his stocks. In August 34% of Axis shipping on the Libyan run was lost and the Panzerarmée's consumption was double its receipts. Of seven tankers urgently needed to provide fuel for the attack at Alam Halfa only three arrived. By night, cruisers and destroyers from the Mediterranean Fleet preyed on shipping making for Derna and Tobruk. In September, six ships were sunk and in October, the month El Alamein started, shipping losses rose to 40%. Even worse, only 4,000 tons of fuel out of the 10,000 despatched arrived. A tanker was sunk just before the battle opened and two more soon afterwards. Lack of fuel severely restricted the use Rommel could make of his armour. Malta had become such a menace to the Libyan supply route that Hitler ordered Kesselring to transfer aircraft back to Sicily from North Africa to suppress it. The attempt was unsuccessful. Malta's 100 Spitfires and 13 Beaufighters broke the German air offensive in nine days of sustained operations in September while its strike aircraft sank three more supply ships.

A month later the relative strengths and logistic conditions of the two armies were to reflect the influence of Malta and the other two Services' contributions. On one hand Rommel's Panzerarmée had eleven days fuel and 21 days fresh bread, but very little fresh vegetables and fruit. Undernourishment took its toll in casualties and lack of spares caused major equipment serviceability problems. The 8th Army on the other hand did not lack for fuel, ammunition, rations or spares. The Panzerarmée's exposure at the end of a long line of communications, 1,420 miles from its main base at Tripoli, together with the failure to capture or suppress the bases at Malta, were at the root of German Army difficulties.

Success in the Mediterranean had depended on all three Services. The use of air power to bomb ports and supply routes had worn down the Panzerarmée's logistic resources in North Africa, above all, the role of Malta in denying supplies and reinforcements of all kinds, particularly fuel and transport, had hamstrung the Axis forces. Of the many factors which contributed to 8th Army's subsequent victory in North Africa co-operation between all arms at every level and co-operation between the three fighting Services at the strategic, operational and tactical levels were amongst the most important.

Bibliography

Addington, Larry H, *The Blitzkrieg Era and the German General Staff*, Rutgers, New Brunswick, NJ, 1971.
Bekker, Cajus, *Hitler's Naval War*, Macdonald, 1974.
Brett-Smith, Richard, *Hitler's Generals*, Osprey, 1976.
Cooper, Matthew, *The German Air Force, 1933 1945*, Jane's, 1981.
Cooper, Matthew, *The German Army, 1933–1945*, Macdonald and Jane's, 1978.
Connell, John, *Auckinleck*, Cassell, 1959.
Cunningham, *Admiral of the Fleet, A Sailor's Odyssey*, Hutchinson, 1951.
Guedalla, Philip, *Middle East 1940–1942, A Study in Air Power*, Hodder and Stoughton, 1944.
Hinsley, F H, *Hitler's Strategy*, Cambridge, 1951.
Howard, Michael, *The Mediterranean. Strategy in the Second World War*, Weidenfeld and Nicolson, 1965.
Jacobsen, H A and Rohwer, J, *Decisive Battles of World War II. The German View*, Chronicles VI and VII, André Deutsch, 1965.
Kesselring, Field Marshal, *The Memoirs...*, William Kimber, 1953.
Kilen, John, *The Luftwaffe, A History*, Muller, 1967.

Macintyre, Donald, *The Battle for the Mediterranean*, Batsford, 1964.
Macintyre, Donald, *The Naval War Against Hitler*, Batsford, 1971.
Macksey, Kenneth, *Kesseffing*, Batsford, 1978.
Shulman, Milton, *Defeat in the West*, Secker and Warburg, 1947.
Smith, Peter, *Pedestal, The Malta Convoy of August 1942*, William Kimber, 1970.
Smith, P, and Walker, E, *The Battles of the Malta Striking Forces*, Ian Allan, 1974.
Stawson, John, *Hitler as Military Commander*, Batsford, 1971.
Trevor-Roper, H R, editor, *Hitler's War Directives 1939–1945*, Sidgwick and Jackson, 1964.
Warner, Oliver, *Cunningham of Hyndhope*, John Murray, 1967.

APPENDIX 10

SUSTAINABILITY

COMBAT SERVICE SUPPORT IN THE GULF WAR 1991

"Desert is heaven for tacticians and hell for admin staff."

ANON. *Note preserved in the El Alamein museum*

The Initial Deployment

It has often been said that logistics are neglected by commanders in peacetime but that in wartime they quickly become a predominant factor in planning and executing operations. This can never be truer than in desert fighting; stretched lines of communication, high rates of ammunition expenditure and rapid manoeuvre all compound the many problems faced by the logisticians.

By the time the first reconnaissance vehicles of the 1st (UK) Armoured Division crossed the line of departure early on the afternoon of 25 February 1991, some 35,000 troops had been flown into theatre on over 1,100 flights, 126 ships had delivered over 2,500 armoured vehicles, 46,000 tonnes of ammunition and thousands of tonnes of essential war fighting equipment. This had been achieved in four months from a standing start into a country many miles from home and lacking the infrastructure normally found in north-west Europe. It was, without doubt, a remarkable achievement and a useful example of the principle of administration in war.

The first task, in September 1990 when Operation GRANBY was being planned, was to form the main logistic headquarters that would be established in theatre. At that stage the logistic requirement was based on 7th Armoured Brigade Group fighting a 12 day battle at intense ammunition rates. The Brigade was planned to be under tactical control of the US Marines and operating approximately 200 km from the main logistic port at Al Jubayl.

The Headquarters staff of the Force Maintenance Area (FMA) formed up at HQ British Army of the Rhine on 7 October 1990 and the pre-advance party flew out to the Gulf on the following day. The FMA was established at Al Jubayl and commanded by Colonel (later Brigadier) White. Its mission was to maintain 7th Armoured Brigade Group, which included the FMA units.

Conditions for those arriving in early October were basic, with the HQ starting its work in a small, single storey administration building at Al Jubayl port. There were few telephones, no proper sleeping accommodation, no catering arrangements and the temperature was in the nineties.

The FMA Commander was responsible for receiving the UK forces into Saudi Arabia through the port of Jubail in the Eastern Province of Saudi Arabia and airports at Dhahran, Jubail and Riyadh, and for its support thereafter. The FMA was initially part of the 7 Armoured Brigade Group. With the deployment of 1 (UK) Armoured Division, the FMA Commander then reported directly to General Sir Peter de la Billière in Riyadh but supported the Division in its operations.

Support for 7th Armoured Brigade Group

To maintain 7th Armoured Brigade Group's stock levels of combat supplies (ammunition, fuel, rations and water) had been worked out on the basis of a defensive battle of 10 days at intense rates of consumption. These were planned, in conjunction with JHQ, for delivery to the Gulf, mainly from Germany by ship, of 30 days at normal rates (intense rates were approximately three times normal rates) with a reserve afloat of a further 12 days. Once deployed to the Gulf, the FMA would have to receive some 13,000 personnel, 5,000 vehicles, 14,000 tons of ammunition and 2,000 containers of materiel and unit stores. Offers of assistance from the United States Marine Corps (USIMC) on the recce were accepted and, as a prerequisite, it was also considered that Host Nation Support (HNS) would be essential from the Saudi Arabian authorities.

The US Marine Corps provided virtually every form of support until the FMA could be established properly in the port area of Jubail. This included all food and accommodation, and it would have been difficult to survive without their advice and guidance. Indeed, the initial links were fostered by a logistic LO who had been left in Saudi Arabia following the recce in September 1990. All he had was a secure phone and the most sketchy instructions.

The LO was joined in Jubail during September by 39 Engineer Regiment, elements of 518 Coy Royal Pioneer Corps (RPC), a local resources section, and postal and communications assets. They were the first British units on the ground and provided a focal point for subsequent operations.

Once the FMA had been established in the area of Jubail and its port, the immediate aim was to integrate the servicemen and women arriving by air with their equipment arriving by sea as soon as possible and to deploy them to the desert for training. The first ship arrived on 18 October and from then on ships and aircraft arrived daily. Much use was made of the huge hangars in Jubail port as temporary accommodation for the servicemen, supplemented by an Engineer constructed 2,000 man tented camp known as Baldrick Lines. The initial build-up went well, it was well balanced and provided, coincidentally, a model for the later deployment of the remainder of 1 (UK) Armoured Division, although this was not anticipated at the time. In those early days, it was planned to support defensive operations in the Eastern province or offensive operations through Khafli into Kuwait. The allies were confident that they could sustain this Line of Communication (LOC) by establishing a Forward FMA (FFMA), although the FMA commander was concerned that this would over extend the limited staff resources, state of training and the communications of his Headquarters. By 14 November, when 7 Armoured Brigade Group was declared operational the FMA had sufficient combat supplies and materiel in theatre to support the Brigade Group.

The tapline road.

Refuelling APC's from a tanker.

The PLOD (Pipeline Over the Desert).

To illustrate what can be done with the proper expertise, the Local Resources Section (LRS) (just six men, under an officer (later increased to 15 men)) provided the interface with local agencies for the provision of fuel, food, rental and vehicles. By the start of the land battle, it had made over 2,300 local purchase orders; in addition 40 contracts had been let for transport hire, laundry and cleaning etc at a cost of over £29 M. This illustrates not only how lucky the staff were to be able to tap into the rather substantial local infrastructure but how necessary this civil military interface is for such operations today.

Support for 1 (UK) Armoured Division

From the logistic point of view the decision to deploy 1 (UK) Armoured Division involved a huge increase in the overall size of the British force in Saudi Arabia. This, together with the resubordination of the UK ground forces from the US Marine Corps to the 7th Corps of the US Army, presented some enormous challenges and created a good deal of 'angst' at the time. One only has to examine the distances involved to gain an impression of the command, control and communications problems that faced the FMA, let alone the necessity to move stock out of Jubail, while conforming to a sophisticated deception plan. However, the FMA commander was an integral part of the decision making process and was consulted frequently by General de la Billière on the feasibility of moving logistic effort in this way

The arrival of the Division meant the reception of over 80 more ships, which strained the facilities in Jubail to the limit, but in harmony both with our Saudi hosts and with the US Marine Corps, who were also receiving their own reinforcements, this was achieved without undue burden. Newly arrived logistic units were put to work as soon as they could marry up servicemen and equipment. As the Division started training to the north of Jubail the shape of the future operation became clear and the FMA staff planned on setting up a Forward Force Maintenance Area (FFMA) 350 km northwest of Jubail at what was known by the Americans as Log Base Alpha. It was now that the Division became responsible for its own integral logistic support (first and second line) leaving HQ FMA/FFMA with a third line role. The Divisional Deputy Chief of Staff for Logistics remained the Division's logistic commander and adviser on all administrative and Combat Service Support (CSS) matters, whilst the Commander FMA retained that role for General de la Billière at the theatre level, an arrangement that worked well but one that had to be set in place early in the planning process.

Forward Deployment

Forward deployment of logistic stocks and units was based on a 21 day time frame and started on 3 January 1991. Major concerns were the limited capacity (number of vehicles and stock holding) of logistic units, the fact that stocks were still arriving at Jubail, the overriding operational security situation, the Nuclear, Biological and Chemical (NBC) threat and the distances and going involved. The main supply route (MSR) along the tapline road (Route DODGE) was about 700 km for the

On the move to the Assembly Area.

A Squadron Assembly Area.

round trip, the time for which varied between 24 and 36 hours, depending on the weather and the density of Allied deployment and logistic traffic. Ammunition stock levels in the FFMA were set at 15 days for artillery, 8 days for tank and infantry, that is 18,000 tons of ammunition, together with 7 million litres of fuel, 6,000 tons of materiel and, of course, rations and water. The logistics staff were constantly checking whether they had got the balance right for offensive operations. Use was made of the two FMA Transport regiments (10 and 27 Regiments (FICT) as well as the two Divisional Regiments (1 and 4 Regiments RCT); tank transporters (7 Regiment RCT) and as many local transporters as could be hired were heavily involved in deploying the Division forward. A fuel pipeline to a point some 100 km north-west of Jubail, designed and constructed by British and American Engineers, helped to shorten the resupply loop for fuel.

This Pipeline Over the Desert (PLOD) was designed and commissioned by British Royal Engineers (RE) of 516 Specialist Team RE. PLOD was commissioned on 26 February 1991 and named the 'Kingham Line' in recognition of the work by Major Kingham (the CC of the STRE) who, tragically, died in a road accident during the construction.

As the inload clock ticked away (towards the 21 day limit), servicemen and assets moved forward and on 17 January Brigadier White moved to command the logistic operations from HQ IFFMA, leaving his deputy, Lieutenant Colonel Bradley (later Colonel Welch), to run the FMA in Jubail. This task remained enormous, with stock continuing to arrive in theatre and elements such as Battle Casualty Replacements (BCRs) and the Prisoner of War Guard Force (PWGF) also arriving and deploying.

At this stage the Division had completed the first part of its training in Jubail and began to move along DODGE using every available tank transporter and as many host nation vehicles as possible. In this latter regard the British found themselves in competition with both the US Marine Corps and US Army.

The Division moved to its Forward Assembly Area (FAA) and the inload to a Divisional Maintenance Area (DMA) providing 10 days of all ammunition natures together with reserve fuel and materiel. Again there were concerns about the logistic balance at this point. In the meantime, the FFMA stock levels were being topped up from Jubail and the third line logistic support for the Division was in place.

The outline logistic concept was to resupply the Division from either the DMA or the FFMA depending on the progress of the battle and the location of Divisional CSS units. A system of Exchange Points (XPs) was, established where individual commodities could be transferred. We had practised this rather complicated operation with the Division and were reasonably content that it would work. The aim was to give the Division the maximum logistic mobility and flexibility possible for their advance. These XPs were simply patches of desert and transport units had to rely heavily on the satellite navigation system to find their location. Incidentally DROPS (Dismountable Rack Off Loading and Pick-Up System) vehicles were employed in this situation solely for the resupply of water and Multi-Launch Rocket System (MLRS) pods. There were no plans for the ground dumping of stocks during the preparatory phase or during the battle itself but, in fact, dumping of artillery ammunition was possible as a result of the subsequent low expenditure rates. This provided a welcome logistic bonus when the Division was projected east towards Kuwait.

At the start of the land battle there were some 5,000 medical servicemen in support of the Division and the FMA. There was a well-established and reasonably well-practised evacuation system, involving the three hospitals, support helicopters and C130 Hercules aircraft as well as co-ordination and mutual support from the US medical services and other Allies. Thankfully, the subsequent casualties were few, but the medical services were kept busy treating Iraqi prisoners, many of who had been left untreated on the battlefield for several days.

From 14–23 February, the Divisional Artillery Group (DAG) took part in the 7 (US) Corps programme of preparatory fire plans known as artillery raids. These had the aim of destroying high value targets, deceiving the Iraqis as to where the main attack would occur, assessing enemy action and allowing for training to continue up to the last moment as units were still deploying.

The Land Battle

The ground war was launched at 0400 hrs on 24 February. Things went well enough, except for bad weather that delayed the initial attack of 101 (US) Air Assault Division. The Divisional Artillery Group supported 1 (US) Infantry Division in the initial breaching and counter reconnaissance battles while the rest of the Division received radio orders to cancel a planned tank transporter move. At 1400 hrs on 24 February, the Division moved forward on tracks to be in the staging area just south of the breach by 2300 hrs on that day.

On 25 February, the Division moved forward behind the Americans, waiting to conduct a forward passage of the lines, which occurred at 1200 hrs. At 1515 hrs, 7 Brigade crossed their Line of Departure. They were in the north of the Divisional area and were followed in the south by 4 Brigade some four hours later. The first major attack was subsequently launched by 7 Brigade at 2000 hrs.

Opposition on the night of 25–26 February was significant as demonstrated by enemy counter-attacks of up to tank company strength. Although it was already clear that the unexpected speed, direction and firepower of the brigades would overwhelm the opposition, it was not until first light on the 26th that the Division effectively dominated its sector. With the divisional recce troops calling for air and MLRS fire, attacks continued during the 26th to clear all objectives up to the Phase Line SMASH which was reached at 0600 hrs on the 27th after 33 hours of action – 15 hours quicker than the operational analysis had predicted.

A number of options were then planned to assist the Corps' main effort in the north against the withdrawing Republican Guard forces. These included a pursuit north-east towards Basra but in fact at 0730 hrs on 27 February, 7 Brigade attacked due east across the Wadi al Batin into Kuwait, achieving their objective on the far side of the Wadi against only light opposition at 1130 hrs. The division was then halted before receiving orders to clear a route south-west down the line of the Wadi starting at 1930 hrs. Counter orders were then received and the Division resumed its advance east at 2110 hrs.

This final advance continued until the ceasefire at 0800 hrs the following morning the 28th the leading battle group of 7 Brigade having reached the Kuwait to Basra road at 0725 hrs. The Division had advanced 290 km in 90 hours, destroyed the best part of at least three Iraqi divisions, and had taken some 8,000 prisoners, including two enemy divisional commanders.

Support for the Land Battle

The divisional and brigade logistic units were heavily involved in supporting the five days of battle. The first elements of FMA transport committed to resupplying the operations were the squadrons allocated to provide artillery ammunition resupply. The plan was to deliver this to artillery XPs. There the ammunition would be cross loaded for forward distribution by divisional transport. The initial resupply of the guns was by divisional transport but, on 22 February, FMA vehicles loaded artillery ammunition in the FFMA and moved forward to a holding area in the DMA. Shortly after this, the vehicles were called forward to an artillery XP just south of the breach, to support artillery operations. Here some of the loads were exchanged and some were dumped on the ground.

It had not been planned to dump stock at the XPs but, because of the lower than expected rate of fire during the breaching operation, approximately three days worth were dumped in this way. This proved a bonus when the Division raced east into Kuwait and, as further XPs were established, transport was able to resupply them from the rear.

During the '100 hour' land battle there was hardly any third line resupply because sufficient stocks were well forward with the fighting echelons and available 'on wheels' or at predetermined dumps but, by the time the Division arrived in Kuwait, it did require further resupply. This was made much easier when the Royal Engineers opened a main supply route running parallel with the Wadi al Batin, and establishing a direct route from Al Jubayl to Kuwait City, thus easing the time taken for resupply.

Once the land battle was over, the task for the logisticians became one of extracting men and equipment from Kuwait and prepare them for their departure back to Germany and the UK.

Bibliography

Addy, Major, *A History of RAOC Operations on 'Op Granby'*.
White, Major General, *Gulf Logistics – Blackadder's War*.

ACKNOWLEDGEMENTS

Textural Quotations

The Ministry of Defence wishes to thank those publishers who have permitted the quotations of extracts from their books. In general the sources of quotations are acknowledged in the appropriate footnotes to the text. It has regrettably not been possible to contact Macdonald and Co (Publishers) Ltd, the publisher of the following two books from which extracts and illustrations have been used in this publication.

Wingate – In Peace and War by Major General D Tulloch, and

War in Peace. A compilation of war journalism by different authors published in 1988.

Illustrations

As this publication is an updated version of the previous publication, many of the same illustrations have been incorporated in this revised edition and are acknowledged again in this version. Every effort has been made to trace the source and copyright holder of new illustrations. The Ministry of Defence wishes to acknowledge and thank those who have permitted these illustrations to be published.

A detailed list of acknowledgements for all illustrations is given below:

The Action at Mirbat Fort, David Shephard
AFM, Vol V, Pt 1, *Peacekeeping Operations*
ASTS Graphic Dept, MOD, Upavon
Broadwater Collection (Sir Winston Churchill)
Camera Press Agency
Central Office of Information
Collins, in conjunction with Times Newspapers
Director Special Forces
Harrap
The History of the SAS Regiment, Secker and Warburg Ltd
P F Holmes MC MA
HQ Commando Forces RM
HQ LAND G3 Media Ops
Imperial War Museum
The Indian Army Book, c/o Lancer International, New Delhi
Israeli Govt Press Office
JWP 01

A Logistician's War (A History of RAOC Operations – Op GRANBY)
Methuen, London
The Middlesex Regimental Association
Mrs Suzanne Miers
MOD Sources
Reproduced from the National Army Museum Publication
Natraj, Dehra Dun, India
Old German and Russia photographs (made available through *Soldier Magazine*)
The Parachute Regiment
Popper Photo
By kind permission of The SAS Regiment
SAS Secret War, HarperCollins Publishers, 1996
Colonel J A Sellers MBE
Suez, Pan Books Ltd
Ten Years On – The British Army in the Falklands War, by courtesy of the Director, National Army Museum, London
The Tanks of Tammuz, Weidenfeld and Nicholson, 1968
Thompson Press, Faridabad, India
United States Dept of Defence
United States Navy Dept
War in Peace, courtesy of Macdonald & Co Ltd
War Since 1945, George Weidenfeld and Nicholson
Wingate In Peace and War, Macdonald & Co (Publishers)

Maps

Maps used to illustrate the historical examples in the Annex are based on a selection of detail from works listed in the individual Bibliography at the end of each Appendix.

The maps and diagrams were drawn by:

Central Graphics Pool, Navy, Empress State Building, London.
CS (Rep S) Pg, Design Studio, MOD, King Charles Street, London.
Directorate of Military Survey, Feltham, Middlesex.
General Staff Map Section, MOD Main Building, London.
Mapping and Charting Establishment, RE, Tolworth, Surrey.
Royal School of Military Engineering, Chattenden, Kent.
RAEC Centre, Beaconsfield, Bucks.
Staff College, Camberley, Surrey.
School of Military Intelligence, Ashford, Kent.
The Graphics Division of ASTS MOD Upavon, Wilts.

ANNEX C

GLOSSARY
SOME ACRONYMS AND ABBREVIATIONS

AAR	After Action Review
ABCA	America Britain Canada Australia (a formal grouping of the armies of these nations to discuss military matters)
ACE	Allied Command Europe
ACF	Army Cadet Force
AD	Air Defence
ADP	Army Doctrinal Publication
ADTN	*Army Doctrine and Training News* (periodical published twice yearly)
AFM	Army Field Manual
AH	Attack Helicopter
AI	Air Interdiction
AMF	ACE Mobile Force
AMF(A)	ACE Mobile Force (Air)
AMF(L)	ACE Mobile Force (Land)
AOCinC	Air Officer Commander in Chief
APC	Armoured Personnel Carrier
ARRC	ACE Rapid Reaction Corps
ATD	Army Training Directive
BAR	*British Army Review* (periodical published twice yearly)
BBGT	Brigade and Battlegroup Trainer
BCR	Battle Casualty Replacement
BDD	British Defence Doctrine (JWP 0-01)
Bde	Brigade
BMD	British Military Doctrine (AC71451)
BRACIS	Biological Radiological and Chemical Information System
BW	Biological Weapons
C2	Command and Control
C2W	Command and Control Warfare
C&AG	Comptroller and Auditor General
CAS	Close Air Support
CATT	Combined Arms Tactical Trainer
CCP	Casualty Collecting Post
CCIR	Commander's Critical Information Requirements
CDS	Chief of the Defence Staff
CFE	Conventional Forces in Europe
CGS	Chief of the General Staff
CinC	Commander in Chief
CIS	Communications Information Systems

CJO	Commander Joint Operations
CMF	Commonwealth Multinational Force
CO	Commanding Officer
COA	Course of Action
COIN	Counter Insurgency
COMINT	Communications Intelligence
CS	Combat Support
CSS	Combat Service Support
CVR(T)	Combat Vehicle Reconnaissance (Tracked)
CW	Chemical Weapons
DAG	Divisional Artillery Group
DCM	Distinguished Conduct Medal
DF	Defensive Fire
Div	Division
DMA	Divisional Maintenance Area
DMO	Director Military Operations
DOP	Defence and Overseas Policy [Committee]
DROPS	Dismountable Rack Off Loading and Pick-up System
DSF	Director Special Forces
DSO	Distinguished Service Order
ECM	Electronic Counter Measures
EFI	Expeditionary Forces Institute
ELINT	Electronic Intelligence
EM	Electro-Magnetic
EOD	Explosive Ordnance Disposal
EPM	Electronic Protective Measures
ESM	Electronic Support Measures
EW	Electronic Warfare
FAA	Forward Assembly Area
FAC	Forward Aid Controllers
FCC	Fire Co-ordination
FFMA	Forward FMA
FIBUA	Fighting in Built Up Areas
FINABEL	France Italy Netherlands Allemagne Belgium and Luxembourg (informal grouping of European armies which meets to discuss military business)
FMA	Force Maintenance Area
FPDA	Five Power Defence Arrangements
FROG	Free Flight Rocket Over Ground
G1	G1 staff in any Army headquarters. Deals with Administration Personnel and Medical topics.
G2	G2 staff in any Army headquarters. Deals with Intelligence.
G3	G3 staff in any Army headquarters. Deals with all aspects of Operations

G4	G4 staff in any Army headquarters. Deals with all aspects of Logistics.
G5	G5 staff in some Army headquarters. Deals with Civil Affairs.
GENFORCE	General Enemy Forces (acronym for describing the type of enemy forces likely to be met in certain situations)
GHQ	General Headquarters
GOC	General Officer Commanding
HFT	Higher Formation Trainer
HNS	Host Nation Support
HQ	Headquarters
IAF	Indian Air Force
ICBM	Inter Continental Ballistic Missile
IDF	Israeli Defence Force
IFOR	Intervention Force (NATO Forces in Bosnia from 1995–96)
IPB	Intelligence Preparation of the Battlefield
IRF	Immediate Reaction Forces
ISTAR	Intelligence, Surveillance, Target Acquisition and Reconnaissance
ITD	Individual Training Directives
IW	Information Warfare
JCRRP	Joint Casualty Reporting and Reception Plans
JFC	Joint Force Commander
JFHQ	Joint Force Headquarters
JHQ	Joint Headquarters
JLP	Joint Logistic Plans
JPS	Joint Planning Staff
JRDF	Joint Rapid Deployment Force
JSP	Joint Service Publication
JTP	Joint Theatre Plans
KP	Key Point
LCL	Landing Craft Logistic
LCU	Landing Craft Utility
LCVP	Landing Craft Vehicles and Personnel
LOAC	Law of Armed Conflict
LOC	Lines of Communication
LPD	Landing Platform Dock
LPH	Landing Platform Helicopter
LSL	Landing Ship Logistic
LRS	Local Resources Section
LST	Landing Ship Tank
MACA	Military Aid to the Civil Authorities
MACC	Military Aid to the Civil Community
MACP	Military Aid to the Civil Power

MAGD	Military Aid to Government Departments
MFO	Multi National Force and Observers (military force in Syria acting on behalf of the UN from 1982)
MHD	Military Home Defence
MLRS	Multi-Launch Rocket System
MM	Military Medal
MND	Multi National Division (term used within NATO)
MNF	Multi National Force (UN sponsored force in Lebanon 1982–84)
MOD	Ministry of Defence
MSMO	Military Support for Mounting Operations
MSR	Main Supply Route
MTB	Motor Torpedo Boat
NAAFI	Navy Army Air Force Institute
NADGE	NATO Air Defence Ground Environment
NAEW	NATO Airborne Early Warning
NAO	National Audit Office
NATO	North Atlantic Treaty Organisation
NBC	Nuclear Biological and Chemical
NCO	Non Commissioned Officer
NEO	Non-combatant Evacuation Operation
NGS	Naval Gunfire Support
OAS	Offensive Air Support
OF	Offensive Fire
OKH	German Army Command (WW2)
OKW	German High Command (WW2)
OOTW	Operations Other Than War
OP	Observation Post
OPCOM	Operational Command
OPCON	Operational Control
OPSEC	Operations Security
OSCE	Organisation for Security and Cooperation in Europe
OTC	Officer Training Corps
PAC	Public Accounts Committee
PfP	Partnership for Peace
PIR	Priority Intelligence Requirements
PJHQ	Permanent Joint Headquarters
PLOD	Pipeline Over the Desert
PMP	Russian Bridging Equipment
PSO	Peace Support Operations
Psy Ops	Psychological Operations
PUS	Permanent Under-Secretary of State
PWGF	Prisoner of War Guard Force
PXR	Post Exercise Report

RA	Royal Artillery
RAF	Royal Air Force
RE	Royal Engineers
RFA	Royal Fleet Auxillary
RM	Royal Marines
ROE	Rules of Engagement
ROK	Republic of Korea
RPC	Royal Pioneer Corps
RPV	Remotely Piloted Vehicle
RRF	Rapid Reaction Forces
RV	Rendezvous
SACEUR	Supreme Allied Commander Europe
SACLANT	Supreme Allied Commander Atlantc
SAM	Surface to Air Missile
SAS	Special Air Service
SAT	Small Arms Trainer
SBS	Special Boat Service
SCUD	Russian built Free Flight Rocket
SEAD	Suppression of Enemy Air Defences
SF	Special Forces
SFOR	Stabilisation Force (NATO Forces in Bosnia from 1997)
SHAPE	Supreme Headquarters Allied Powers Europe
SIGINT	Signal Intelligence
SNMF	Standing Naval Mine Counter Measures Force
SOFA	Status of Forces Agreement
SOP	Standing Operations Procedures
SPKP	Specific Key Point
STANAVFORLANT	Standing Naval Force Atlantic (NATO Naval Forces)
STANAVFORMED	Standing Naval Force Mediterranean (NATO Naval Forces)
STAP	Surveillance and Target Acquisition Plan
STRE	Specialist Team Royal Engineers
STRIKE	HQ STRIKE Command RAF
TA	Territorial Army
TACOM	Tactical Command
TACON	Tactical Control
TES	Tactical Engagement Simulation
TEWT	Tactical Exercise Without Troops
TIC	Toxic Industrial Chemicals
TLB	Top Level Budget
UKSF	United Kingdom Special Forces
ULTRA	Signals Intelligence Codeword (WW2)
UN	United Nations
UNIFCYP	United Nations Forces in Cyprus (since 1974)

UNPROFOR	United Nations Protection Force (UN Force in the former Yugoslavia 1992–95)
UNTAC	United Nations Transitional Authority in Cambodia 1992–93
US	United States
USMC	United States Marine Corps
WEU	Western European Union
WMD	Weapons of Mass Destruction
WO	Warrant Officer
XP	Exchange Point
ZSU	Russian SP Air Defence Gun